U 26

U-Boats
Under the Swastika

U-boats Under the Swastika

An Introduction to German Submarines 1935—1945

J. P. Mallmann Showell

ARCO PUBLISHING COMPANY, INC
New York

Published 1974 by Arco Publishing Company, Inc.
219 Park Avenue South, New York, N.Y. 10003

Library of Congress Catalog Card Number 73-93-152
ISBN 0-668-03457-2

Printed in Great Britain

Contents

Acknowledgements

I should like to express my sincerest thanks to Kapitän zur See Otto Köhler for all the help and encouragement he has given me. I am also especially grateful to Fritz Köhl, who sailed on U 765 and U 1203, for supplying me with plans, technical information, hundreds of photos and exceptionally long accounts about his experiences. Without their help this book would never have been completed.

My grateful thanks also go to the following, who have kindly helped with this book:

Buckinghamshire Public Library Service; particularly Miss Iris Loe and Miss Magaret Mackenzie of the Beaconsfield Branch.
Michael P. Cooper for helping to check numerous facts and also for reading through part of the manuscript. I am grateful to Admiral a.D. Godt and Korvettenkapitän a.D. Adalbert Schnee for corresponding with Mr Cooper to help clear up several problems.
Grossadmiral a.D. Karl Dönitz for reading the proofs and for making invaluable comments.
Roel Diepeveen for kindly helping with "schnorkels" and "Dutch U-boats". I should also like to thank him for selecting a few photographs from Dutch archives.
Ray A. Freeman of the Imperial War Museum for allowing me to photograph a Dräger lung and for helping with several other points.
Hanni Fletcher for providing a great deal of information.
Jack Fletcher for reading through the manuscript.
Heinz Kurt Gast for sending a long list of places where I might obtain information about U-boats.
Ilse Hegewald for information about her husband Wolfgang Hegewald, who died as commander of U 671.
Bodo Herzog for kindly helping to clear up a few points about Type VII D and VII F boats.
Imperial War Museum; particularly Mr M. Brennan, Mr R. E. Squires, the staff of the Photographic Library, the staff of the Reference Library and the staff of the Documents Section.
Fregattenkapitän a.D. Max Kaluza for corresponding with Fritz Köhl and sending details of U 995.
Friedrich Kiemle for information about the *Grundausbildung* and the last days of the German bases in France.
National Maritime Museum; particularly Dr M. W. B. Sanderson, Mr Stonham and Mr G. A. Osbon.
Fregattenkapitän K. H. Nitschke for information about U 377 and for helping to identify photographs.

Mr A. Pitt, a retired British submarine commander, for helping to sort out many problems about U-boat warfare.
Karl, Adele and Heidi Prawitt for dealing with numerous problems that cropped up in Germany.
Kapitän zur See K. T. Raeder, the Federal German Naval Attaché in London, for help and advice.
Christiane Ritter for kindly corresponding with me about her deceased husband (Oberleutnant Ritter) who helped to set up the secret meteorological stations in the Arctic.
Dr Jürgen Rohwer for help and advice.
Colonel G. Salusbury for reading through part of the manuscript.
Science and Industry Museum in Chicago; particularly Mr J. E. Irwin, Administrative Assistant to the President, for sending information about U 505.
Staatliche Landesbildstelle in Hamburg; particularly Dr Diederich and his staff for searching through their archives. (Unfortunately no U-boat photos were found.)
Herr J. Staus, who sailed on U 377, for helping with the identification of photos.
Ulfert Tilemann, who sailed on several U-boats, for devoting an afternoon of his holiday in London to talking to me about his wartime experiences.
Anthony J. Watts, BNRA, for help and advice.
Oberleutnant zur See a.D. Herbert A. Werner for answering several questions about the last days of the German bases in France.

The following have kindly helped with finding information or addresses and passing this on to me; I should like to thank them very much for their assistance:

R. Anderson of Arthur Baker Ltd
Henry Birkenhagen
Fräulein M. Elsner
Dr Wolfgang Frank
Kapitänleutnant a.D. Wilhelm Spahr
Commander G. A. M. van Wermeskerken (Royal Netherlands Navy)
George Allen & Unwin Ltd
Walter Kabisch of Verlag Ullstein G.M.B.H.
Schulte & Bruns, Emden
Herr G. Vannotti

I should like to emphasize that these people helped by passing on information and that the opinions and mistakes in this book are my own.

J.P.M.S.

Photo Credits

I am grateful to the following for supplying photographs:

Imperial War Museum, London; 13 bottom, 21 top, 30 bottom, 32, 33, 35 top, 44 left & right, 45, 46 top, middle, bottom & right, 54 top left, 71 right, 73 top, 78 top left, 90 middle & bottom, 91, 98, 99 left & right, 115, 116 top, middle & bottom, 117 top, middle & bottom, 118 left & right, 119 left & right, 121 top, 128 bottom left & bottom right, 130 top left, top right & bottom, 133 top & bottom, 138 middle, 141 top & middle, 142 top & bottom, 143 top left & top right, 152, 154, 155 top & bottom, 156, back endpapers.

Foto-Drüppel, Rheinstrasse 50, 2940 Wilhelmshaven, Germany; Front endpapers, 13 top left, 17 middle & right, 18 top, middle & bottom, 20 top & bottom, 145 top & bottom.

The Editor, 'The Motor Ship', London; 30 top & middle, 48 left & right, 49 left & right, 51 bottom, 138 top.

The Royal Institution of Naval Architects, London; 135 top & bottom, 136 left & right, 138 bottom, 141 bottom.

Aerofilms Ltd., London; 88.

J. F. van Dulm, MWO, Commandeur b.d., Bur. maritieme historie, Den Haag, Holland; 134 top & bottom.

L. L. von Münching, Middleweg 85, Wassenaar, Holland; 17 top left.

Deutsches Museum, Munich; 143 bottom.

J. Staus, Germany; 35 bottom right, 69, 84 bottom.

F. Köhl, Switzerland; 55 top, middle & bottom, 57 top left & top right.

Photos not listed above have come from Kapitan zur See Otto Köhler and Jak P. Mallmann Showell's private collection.

German Rank Equivalents

Grossadmiral (Admiral of the Fleet)
Generaladmiral (Admiral)
Vizeadmiral (Vice Admiral)
Konteradmiral (Rear Admiral)
Kapitän zur See (Captain)
Fregattenkapitän (Commander)
Korvettenkapitän (Lieutenant Commander)
Kapitänleutnant (Lieutenant-Senior)
Oberleutnant zur See (Lieutenant-Junior)
Leutnant zur See (Sub Lieutenant)

1
The Birth of the U-boat Arm

Germany became a republic in 1918 after the abdication of the *Kaiser* (Emperor) and the termination of World War I. The Weimar Republic, as it was called, was governed along lines set out in the Treaty of Versailles, which imposed difficult financial restrictions on Germany. This treaty was not negotiated, but dictated by the victors of the war, who also placed numerous limitations on the armed forces. For example, in many cases the total strength of units was laid down; Germany was not permitted to station troops west of the river Rhine; neither was she allowed to build or own heavy artillery, tanks, military aircraft, aircraft carriers or *submarines*. All the weapons in these categories were scrapped by order of the Allies after World War I. This made a great contribution towards Hitler's armed forces because it took away most of the old weapons and he started with a clean sheet to build new and modern equipment. Thus, at the beginning of World War II, Germany was not in the same predicament as the British Royal Navy of having 'heaps of obsolete junk floating about'.

Ever since its foundation Hitler's Party, the *Nationalsozialistische Deutsche Arbeiterpartei* (*NSDAP*—National Socialists German Workers' Party: Socialists at this time were nicknamed 'Sozis', thus the *NSDAP* became 'Nazis') had advocated the abolition of the Versailles Treaty. Shortly after being made Chancellor, on January 30th, 1933, Hitler called together the important military leaders to outline to them, in secret, what he had in mind for the armed forces of the future and what role he expected these to play in the new Germany. Hitler informed the leaders that the armed forces would soon be allowed to develop beyond the restrictions of the Treaty of Versailles, and he asked them to plan for this increase in strength.

Trade unions were abolished in the summer of 1933 and replaced by a single union called the *Deutsche Arbeitsfront*. Every person who worked, whether small employee or mighty employer, had to be a member and paid at least a few marks subscription each week, thus giving the *NSDAP* a large, regular income. Some of this money was given to the *Kriegsmarine*, making it possible to expand the force by several thousand men, without anyone, except the Admiralty, being aware of this increase. In addition the navy had also built up, over the years, a secret fund, which had been obtained by overcharging on normal bills and filtering off the excess cash.

When Hitler had been Chancellor for just over two years the Versailles Treaty was officially repudiated with great publicity and ceremony, but to many people's astonishment large parts of the previously prohibited forces were already in existence. The *Luftwaffe* (Air Force) had been functioning as a civil flying club; officers had been trained in groups that posed as sport clubs; barracks had been built in previous years under the disguise of factories. This repudiation also triggered off a new era of submarine construction in Germany, but it was by no means the beginning of the story because submarine development has been in progress secretly since 1922, some ten years before Hitler came to power.

At that time, in 1922, the German Admiralty had encouraged the formation of a 'Submarine Development Bureau' in Holland by financing a great part of the concern and by putting naval facilities at its disposal. This Bureau, employing the best German submarine designers, was based in Den Haag, where it posed as a normal Dutch ship-building firm under the name of 'Ingenieurskantoor voor Scheepsbouw'. Its task was to keep up-to-date with submarine development and possibly even to build boats for other countries.

Fregattenkapitän, later Admiral, Wilhelm Canaris had personal connections with the King of Spain, King Alfonso, and he managed to arrange for the Submarine Development Bureau to build a submarine in Cadiz for the Spanish Navy. However, these plans were interrupted by Spanish Civil War, although the Bureau did supervise the building of a sea-going submarine at Cadiz, which was later sold to Turkey and became known as *Gür*. In addition to this, Crichton-Vulcan, a firm in Finland under German influence, had constructed two submarines in Turku, using German plans and help from the Development Bureau, and two further boats were developed in Holland.

The men of Germany's new U-boat flotilla were too young to have fought during World War I and they had no experience of fighting in submarines. This gap was also filled by the Development Bureau as all these submarines were taken for extremely long tests by specially selected personnel, some of whom later helped to form the new U-boat flotilla.

The individual parts needed to assemble about ten submarines had been built in Spain, Holland and Finland, and were stored in Kiel by the autumn of 1934; some five months before the 'official' repudiation of the Versailles Treaty. Grand Admiral Erich Raeder, Chief of the German Admiralty, asked Hitler in November of that year whether it might be possible to assemble a few of these hulls, but Hitler did not permit this as he did not wish to provoke foreign powers. However, submarines were constructed at an exceptionally fast rate after the repudiation. Three different types, totalling well over twenty boats, had been laid down by the end of 1935. The plans for the construction of these craft were a direct product of the work carried out by the Submarine Development Bureau. The first Type II boats, for example, were identical to the Finnish *Vesikko;* only the conning towers differed and the new German boats were welded instead of being riveted to save weight. Type I boats were based on the Turkish *Gür*, which had been built in Spain. This was a poor design, and only two of these, U 25 and U 26, were ever constructed. The third U-boat type was developed from a successful World War I Submarine and a prototype had been made in Finland.

Some of these new submarines were formed into a training group and attached to the submarine school and the others became Germany's first new operational flotilla, known as the Weddigen Flotilla, after Otto Weddigen, a World War I submarine hero.

At this time it was Hitler's aim to join Britain in some type of European defence league and because of these political ambitions the Anglo-German Naval Agreement was signed during June 1935. With this agreement Hitler hoped to show that he seriously wished Britain to be an ally. This is why Germany volunteered to restrict her navy to about one-third of the total strength of the British Navy. (This strength was measured in displacement tonnage.) She wanted to build up her U-boat strength to just under half that of the Royal Navy. Possibly later, after mutual agreement, Germany would wish to increase this to 100 per cent, but would then sacrifice tonnage on the other categories. Today it may appear strange that the Admiralty in London agreed to this, but several points must be remembered.

First, the British submarine fleet consisted of only about fifty boats at that time. Secondly, for numerous reasons the British Admiralty saw only a limited future in submarines: years of tradition and experience had gone into the evolution of the Royal Navy, whose main task had been to protect the trade routes. So the ships that had been developed were powerful, impressive battleships, backed up by squadrons of fast, well-armed cruisers. Submarines were regarded as having no great future because it was thought difficult to defend anything with them; they were primarily attacking weapons. Britain had also experimented with several unsuccessful ideas, such as mounting battleship-sized guns on submarines or fitting them with hangers to carry aeroplanes; and in addition there had been a whole series of disasters with the 'K' Class vessels, making submarines less desirable in the eyes of officialdom.[1] At the same time Britain had been developing new underwater detection devices and was becoming more

[1] (See *The K-Boats* by Don Everitt, published by George Harrap, London 1963).

The Early Tenders

The first U-boat tenders were boats which had survived the First World War and were not scrapped as a result of the Treaty of Versailles. M 61, M 136, T 23, T 156, T 157 and T 158 belonged to this group.

Left: *An "M" boat running into Swinemünde.*

Below: *U-boat tender T 157 at sea.*

In The Beginning. . . . . .

Below left: *The 1st U-boat Flotilla–Flotilla Weddigen–with the 2,710 ton depot ship* Saar.

Bottom: *Kiel during the summer of 1939. Next to the tender is U 33. To the right of the pier, U 34; to the left, U 27 and in the background is another Type VII A and probably U 26. Note the* Spatz *(Sparrow), the striped rescue buoys with light bulbs. These can be seen just behind the conning tower and a short distance forward of the 88mm gun. The above water torpedo tube can also be seen at the back of U 33. (Identification feature for Type VII A – The only Type with torpedo tube above water)*

Below right: *Grand Admiral Erich Raeder, Adolf Hitler and Field-Marshal Werner von Blomberg. (Blomberg was Defence Minister and Commander-in-Chief of the OKW* (Oberkommando der Wehrmacht). *He was supposed to co-ordinate all the various branches of the armed forces. The lack of this co-operation contributed to Germany's downfall.)*

confident that this apparatus would diminish the operational value of submarines since their presence, below the surface, could easily be detected.

In September 1935, Kapitän zur See Karl Dönitz, commander of the cruiser *Emden* and a submarine commander during World War I, was appointed Commanding Officer for U-boats. Contrary to generally accepted doctrine his primary job was to develop fighting tactics with the Weddigen Flotilla. He was not made Rear-Admiral until after the start of the war. His promotion to Head of the Admiralty only came about in January 1943. So during these early days he was by no means responsible for the submarine defence policy or for U-boat construction, in fact he had numerous personal difficulties with the Naval High Command about submarine warfare.

Germany had not owned any submarines since the end of World War I, so when Dönitz took over command he was not confronted with a book of rules, and he was free to develop his own ideas. Already during World War I he had learned that submarines had little effect when working as members of the fleet and that they could be better employed operating on their own against merchant ships. Dönitz was also one of the first Germans who realised that Germany's future enemy would be Britain, in which case he felt certain that the Royal Navy would resort to the same convoy tactics that had been developed during the previous war. This meant that merchant ships would sail in groups, escorted by armed vessels of the Royal Navy. A lone submarine had little impact upon such a convoy because they were difficult to find and even if the escorts did not sink the submarine they could, at least, keep it at bay until the convoy escaped with its superior speed.

To meet such a convoy, Dönitz organised the U-boats into groups, which would hunt like a wolf pack, thus having a great hitting power while putting the greatest possible strain on the escorts. The idea was that this group would spread out in the shipping lanes and when one of the U-boats spotted a convoy it would drop behind these ships radioing its position, so that the other submarines could race to the scene and attack en masse. This method was proved to be successful long before the war started, when it was discovered that it was relatively easy to attack a convoy. The main difficulty lay in finding such a convoy in the first place, because practical radar did not exist and even a group of submarines had a very limited field of vision. The only way in which U-boats could detect their enemy was to position lookouts on the conning tower, who would scour the horizon with binoculars. It must be emphasised that these German binoculars were far superior to the British equivalent – so much so that the few that fell into British hands became highly treasured war prizes. Donald Macintyre, who captured Otto Kretschmer after sinking U 99, retained Kretschmer's glasses and used them throughout the war in preference to British binoculars; in fact Macintyre is still using them today.

By the time war started in 1939 Dönitz had set up an efficiently organised information room, where the position of all U-boats, as well as reconnaissance information was marked on large maps. This room had excellent radio contact with all U-boats and also monitored Allied radio, so that it was possible to direct the boats to areas where they would have maximum impact. Dönitz approached the Nazi High Command, through his chief Admiral Raeder, to ask whether some long range planes might be attached to the U-boat Arm for reconnaissance purposes. The request was promptly refused by Hermann Göring, Commander-in-Chief of the *Luftwaffe*, who said all *his* planes were needed for far more important jobs elsewhere. One of Göring's favourite comments was 'Everything that flies belongs to me.'

It was not until much later during the war that Hitler, after hearing of U-boat successes, gave a direct order that Dönitz should have his own planes. Dönitz had estimated that some ten to twelve planes would be needed in the air each day to have any significant effect, but even with Hitler's special order only two were available for duty. Göring was absent on a hunting trip as Hitler issued this order, and on returning he asked Dönitz to return the aeroplanes to the *Luftwaffe*. As Dönitz refused, Göring tried another way of retaining command of the planes by creating a new post in the Luftwaffe of

'Commander for Aircraft for the Atlantic'. These planes did not have an immediate impact. On spotting the enemy they could not always accurately pin point the position on the water.

This lack of co-operation between Dönitz and the *Luftwaffe* must be stressed because it was not just restricted to these spheres. During the entire reign of the Third Reich essential co-operation between different departments of the armed forces was very limited or non-existent and this certainly contributed to Germany's downfall.

Göring's hate of anything naval was probably due to his characteristic love of himself and dislike of everybody else. He never had much respect for any of the armed forces, except *his* Luftwaffe. His small liking for the *Kriegsmarine* was completely destroyed while he attended the naval exercises in 1937. Göring was aboard the cruiser *Königsberg* and feeling rather sea-sick, whereat a wit among the officers, Leutnant zur See (Ingenieur) Fischer, dubbed him *Reichsfischfuttermeister* (The Reich's master for feeding fish). This was too much for Göring's composure and he immediately signalled to a tender to take him ashore.

In the autumn of 1937 Dönitz submitted several major proposals to the *Oberkommando der Marine* (*OKM* – Naval High Command). He suggested that, in view of the successes with the wolf pack methods, no more Type II boats should be produced, because their range and hitting power was too poor. Three-quarters of the permitted tonnage should be taken up with the successful Type VII craft, which had plenty of modification potential. The remaining quarter of the permitted tonnage should be filled with large, 1000 ton, submarines, which would be capable of operating in distant seas. Unknown to Dönitz at the time, these proposals were totally rejected by the *OKM*, who was still not convinced that the submarine was a first-class torpedo carrier and useless as reconnaissance craft or as a gun platform. The *OKM* argued that wolf pack tactics were unsuitable and that U-boats would have to be capable of operating with the surface fleet. The gentlemen of the *OKM* also stated that powerful guns were needed, as these were more important than torpedoes. The *OKM* therefore planned huge, 2000 ton, submarine cruisers. However, the war started before these could be built and none ever appeared.

It should be remembered that Hitler and his 'inner circle' had grown up in Austria/Bavaria, where they did not develop any great maritime sense. Hermann Göring kept impressing on Hitler that any future war would be won in the air and so Hitler saw no urgency to build up a U-boat fleet, since impressive battleships appeared to be far superior symbols of his might. Grand Admiral Raeder kept urging Hitler that naval development was too slow, but Hitler replied that the *Kriegsmarine* would not be needed until 1946 at the earliest. Hitler had given highest priority to the 'Z' Plan only some nine months before the start of the war, but this development plan was not due to be completed until 1948. The total number of U-boats to be completed by then, might look impressive, but these were only a very small part of the *Kriegsmarine's* expenditure. The *Bismarck* and *Tirpitz* cost around 200 million Reichsmark each and only 4 million RM were needed to build one Type VII U-boat. This meant that about 100 U-boats could have been built for the price of these two battleships. However, there was a dramatic change in naval opinion after the start of the war and this entire 'Z' Plan was dropped. Ships that were nearing completion were finished, but the rest were scrapped, so that all energy could be concentrated on the production of U-boats.

During these years, while Dönitz was developing the wolf pack tactics and trying to make his superiors see that a completely new era of submarine warfare was being born, the British Navy was also attempting to find out what future submarines might mean to the nation. Large-scale exercises were held to attempt to establish the importance of submarines. During these experiments Britain assumed that submarines of the future would hunt on their own and attack from below the waves. This resulted in the Defence Advisory Committee stating that Britain would never again be cut off by submarines, as had almost happened during World War I. When World War II began Britain was taken completely by surprise by the wolf pack tactics and by U-boats attacking at night on the surface, like torpedo boats. Both these facts contributed greatly to the early U-boat successes.

The 'Z' Plan

This plan was drawn up for the 10 years 1938-1948.

Type	*Number Planned*	*Completed or almost completed at start of war*	*Under construction at start of war*
Aircraft carriers	4	Graf Zeppelin	Design 'B'
Battleships & Battlecruisers	10	Tirpitz Bismarck Scharnhorst Gneisenau	'H' 'I'
Heavy cruisers/ Pocket battleships	20	Admiral Scheer Admiral Graf Spee Deutschland Blücher Admiral Hipper Prinz Eugen Seydlitz Lützow	
Light cruisers	48	Nürnberg Leipzig Köln Karlsruhe Königsberg Emden	'M' 'N' 'O' 'P' 'Q' 'R'
Reconnaissance cruisers or heavy destroyers	22	None	
U-boats	249	57	
Destroyers	68	30	
Torpedo boats	90	35	
Minesweepers	10	3 or 4	
Small boats	over 300	190	

Simultaneously with this U-boat development in Germany it became necessary to build up the great machinery needed to maintain the fleet. Early U-boats could not defend themselves against air attack, nor were they armoured, so they needed special protection while in port. For this purpose huge docks were constructed at the important bases. Eventually these U-boat bunkers developed into terrific concrete structures, some of them being, at that time, the largest pieces of man-made concrete on earth. The roofs and walls were somewhere around five to eight metres thick and being composed of reinforced concrete were capable of withstanding any air attack. It was not until just before the end of the war, when RAF Squadron 617 was equipped with the special 'Blockbuster' or 'earthquake' bombs, designed by Barnes Wallis, that these bastions were challenged.

Dönitz, visualising a war against Britain noted that it must be possible for the U-boats to operate far out in the Atlantic. For maximum effect they would have to remain there for a long time and not spend too much time travelling backwards and forwards from their bases and war stations. So it was necessary to establish good supply facilities. The U-boats experimented with several methods of passing stores from one boat to another, but had still not discovered a really efficient method by the end of the war. At first several boats left over from World War I were converted into tenders and attached to the U-boat Arm. The *Memel*, just under 1000 tons, was launched in 1937, and as a new, specially-designed supply ship it became the parent boat for the Weddigen Flotilla. Later, at the beginning of 1939, several long-distance supply ships, of about 3000 tons, were completed to act as supply tenders for merchant raiders and U-boats.

Dönitz was not content with surface supply ships, but it was not until the events of the war pressed the *OKM* that they started to experiment with submarine supply boats. The first of these supply U-boats was completed in 1940, being specially designed not to fight, but to supply front line submarines with provisions and munitions. These U-boats carried some 440 tons of oil to keep five to twelve ocean-going submarines at sea for an additional four to eight weeks, thus increasing the fighting U-boats' range so that they could easily operate along the American coast and in the Caribbean. These 'Milk Cows', (this has been translated as 'Milch-cow', but the Germans called them *Milchkuh* so 'Milk Cow' is a better translation), as they were called, had the great advantage of being able to dive and hide on spotting the enemy, making it possible to approach the secret rendezvous completely unseen. Unfortunately they only had a short history, as all ten that were ever built were sunk very quickly and before planned experiments with underwater refuelling had been carried out to any great extent.

Several European political developments between the abolition of the Versailles Treaty and the start of the war influenced the U-boat Arm. In February of 1938 Hitler, who had been a corporal in the army during World War I, promoted himself to Commander-in-Chief of *all* German Armed Forces and sole leader of the German Reich. Members of the armed forces had to take a new oath; an oath whereby they promised to be faithful to one man – Adolf Hitler; not to the German people, the govern-

Top left: *Probably the Dutch submarine O 25, which fell into German hands in 1940 and was commissioned into the* Kriegsmarine *as UD 3.*

Above: *One of the submarines the Germans obtained from Italy, UIT 21. Notice diagrams representing ships claimed as sunk.*

Middle left: *Type I. U 26. This type proved to be unseaworthy and only two were completed. In front of the conning tower is a 105mm quick firing gun.*

Bottom left: *Type II A. U 3. Only six of this type were built.*

Type II B boats. These were modified from Type II A. From left to right: U 23, U 15, U 16, U 12, U 14. U 20 can be seen in the background, just to the right of U 12's conning tower. U 12 is fitted with a circular radio direction finder aerial. The 'horseshoes' on the conning towers are lifebelts.

Rear view of Type II B boats. From left to right: U 9, U 8 and U 11.

Type VII A boats. (The numbers on the conning towers and most of the hand rails were removed from operational boats after the war started)

ment, or to the constitution, but to Adolf Hitler alone. As Supreme Commander of the Armed Forces he had overall control and could issue direct orders to individual units of the *Kriegsmarine.* These orders often contradicted Admiral Raeder's ideas and forced him into difficult situations. Dönitz too was obliged to obey the wishes of the *Führer*, who on numerous occasions gave U-boats tasks to perform for which they were completely unsuited. Several U-boats, for example, were ordered to sea to act as mid-ocean weather stations for the *Navy* and *Luftwaffe*; others were required to transport people and goods, while some had to refuel long distance aeroplanes at sea – all tasks for which submarines are highly unsuited and which they were never designed to perform.

Hitler's aggressive action in Europe shortly before the start of the war affected the U-boats to such an extent that they were ordered to war in September 1938, one year before World War II actually started. The U-boat commanders were informed that Hitler was going to Munich to hold an important meeting with other heads of state, and that there was a possibility of this meeting not coming to a peaceful conclusion, in which case they had to prepare for a conflict with Great Britain. The commanders were issued with sealed envelopes, containing their secret instructions and ordered to their war stations, so that they would be ready to strike at a moment's notice. This was announced by the newspapers as a grand naval manoeuvre. It was from this meeting that the British Prime Minister, Neville Chamberlain, returned triumphantly to England, waving a small piece of paper and making the famous announcement 'Peace in our time.'

After the peaceful conclusion of the Munich meeting the U-boats were recalled over their efficient radio network. On returning to base, Dönitz ordered the commanders to open their secret instructions and to discuss them with their officers. The general opinion was that most of these instructions were too difficult to carry out since it meant approaching too close to British harbours and main shipping centres. It was feared that Britain would not only have some efficient underwater and surface detection apparatus, but that these waters would be heavily guarded. Dönitz and the *OKM* appear to have contributed to this view as well because they did not scrap the 'Z' Plan until they were convinced that Britain did not have such a weapon.

By the spring of 1939 the U-boat Arm had been welded into an efficient fighting force, but it was by no means strong enough to take on Britain. Only very few people in the *OKM* had realised that they might have to fight Britain, and the *Kriegsmarine* had not been developed for this task. Hitler kept impressing upon Admiral Raeder that Germany would *not* go to war against Britain and only in 1938 did he give a hint that the Navy might, in the far distant future, have to meet the Royal Navy in battle on the high seas. The officers of the U-boat Arm were worried at their insignificant strength and although Dönitz was only a Captain in rank he asked that these anxieties should be made known to Hitler. Dönitz stated that the U-boats could not inflict any significant damage upon Britain. On July 22nd, only some six weeks before the start of the war, the high ranking officers of the U-boat Arm met Admiral Raeder aboard the *Aviso Grille*, where they were informed that Hitler had said that under *no* circumstances would Germany go to war against Britain. Four weeks later Dönitz was recalled from leave, so that he could personally direct war preparations against Britain!

The pocket battleships *Deutschland* and *Graf Spee*, as well as 21 U-boats were ready to sail to war during the first fortnight of August 1939. The German fleet actually sailed between August 19th and 31st, so by the time the conflict started, some 40 U-boats were waiting at their war stations around Britain. Owing to the apathetic attitude of the Nazi High Command towards U-boats, Germany only had a total of 57 submarines, of which merely half were capable of operating in the Atlantic.

As far as Britain was concerned her Admiralty had been asking for more new ships since the end of World War I, but only a fraction of these requests had been granted. It appears utterly astonishing today that although Hitler had disregarded several treaties, which he had signed, and also carried out numerous acts of aggression, that there were still high-ranking people in Britain who strongly believed that Hitler would not force a war. It was not until the spring of 1939, only some six months before the war, when

Hitler repudiated the Anglo-German Naval Agreement and ordered the armed forces to invade Czechoslovakia that these people were convinced that Britain must re-arm herself.

The Royal Navy at that time was in an atrocious mechanical state. Not only was it greatly under strength, but also equipped with old ships and obsolete armaments. Britain had to pay a heavy price for this neglect of her Royal Navy because as the war started modern German equipment scored too many victories. During August, 1939 the Admiralty assumed control of all merchant shipping in British waters and planned to re-introduce the convoy system. About fifty passenger liners were requisitioned to be converted into armed merchant cruisers so that they could supplement the Royal Navy cruiser fleet; but only guns and equipment removed from obsolete vessels scrapped after World War I were available, making them completely unsuitable for this task. Many of them were sunk during the early months of the war and those that

Above: *U 570 (Type VII C) under the White Ensign as HMS* Graph. *This boat was captured in the North Atlantic.*

Right: *The conning tower of U 377 (Type VII C) is painted white for service in the Arctic. On the rear gun platform (Wintergarden) is a single 20mm AA gun. The small projection, at deck level on the front of the tower, houses a magnetic compass. The lip at the top of the tower was called "wind deflector" and half way up is the "spray deflector".*

Opposite page top: Left: *U 873 (Type IX D_2).* Right: *U 234 (Type X B). U 873 was one of the large boats used for operations in far distant waters. Type X B was a large minelayer. Three of the side mine hatches can be seen just forward of the conning tower. The raised section, where the men are sitting, housed another six mineshafts. (The photo was taken after the war, when the boats had surrendered.)*

Bottom: *U 47 (Type VII B), commanded by Günther Prien, returning to port after the famous Scapa Flow raid.*

survived were later converted for use as troop transports. Britain did not, at this time, worry about foreign ships in her waters because it was thought that Hitler would not allow these to be attacked for fear of drawing more countries into the conflict.

By the end of August 1939 the two navies were waiting patiently on the high seas; then on September 1st the German Armed Forces invaded Poland. Britain was bound by treaty to give assistance to Poland and this forced her to declare war on Germany – so World War II started on September 3rd, 1939.

Above: *U 377. The metal structure on the top of the conning tower and the cradle in the foreground are used for loading torpedoes. These would be dismantled when not required. The gun fires 88mm shells.*

Above left: *U 377.*
1. Korvettenkapitän Otto Köhler (Commander). The commander was usually the only person on the boat to wear a white peak cap. 2. Leutnant zur See (Ingenieur) Karl-Heinz Nitschke (L.I.) 3. Stbs. Ob. Masch. Jak Mallmann (Chief Engineer for Diesel Engines.)
4. Leutnant zur See Langenberg (II.W.O.) Later Commander of U 336.
5. (?) 6. Stbs. Ob. Masch. Rienecker (?) 7. Oberleutnant zur See Pietschmann (?) (I.W.O.) Later commander of U 762 and U 712.
8. Leading Boatswain Albert Jungclaus.

Left: *U 377 in Norway. The cradle for lowering torpedoes can be seen in front of the gun barrel. The 'T' shaped stalk (arrow pointing to it) at the front of the boat is the head of underwater sound detection apparatus.*

2
The War Starts

As far as the men in the U-boats were concerned September 3rd, 1939 merged into the previous day, just like every other day of the year. In any case *days* are insignificant aboard a submarine, because such vessels must remain fully operational all the time; so the men slept when they were not on duty, whatever hour of the day it was. Most of the U-boats had been on their war stations for over a week. Only a few people really anticipated a war. There had been tense political situations in Europe on many previous occasions and the U-boats had even been sent to war before. Each time the European Powers gave way to Hitler's demands and nothing developed. None of the U-boats had been involved in serious battle, a few had seen some action during the Spanish Civil War, but no-one really knew what war was. However, they had *played* war on many occasions and the days leading up to September 3rd were considered by many to be just another such exercise and a boring one at that: as the boats had been given no special objective, they could only float around in a vast wilderness of water, endeavouring to remain undetected and to use the minimum of fuel. Such a waiting game is not only monotonous for the officers, but also a little disturbing for the crew, because on such occasions the officers go out of their way to find them odd jobs, which always means extra work.

The waiting game was broken at just past eleven o'clock in the morning of September 3rd when all units of the *Kriegsmarine* received a signal from the *OKM*. This signal was not dramatic; it merely stated that Britain had declared war on Germany and that all German naval units at sea were to carry out their prearranged instructions. Some ten minutes later there followed a signal from Dönitz, which enforced the previous order and added some details about Prize Ordinance Regulations. After that the situation was the same as before, only now the officers were planning their new tasks. This was also the time for several commanders to read carefully their General Instructions for Warfare. Such documents, although important, had been irrelevant before and were only read as a matter of duty. Now, suddenly, the regulation took on a new light.

The most important documents were orders referring to the Prize Ordinance Regulations, which was an agreement signed by several maritime nations long before the start of the war in order to establish a code of conduct for submarine warfare. To summarise the main points of this protocol:

Submarines were not allowed to sink merchant ships, unless these were directly helping the war effort. Submarines were not allowed to make surprise attacks on merchant men from below the surface; it was necessary for them to surface, stop their quarry and inspect the ship's papers. A long list of contraband was compiled and only ships carrying such articles were allowed to be sunk, and then not until the submariners saw to the safety of the merchant crew. The agreement regarded lifeboats as unsuitable on the high seas and the crews of merchant ships had to be taken on board the submarine or passed on to another vessel. This was, of course, completely impossible, for on most submarines there was hardly sufficient room for the crew. Even armed merchant ships had to be treated according to the regulations. Submarines were expected to surface in front of the guns and then ask the ships to stop! There were a few categories, such as merchant ships sailing in convoy, or those being guarded by vessels of a fighting

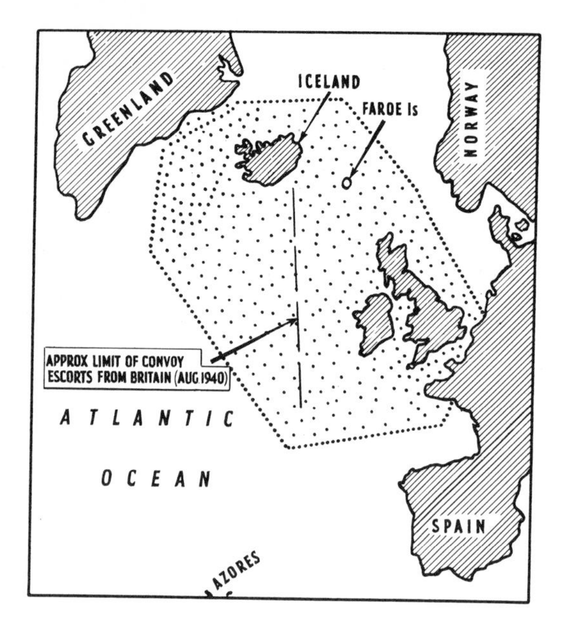

German Blockade Area Around Great Britain

navy, which one was allowed to attack without warning.

The rules of this protocol rendered submarines more or less useless. In fact the whole agreement was meaningless and ridiculous, to such an extent that Britain did not expect anybody to adhere to it and the Admiralty in London issued instructions as early as 1937, which completely contradicted the rules and broke the code of conduct. However as the conflict started, Hitler did not wish to draw more countries into the war, so he issued strict orders that these regulations were to be obeyed to the fullest degree.

Unfortunately the first ship to be sunk by a U-boat was a tragic case of mis-identification. Fritz Lemp, commanding U 30, identified the passenger liner *Athenia* as a troopship – a category which could be sunk without warning! Lemp later realised what he had done and on returning to port he admitted sinking the *Athenia* to Dönitz. Several weeks had passed between his return and the sinking, during which

Above: *Type VII C boats with 88mm guns.*

Right: *U 377 with circular radio direction finder aerial extended. The white symbol at the side of the tower is a tactical mark and not an insignia. Below this is a navigation light. At the front, above the spray deflector, is the intake for the radio aerial.*

both Germany and Britain had used this incident as propaganda. Britain accused Germany of waging unrestricted warfare on the high seas and the Nazi Propaganda Ministry, who had no information and were unsure of what had happened, stated that Winston Churchill had deliberately sabotaged the *Athenia* to give the Royal Navy an excuse for attacking German ships without warning. Dönitz threatened Lemp with court-martial, but after listening to Lemp's report came to the conclusion that U 30 had acted in good faith and that the incident had been a genuine mistake. The Nazi Propaganda Ministry did not wish to publicise acceptance of responsibility, so Dönitz was ordered to keep the matter secret, by ordering the crew to keep quiet and to eradicate all other evidence of the *Athenia* from the U 30's logbook.

Meanwhile the Admiralty in London was more or less certain that the ship had been sunk by a U-boat and thought that Germany had issued an order for unconditional sea warfare. Instead of this Hitler put further restrictions on the U-boats, by preventing them from sinking anything that looked like a passenger liner, whether it was being escorted by armed ships or not. The British Admiralty, being unaware of these moves from the German side, stepped up their campaign and further lifted restrictions so that their ships had a freer hand in possible combat.

Some U-boat commanders obeyed Prize Ordinance to almost ridiculous lengths. Herbert Schultze in U 48, for example, radioed the Admiralty in London giving them his exact position and informed them "that he had just sunk a merchant ship which did not have time to send an SSS call, and would Winston Churchill please come to pick up the survivors?" The SSS call, incidentally, replaced the normal SOS when a vessel was being attacked by a submarine. This way the Royal Navy or Royal Air Force could race to the scene and perhaps help the stricken ship.

On another occasion U 48 attempted to stop the ss *Royal Sceptre*, but her shot across the

Gun drill on U 377. Operating this large 88mm gun in heavy seas was not easy. When not in use the end of the barrel was sealed with a watertight tampion, which can be seen in other photos.

Opposite page: *U 377 after the major refit of 1943. She is armed with two twin 20mm and one quadruple 20mm AA guns. Note the radar warning device which is visible next to the attack periscope. For identification of other important features see the diagram of a Type VII C on page 106. The commander, on tower at extreme left is Oblt. z. S. Gerhard Kluth.*

Inset: *U 377's quadruple 20mm AA gun. The circular lids of watertight ammunition containers are visible in front and behind the gun.*

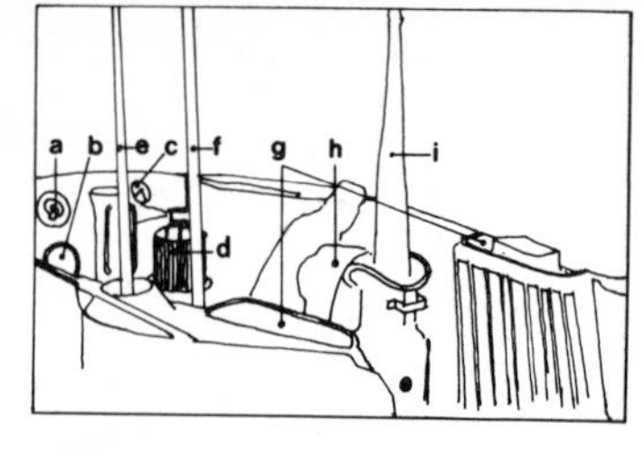

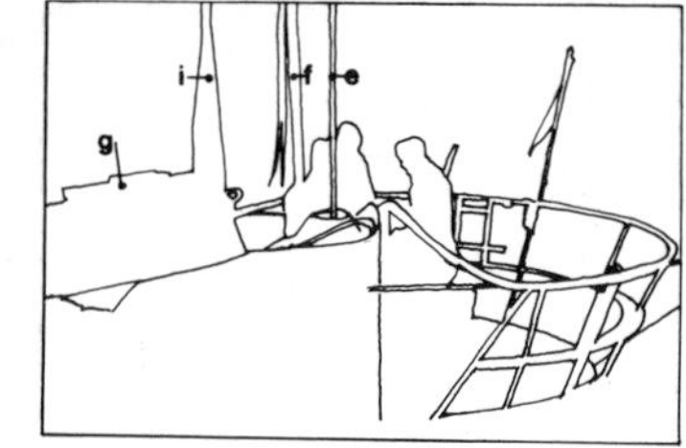

Close up of U 377's conning tower as it appeared before the major refit in 1943.
A Compass at the main steering position. B Dial for engine room telegraph. C Speaking tube with whistle. D Torpedo aiming device. E Rod aerial which could be raised and lowered. F 'Commander's flag pole'. G The ends of ventilation shafts. H Compass (covered with a coat). I Attack periscope.

bows resulted in the ship's increasing speed and instantly sending the SSS call. U 48 punched another shell into the engine room, bringing the ship to a halt. Herbert (nicknamed 'Vaddi') Schultze did not wish to injure the crew with more artillery fire, so he waited until everybody had abandoned ship and then fired a torpedo into her side. By this time U 48 was in an exceptionally dangerous position because ss *Royal Sceptre*'s radio officer did not abandon ship and had been sending the SSS call all the time. The use of radio, after being stopped, was against the rules of Prize Ordinance and Schultze could have sunk the merchant ship instantly. These radio signals forced U 48 to sail as quickly as possible away from the scene, in case British forces turned up, but Schultze was distressed at seeing all those men in the small lifeboats. Shortly after this incident the lookouts spotted another merchant ship, the ss *Browning*. A shot across her bows brought it to a standstill and the crew scrambled over the decks into the lifeboats. The men were surprised to see the U-boat closing in, but not for the kill, instead Schultze bellowed at them to get back on board. They were given ss *Royal Sceptre*'s last position and told to go and pick up the survivors! Very often, during the early months of the war, shipwrecked sailors found that they were chased by U-boats, who gave them clothing, food or charts. Unfortunately, as the war progressed, air-cover became too efficient and these humane operations had to be given up.

The Royal Navy blocked the English Channel with minefields and with regular patrols, barring the route to German vessels. This meant that the only route into the Atlantic was through the North Sea and around the north of Scotland. The Royal Air Force quickly organised regular patrols over these waters, making them dangerous to negotiate. The German Navy renamed the North Sea from the German *Nord See* to *Mord See*, meaning 'Murder Sea'. (There was also a British minefield between Scotland and Norway, but this accounted for only one German ship.)

Even in spite of this long voyage around the north of Scotland, U-boats managed to operate further west in the Atlantic than the Royal Navy could escort convoys. Air cover in the Western Approaches did not become established until 1940 and even then it was limited to coastal waters. Britain urgently needed naval bases as far west as possible to protect shipping in this area. The Royal Navy had given up its bases at Lough Swilly and Berehaven in the Republic of Ireland during 1938, without making provisions for their re-occupation in time of war, and Britain urgently needed bases in this area. Negotiations were therefore started in 1939 between the United Kingdom and Ireland to obtain the use of bases on the western coast, but the Irish Government did not help a great deal and Britain only had the use of bases at Londonderry and Belfast. Both were on the east coast and not very much further west than the Scottish, Welsh or English coast. However these two bases made it possible to extend the escorts for convoys from the 15th to the 19th Meridian, but the U-boats were already operating further west than this. After the fall of France, during June 1940, U-boats quickly made use of the French Atlantic ports and were thus enabled to operate still further out in the Western Approaches.

During this time the U-boats scored numerous individual successes, but this did not have a great impact upon the people of Great Britain. First, as there were only a few U-boats at sea, most merchant ships reached their destinations; secondly, Britain managed to sink U-boats faster than Germany replaced them; and thirdly, of more immediate concern to the people in Britain, the *Luftwaffe* was trying to win air superiority over the eastern part of the country, in preparation for an invasion. These frequent bomber raids over the English cities were causing far more havoc to the population than were the few U-boats. The Admiralty in London were not worried about U-boats at this stage of the war, because the new German magnetic mine was presenting them with far more serious problems.

There were also many Germans, including many members of Hitler's inner circle, who considered the U-boat arm to be an additional novelty, rather than a serious fighting force. To focus attention on to the U-boats, Dönitz planned a special raid – one which would not necessarily inflict a great strategic blow against Britain, but would let the world know that nothing was safe from his U-boats. This raid was probably the most remarkable U-boat mission of the war; perhaps it was even the most daring

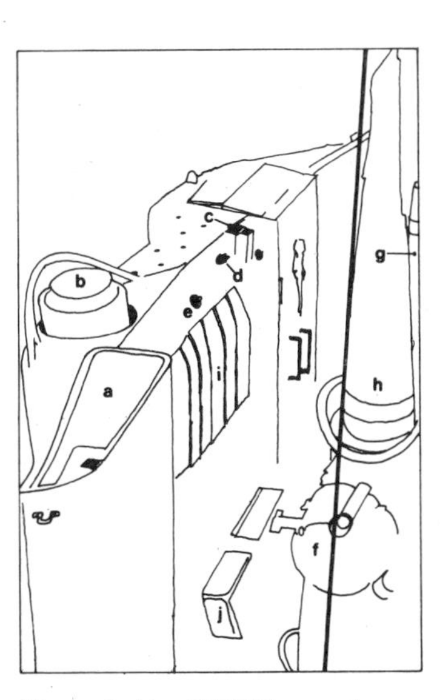

The port side of U 377's conning tower; looking forward. Features not clearly identified elsewhere are :–
A Grid over top of ventilation shaft. B Housing for extendable rod aerial. C Bracket for attaching grips and rails. (?) D Bullet holes made by cannon fire from a Liberator. E Brackets for attaching safety belts. F Portable signal lamp. G Radar detection aerial, just visible between edge of photo and periscope. H Attack periscope. The screw like threads are wires, firmly screwed to the side to prevent the head from vibrating and from creating too much of a wave, when in use. I Wooden planks attached to the metal walls. These were warmer to touch than metal and made the lookouts' life a little more comfortable. J Foot rests, above them are folding seats.

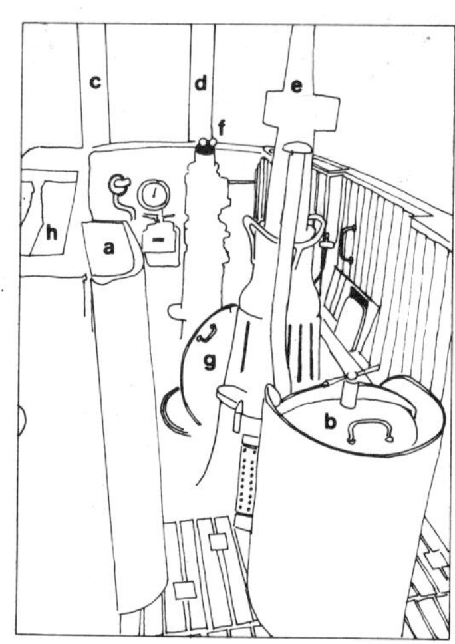

The bridge of U 776, looking forward. (1945)
A Grid over the top of a ventilation shaft. B Water and pressure resistant container, probably for AA ammunition. C Schnorkel. D Sky/navigation periscope. E Attack periscope with radar detection aerial. F Torpedo aimer with special binoculars in position. G Hatch. H Hohentwiel radar aerial. (Housed in the large slot.)

The conning tower of U 776. (1945)

The U-boat pens at Trondheim with U 953 (Type VII C) on the left and U 861 (Type IX D_2) next to the quay. Both boats were fitted with a 37mm AA gun on the lower platform and with two twin 20mm AA guns on the upper platform. The twins appear to have been dismantled on U 953 and on the other boat they are pointing directly at the camera, so that they are hardly visible. Note that the protective shield of the guns could be folded backwards and that U 861 has a circular radar detection aerial on the conning tower.

raid in submarine history. U 47 penetrated the defences of Scapa Flow and sank the British battleship HMS *Royal Oak.*

Scapa Flow, one of Britain's main anchorages, must have ranked among the most heavily guarded waters in the world. The possible entrances were guarded by mines, nets, sunken ships, regular patrols by the Royal Navy and by exceptionally strong adverse currents. These currents were faster than the top underwater speed of a submarine, thus making submerged attacks impossible. The story of Scapa Flow and U-boats really started during World War I as Korv Kpt von Henning and Kptlt Emsmann were lost, together with their boats and crews, while attempting to break into the Flow. Already before World War II several U-boats (particularly U 16, commanded by Kptlt Wellner), had patrolled the Orkney waters. U 16 managed to collect valuable information about currents, tides and Royal Navy patrols, which together with air photos made Dönitz think that a U-boat might just slip through the narrow Kirk Sound. There the navigable channel was only just over 15 metres wide and only about 3½ fathoms at its deepest point, but there were no visible obstructions and there was a chance to get through during slack water.[1]

For U 47 the story started as she was lying in port, ready to sail and only awaiting orders for her next voyage. Günther Prien, the commander, gathered that something was afoot when he was called to see the Commander of the U-boat fleet on a Sunday morning. On entering Dönitz's room he was faced with a map that had the name SCAPA FLOW printed at the top. At first Prien did not fully comprehend what was being said, he could only focus his attention on that well known name. After some general conversation, Dönitz asked whether Prien thought it possible to penetrate the defences of Scapa Flow and sink shipping there. Dönitz did not want an immediate answer. He told Prien to go away, take the maps with him and consider the matter in detail. He made it quite clear to Prien that nothing would be held against him if he considered the task impossible; he wanted his truthful and genuine answer.

Two days later Prien returned and said, "Yes". At that stage the officers and crew of U 47 had no clue as to their next mission. They must have guessed that they were about to embark on a short special operation, as fuel, fresh water and provisions which had already been carefully stored on board for the usual long trip, were unloaded. Eventually, after a special last minute check, U 47 slipped from her mooring and nosed through the North Sea. The crew's suspicions about something special lying ahead of them were further aroused as the lookouts spotted a good target and instead of attacking, U 47 slipped below the waves to hide. One dark night, while U 47 was lying on the surface recharging her batteries the IWO (First Watch Officer), Oblt z S Endrass, asked whether they were heading towards the Orkneys. "Yes!" answered Prien. "Hold on to something Endrass . . . we're going into Scapa Flow."

There was a moment of absolute silence. Endrass looked at Prien; only the gentle murmur of the diesels and the lapping of the water against the hull could be heard. "Oh – yes – that'll be OK," said Endrass, and then after further thought. "That'll be OK Herr Kaleu."[1]

Later, when the batteries had been charged and compressed air bottles filled, Prien ordered the boat to dive and all the men to assemble in the crew's quarters, where he informed them of their mission. He might have announced that they were going to watch a good football match, for his speech was met with great enthusiasm and everybody worked hard during the following hours to see that the machinery, for which they were responsible, functioned without a hitch. Meanwhile, U 47 had settled on the sea bed and after the work was completed everybody was ordered to their quarters and to keep completely silent, for Prien still expected the Royal Navy to have some secret submarine detection apparatus. So much attention was paid to silence that those who had to walk about the ship wrapped their shoes in rags.

The boat remained on the sea bed until the afternoon of October 13th, when the crew was woken up to consume a special meal, which could have been their last. Slowly the machinery

[1] Slack water is the period between the tides, when there is little or no current.

[1] Short for Kapitänleutnant.

was prepared for battle and everything given a final check, to make absolutely sure that it functioned. Shortly before 20.00 hours the boat was brought up from the sea bed to periscope depth. A quick look revealed nothing, so U 47 surfaced. The weather was absolutely perfect, but there was a magnificent display of northern lights in the sky, which was beautifully reflected in the mirror-smooth water. Prien considered postponing the raid until a darker night, but he thought that this would fray the nerves of his crew too much and it would be better to act while morale and reflexes were still strong. Quickly he came to the conclusion – now or never!

Unknown to Prien the Royal Navy had not been satisfied with the defences at Scapa Flow and was planning to sink an old ship on October 14th in the very channel that U 47 was heading for. So had Prien waited, it would probably have been 'never'.

Just before entering Kirk Sound one of the Chief Engineers reported to Wessels, who was LI, that the lubricating oil in one of the diesel engines contained an unusually high proportion of salt water. Wessels immediately informed Prien, who did not understand such technical matters and suggested that they should look at it when they got back home. Wessels insisted that it would be suicidal to continue, so Prien asked what had to be done. Wessels went to investigate. He found a small hole between the section containing cooling water and that containing lubricating oil. After some discussion the men came to the conclusion that the fault might temporarily be remedied by fitting a kind of gutter to drain the water through the oil section into the bilges. This idea worked and was in later years even installed as a standard fitting.

After this episode U 47 continued on her way. Prien had memorised the chart and he guided the boat through the narrow channel without reference to it. This is an exceptionally difficult task in daytime, so it is perhaps no wonder that the boat ran aground in the dead of night. U 47 was easily freed and eventually they were inside the British anchorage. Unfortunately for U 47,

Left: *Another view of U 953 and U 861. The rigid schnorkel has a 'beer barrel' head valve, which was a new design and only in limited use. The bracket to hold this mast can be seen on the conning tower, just below the wind deflector. (A circular air raid shelter is just visible in the background, above the conning tower of U 953. Sticking up from the deck, behind the two bollards, is an electric winch, which could haul ropes or anchor chain.)*

Right: *The periscopes of U 570.*
Left: *Surface or attack periscope.*
Right: *Sky periscope.*
The circular loop is a radio direction finder aerial. The size of the periscope heads is slightly distorted, with the sky periscope appearing smaller than it actually was because it is further away from the camera. Compare with later photos. Usually the sky periscope was not used in day time because it was so conspicuous.

most of the British fleet had departed and there were very few targets. The lookouts did, however, spot two shadows; one was a battleship lying in front of what looked like an aircraft carrier. The further ship presented a difficult target because it was shielded by the nearer one. U 47 shot a salvo of torpedoes towards this double target, but only one torpedo exploded and this, on hitting an anchor chain, did not cause any damage. The men aboard U-Prien expected the harbour to immediately erupt into activity, but after the explosion everything was as peaceful as before. Prien decided therefore to reload and have another shot. This second attempt had the desired effect. He was rewarded with a deafening roar and by seeing parts of the battleship blown into the sky. For a time Prien stared at the chaos; then, remembering that he was inside a British harbour, he ordered a quick retreat.

Both the diesel engines and the electric motors were used to push the U-boat as fast as possible along the surface. Suddenly a car was spotted on the black Mainland. It stopped, turned so that its headlamps were pointing towards U 47, and then chased back the way it had come. Had they been spotted? Detonating depth charges were heard, and then, just as they were slowing down to negotiate the narrow Kirk Sound, a destroyer was spotted rapidly closing in behind them. U 47 was already straining with all available power turning the propellers and the boat could not go faster. Prien therefore prepared to stop, in order that the crew might have a chance to leave the boat before it was turned into an iron coffin. Suddenly, surprisingly, the destroyer stopped, leaving U 47 in peace to thankfully negotiate the dangerous channel that separated them from the open sea.

Whilst reloading the torpedoes in Scapa Flow there had almost been another fatal calamity as one of the torpedo doors had sprung open, admitting vast quantities of water. The boat was on the surface and the low water pressure permitted the crew to seal off the leak. U 47 seemed to have been accident prone that night, because just after leaving Kirk Sound there was a noticeable lack of power, with one of the propellers losing revolutions. LI Wessels went to investigate and found that one of the joints on the propeller shaft had worked loose and needed urgent repair. It was impossible to go on, so there was no choice but to put the boat on the sea bed until the repairs were complete. Eventually the boat continued on its way.

The following day, on October 14th, the BBC in Britain announced that the battleship HMS *Royal Oak* had been sunk with 833 men on board and that the U-boat responsible had been destroyed by units of the Royal Navy. However as the broadcast was being made that U-boat was in fact already approaching the minefield that was guarding the low north German coastline, to return safely and without loss of life! Raeder and Dönitz met U 47 as the boat docked. It was aboard U-Prien that Grand Admiral Raeder announced that her commander had been awarded the Knight's Cross and that the whole crew was to fly to Berlin for an interview with the Führer. At the same time he made it known that Dönitz had been promoted from *Kapitän zur See* to Admiral. The raid certainly focussed attention on the U-boats; and they rose greatly in Hitler's esteem, at the same time becoming the main talking point throughout Germany.

Prien was by no means the only commander to take his boat into a British harbour. 'Vaddi' Schultze took U 48 into Portland harbour to 'lay eggs' (mines) and Kptlt Rollmann sailed U 34 into Falmouth harbour for another mining operation. Such undertakings were considered important, because even if no ships were sunk by the mines (usually they were quite successful), it did mean that the harbour would be out of use for a few days until the 'eggs' were cleared away. The U-boat men did not like mining operations because they received little credit for the sinkings, whereas with torpedoes they could add to their tonnage totals. Mining was also a little unnerving because British harbours were themselves guarded by minefields, which meant that navigation had to be absolutely faultless. Rollman considered his task of mining Falmouth more or less impossible and prepared to destroy his boat before the operation. The device for coding their signals was taken to pieces and the parts distributed among the men, who were told that they would be kicked in heaven if one piece was left in their pockets by the time they were captured.

U 34 approached Falmouth from the Atlantic and the entire operation was carried out from below the surface, with Rollmann not even daring to raise the periscope in case the motor noise was picked up by some British listening device. Entering the harbour is no easy matter on the best of days and it is a small miracle when such a task is carried out when totally 'blind' in a huge submarine. U-Rollmann successfully carried out its mining operation and managed to return safely to the open sea. The undertaking had been such a strain on the crew that many men jumped out of their places as Rollmann raised the periscope. Normally the periscope motor noise is taken for granted.

One might wonder where the detailed information for such delicate navigation came from. In the case of Falmouth this was probably collected by a visiting 'student' some years before the war. A colleague, Mrs D. Cook, who did not know that I was working on this book, once mentioned during a discussion on 'spying' how she had met a German student at Falmouth before the war. They had met at a sailing school there and she had noticed this fellow because he spent most of the time photographing the harbour and coast line. It is quite possible that a fair amount of information about Britain was gathered this way.

One of the major problems which faced the U-boat arm during the first months of the war was the quality of its torpedoes, which were most unreliable and often failed to function. During the Norwegian campaign of spring 1940, for example, at least 42 out of a total of 48 U-boats came in contact with the enemy. On these occasions more than thirty attacks were failures because the torpedoes failed to do their job. The U-boats attacked some 25 fighting ships, but managed to sink only one British submarine. U 47 attacked two cruisers, the battleship HMS *Warspite*, and several transports, but all these escaped because of faulty torpedoes. HMS *Warspite* was also attacked by U 46 (Sohler), U 38 (Liebe) and by U 37 (Hartmann), but was not even seriously damaged. U 25 (Schütze) attacked an entire destroyer flotilla near Narvik without success! U 30 (Lemp) attacked the 31,000 ton battleship HMS *Barham*, his crew heard the torpedoes hit, but there was no detonation. Perhaps the most disappointing failure was when U 56 (Zahn) attacked the huge battleships HMS *Hood*, HMS *Nelson* and HMS *Rodney* on October 30th, 1939—and none of the battleships sank. Adding to their disappointment was the rumour that the British Prime Minister

Right: *A Type VII in France during 1941. This shows how little of the actual boat is normally visible, even when fully surfaced.*

Below right: *Funkobermaat Paul Czinczoll coming out of the 'Galley Hatch' of U 377.*

Below: *U 377's Diesel Obermaschinist, Jak Mallmann, on duty in the engine room. Autumn 1943.*

had been aboard HMS *Nelson*—but from Winston Churchill's Memoirs one learns that this was not true.

Not all these failures were straightforward disappointments. Prien gave everybody aboard his ship one of their most hair-raising moments of their lives and almost lost his U 47 as a result. It happened when he had become fed up with patrolling the seas and decided to try his luck inside a fiord. After a fruitless search the boat was laid on the bottom to wait for darkness. Towards afternoon a strange noise, which no-one had heard before, was picked up. Investigating Prien discovered that an entire supply convoy had moored not very far away, and that the strange noise had been made by the anchor chains. This was not only the target every U-boat man dreamed about, but also a golden opportunity of perhaps crippling the entire British land forces by removing their supplies. It had not been all that long ago since Prien had failed to sink a British cruiser owing to torpedo trouble and at the same time jamming the boat into the fiord bed; luckily U 47 was submerged at the time and was not discovered. This therefore was the chance to bring new life and instil better morale into his jaded crew.

U 47 shot a salvo of torpedoes at the convoy, but again nothing happened, except that the boat became stuck on the fiord bed. Being on the surface this time, U-Prien was now in a difficult predicament, especially as one of the torpedoes missed the convoy and exploded with a loud roar at the far end of the fiord. All the tricks he knew failed to free the boat. The IWO jumped below to destroy secret papers while Prien ordered the crew on deck, not to abandon ship, but to walk, as a group, from one end of the boat to the other, so that it would start rocking and perhaps prise itself from its firm grip of terra firma. While this was going on they received a message via flashlamp from a British destroyer. "Shall I send a confusing signal?" asked the radio officer. "For God's sake no!" cried Prien. "They probably think we are a rock or pensioned-off lighthouse." U 47 was eventually freed and it managed to depart from the scene.

It is no wonder that Prien and many other commanders were bitterly complaining to Dönitz about such incidents and that some of them were threatening not to go to sea if the failures continued. Prien pointed out that the *OKM* could not expect him to 'fight with a dummy rifle'. Dönitz was just as troubled as the commanders about the failures and a full-scale court of inquiry was set up. This resulted in a court martial of technical staff. It appeared that the high air pressure which built up inside the submarine when submerged for any length of time was responsible in that it upset the delicate torpedo mechanism.

But the 'kindness' of shooting *dead* torpedoes at British ships was being returned by Coastal Command of the Royal Air Force, who were in turn throwing *dead* bombs at the U-boats! During November 1939 reconaissance aircraft were issued with bombs so that the crews could attack any U-boats they met during their patrols. Contrary to the general opinion of the day, submarines are difficult targets to hit with bombs, because they are highly mobile and can easily move out of the way before the missile hits them. This point was eventually brought home by irate Royal Navy Submarine commanders, who complained that Coastal Command should be able to distinguish between German and Allied submarines before dropping 'things' that might accidentally go 'bang'. Eventually Coastal Command was issued with a far superior weapon, an aerial shallow-set depth charge. These were fitted with a special break-off nose and tail, so that they would follow a good path through the air like a bomb, and on hitting the water would behave like a depth charge, meaning that a direct hit was not necessary because a near miss would still damage the boat.

By the end of 1940 there had been a drastic change in the war. U-boat operations in the North Sea had become more difficult and most of them had moved far out into the Atlantic. After the fall of France, during June 1940, it became possible for the U-boats to use the French Atlantic ports and thus roam further west. These bases would have made it possible for small (Type II) coastal boats to operate on the important shipping routes, but their range would still be far too limited and they were rapidly replaced by larger, more efficient Type VII boats. Most of the Type II were moved to the submarine schools in the Baltic.

The *OKM* was also slowly revising the Prize Ordinance Regulations, each step making the U-boats more deadly, until eventually in August 1940, Hitler declared a total blockade of the British Isles. This meant that any ship in that area could be attacked on sight, without warning. This declaration was followed up with an extensive amount of propaganda in Germany, giving the impression that the U-boats were controlling the entire Atlantic. Newsflashes of U-boat successes would often interrupt normal radio programmes. For Britain this period was certainly a grim time, with barely sufficient supplies getting through to keep the island from disaster. Although the United States had not yet come into the war, they were already helping Britain by operating a type of cash-and-carry general stores, meaning that anybody could buy war supplies from them, provided the goods were paid for and fetched. The Royal Navy was preventing the few German ships from crossing the Atlantic, so the service was only of use to the Allies.

Because of this assistance, several influential Germans urged Hitler to declare war on the United States, which he avoided at all cost. Although it was Britian's 'darkest hour', the German economy was also struggling hard for their greater stability. Conflict with the United States was avoided to such an extent that U-boats received instructions not to attack American ships, even if these appeared in the blockade area. The first major confrontation occurred on June 20th, 1940 when U 203, commanded by Kptlt Mützelburg, sighted the USS *Texas*. Not being sure about procedure, U 203 radioed for permission to shoot. Dönitz guessed that this was a direct challenge by the United States and consulted Hitler before sending an answer. The reply took the form of a general signal to all U-boats that conflict with America was to be avoided and that only hostile ships could be attacked. The signal stated that ships sailing without lights at night time were not necessarily hostile.

The United States at this time was making little attempt to avoid conflict with Germany. This was not kept secret for President Roosevelt stated quite openly, while discussing the Battle of the Atlantic, that one does not wait for a rattlesnake to bite before hitting back. Seeing that they were probably going to be involved in the war sooner or later, the United States obtained permission from Britain to establish bases on British territory. In return the USA gave Britain 50 old-fashioned destroyers. These were far from being in good condition, but they were better than no destroyers at all. Crewed by the Royal Navy they became a familiar sight along the Atlantic shipping routes.

The German methods of attack also changed as time went on. The initial fear of Britain having some secret detection apparatus finally dissolved when Prien penetrated Scapa Flow and after that U-boat commanders were happier to approach close to British units. Eventually these fears disappeared completely after several U-boats had passed accidentally within 100 metres of British warships, without being detected. The commanders also learned that they could even outrun some Royal Navy ships on the surface. These factors contributed to the different methods of attack, so that instead of firing a salvo of, say, three torpedoes, the U-boat would approach so closely that it could guarantee a hit with only one. These attacks became so daring that some U-boats actually penetrated into the columns of the convoys and picked out the fattest targets at point-blank range.

The struggle in the Atlantic evolved into a fierce and ruthless battle for superiority in the shipping lanes and the Atlantic became one of the most important battlefields during World War II. Lengthy volumes have been written about this theatre of war and the majority of U-boat publications describe this involved conflict. In view of the magnitude of the subject and the abundance of literature already devoted to it, it is felt unnecessary to evaluate the Battle for the Atlantic in this book. The vital statistics of the battle, however, are shown on the following pages. For further information the reader is asked to consult the books listed in the bibliography.

Looking from the commander's attack position upwards through the hatch. U 377, with Otto Köhler on the left.

3

The Essence of the Battle of the Atlantic

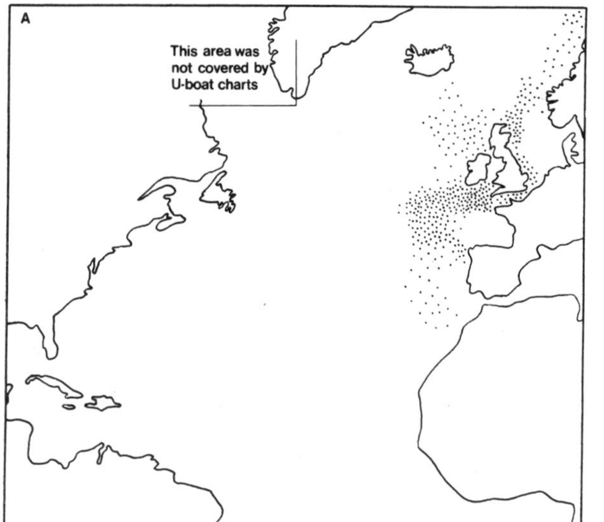

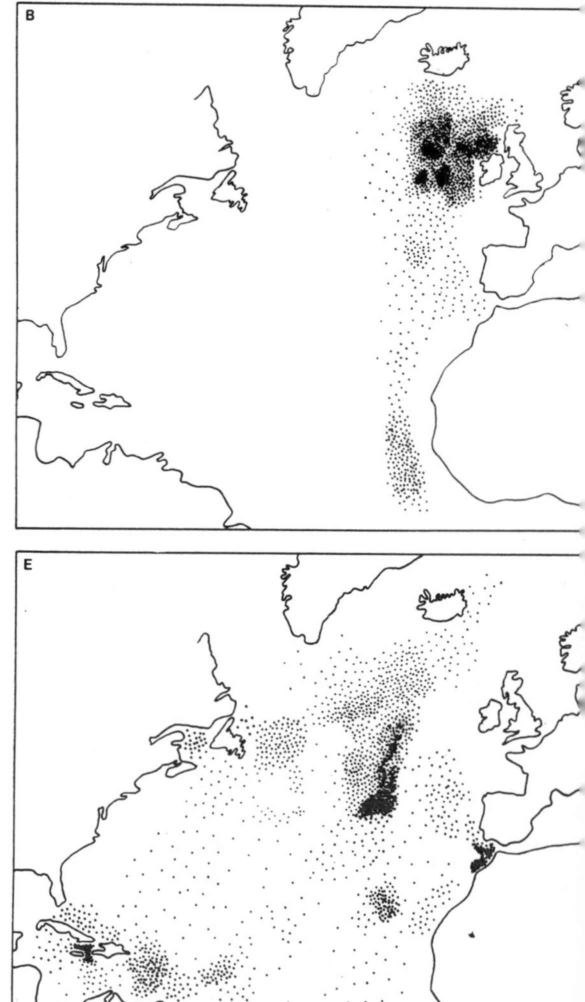

The Battle ot the Atlantic in Maps.

One dot represents one sunk merchant ship

Months covered by the maps.

Atlantic Map A September 1939–July 1940
Atlantic Map B August 1940–April 1941
Atlantic Map C May 1941–January 1942
Atlantic Map D February 1942–October 1942
Atlantic Map E November 1942–July 1943
Atlantic Map F April 1943–May 1944
Atlantic Map G June 1944–May 1945

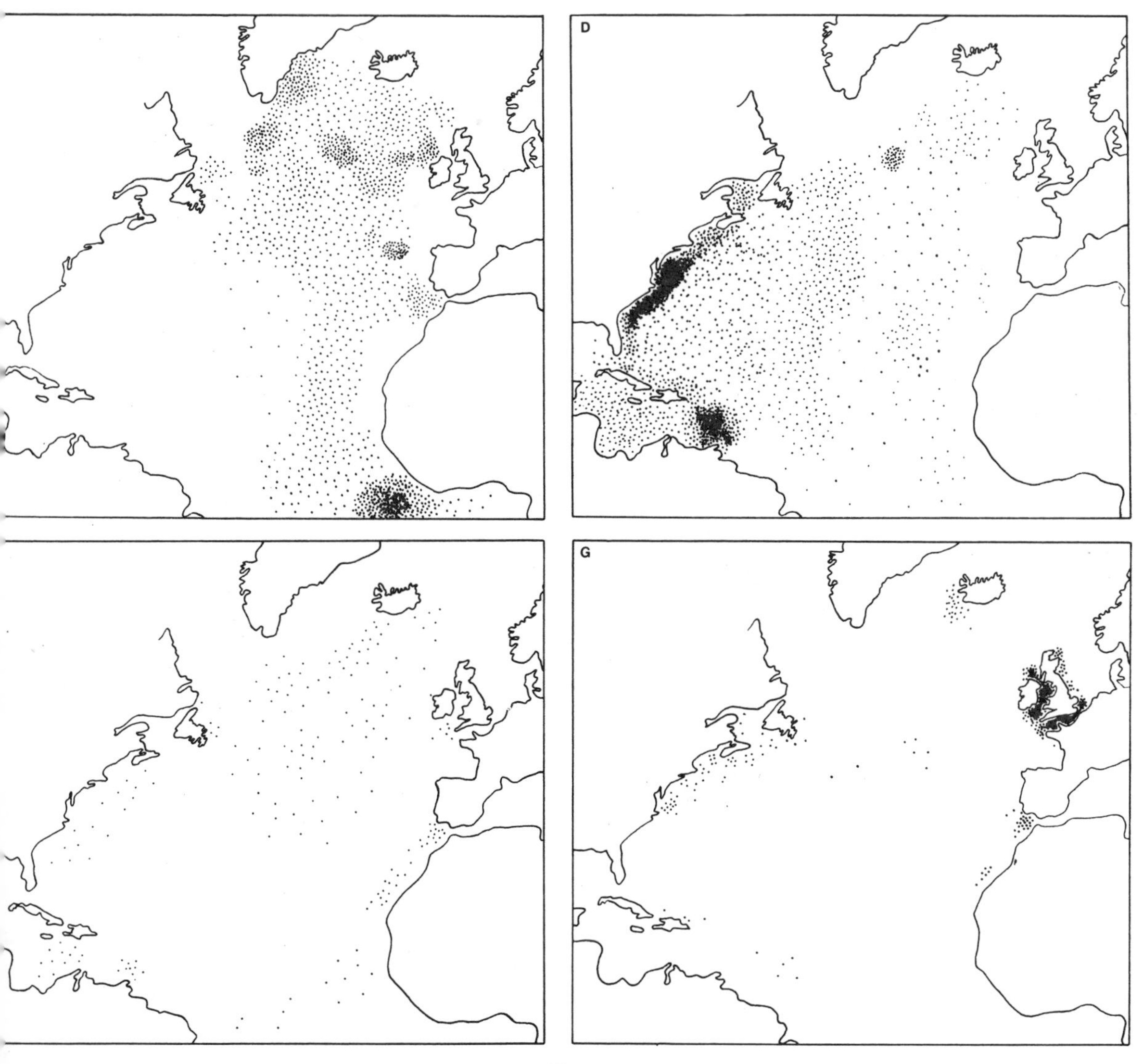
D
G

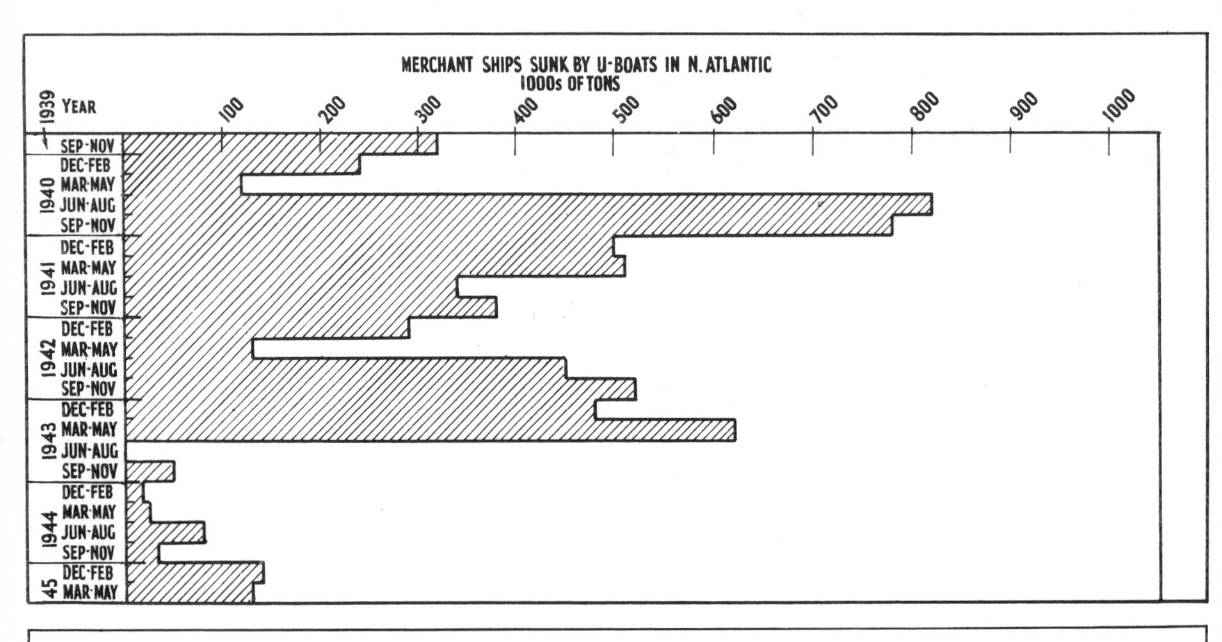
MERCHANT SHIPS SUNK BY U-BOATS IN N. ATLANTIC
1000s OF TONS
YEAR
100
200
300
400
500
600
700
800
900
1000
1939
SEP-NOV
1940
DEC-FEB
MAR-MAY
JUN-AUG
SEP-NOV
1941
DEC-FEB
MAR-MAY
JUN-AUG
SEP-NOV
1942
DEC-FEB
MAR-MAY
JUN-AUG
SEP-NOV
1943
DEC-FEB
MAR-MAY
JUN-AUG
SEP-NOV
1944
DEC-FEB
MAR-MAY
JUN-AUG
SEP-NOV
45
DEC-FEB
MAR-MAY

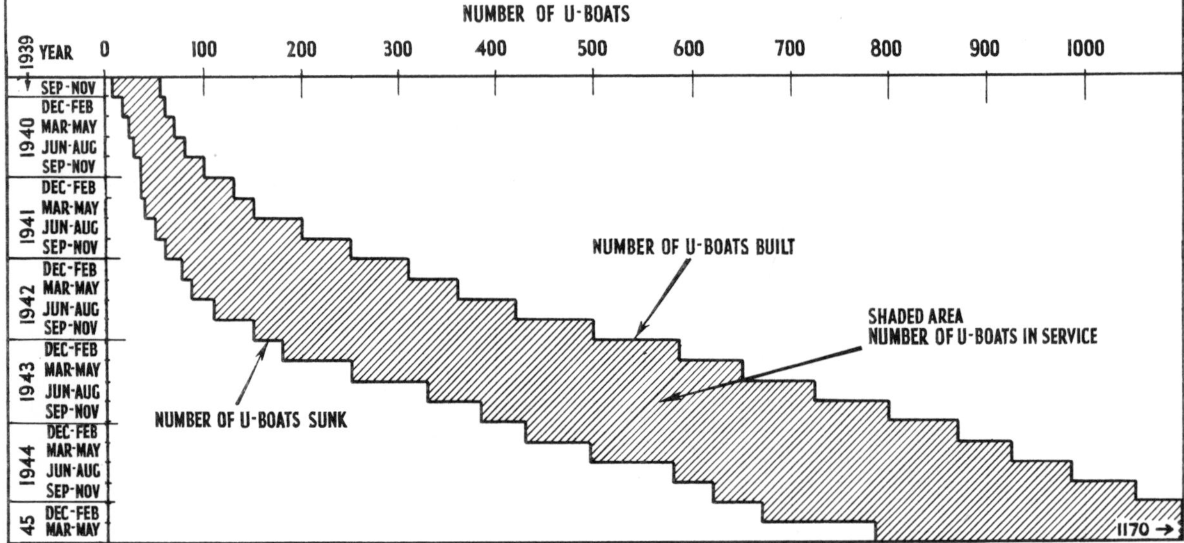
NUMBER OF U-BOATS
YEAR
0
100
200
300
400
500
600
700
800
900
1000
1939
SEP-NOV
1940
DEC-FEB
MAR-MAY
JUN-AUG
SEP-NOV
1941
DEC-FEB
MAR-MAY
JUN-AUG
SEP-NOV
1942
DEC-FEB
MAR-MAY
JUN-AUG
SEP-NOV
1943
DEC-FEB
MAR-MAY
JUN-AUG
SEP-NOV
1944
DEC-FEB
MAR-MAY
JUN-AUG
SEP-NOV
45
DEC-FEB
MAR-MAY
NUMBER OF U-BOATS BUILT
SHADED AREA
NUMBER OF U-BOATS IN SERVICE
NUMBER OF U-BOATS SUNK
1170 →

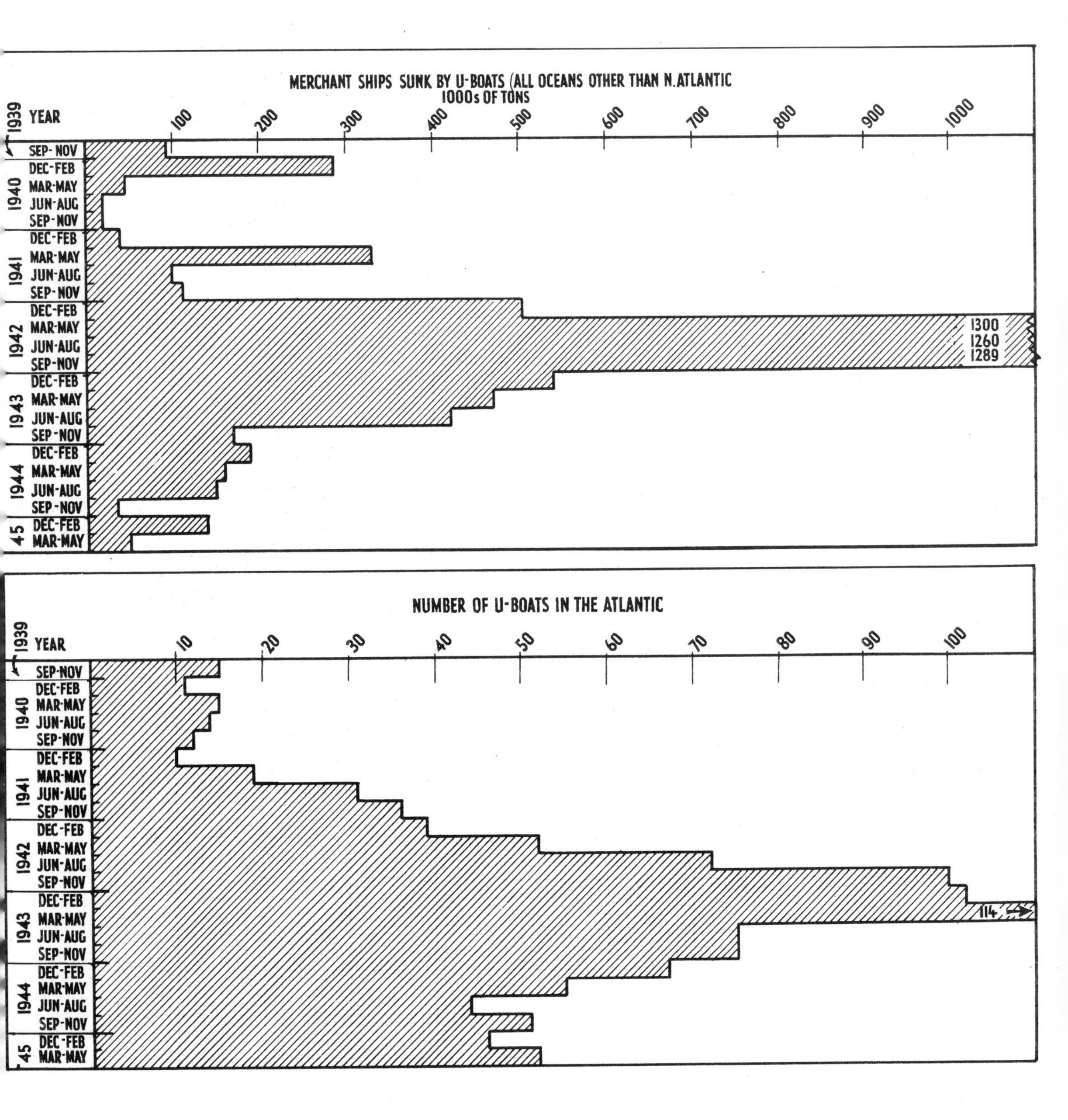
MERCHANT SHIPS SUNK BY U-BOATS (ALL OCEANS OTHER THAN N. ATLANTIC
1000s OF TONS
YEAR
100
200
300
400
500
600
700
800
900
1000
1939
SEP-NOV
1940
DEC-FEB
MAR-MAY
JUN-AUG
SEP-NOV
1941
DEC-FEB
MAR-MAY
JUN-AUG
SEP-NOV
1942
DEC-FEB
MAR-MAY
JUN-AUG
SEP-NOV
1300
1260
1289
1943
DEC-FEB
MAR-MAY
JUN-AUG
SEP-NOV
1944
DEC-FEB
MAR-MAY
JUN-AUG
SEP-NOV
45
DEC-FEB
MAR-MAY
NUMBER OF U-BOATS IN THE ATLANTIC
YEAR
10
20
30
40
50
60
70
80
90
100
114
1939
1940
1941
1942
1943
1944
45

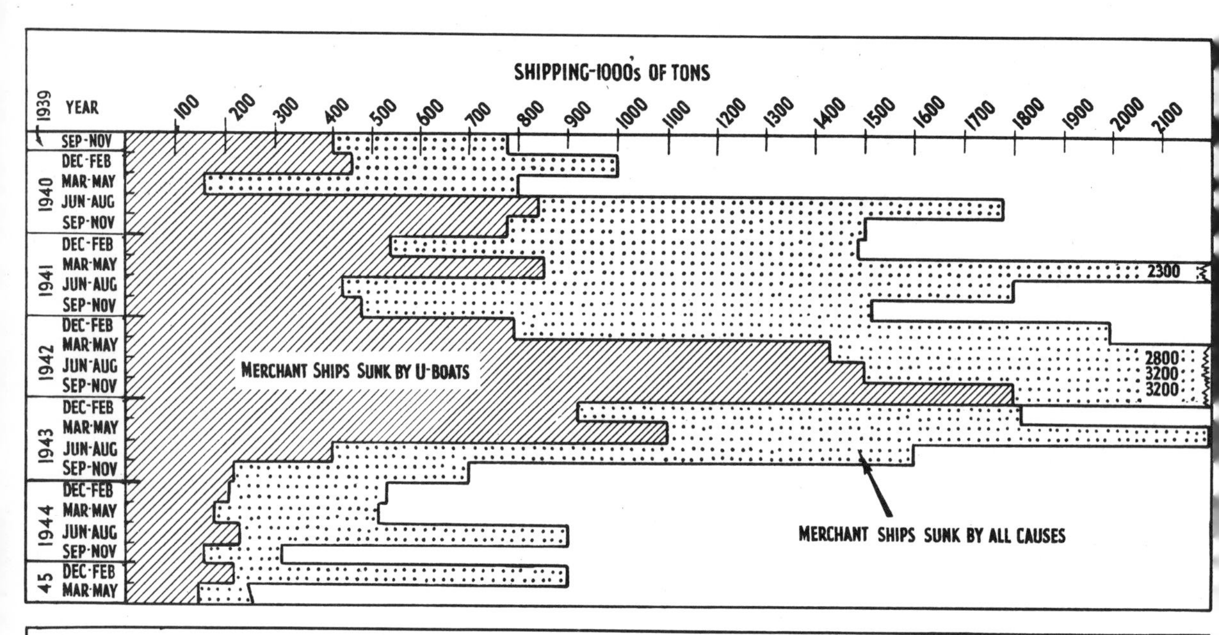
SHIPPING-1000's OF TONS
YEAR
1939
100
200
300
400
500
600
700
800
900
1000
1100
1200
1300
1400
1500
1600
1700
1800
1900
2000
2100
SEP-NOV
1940
DEC-FEB
MAR-MAY
JUN-AUG
SEP-NOV
1941
DEC-FEB
MAR-MAY
JUN-AUG
SEP-NOV
1942
DEC-FEB
MAR-MAY
JUN-AUG
SEP-NOV
1943
DEC-FEB
MAR-MAY
JUN-AUG
SEP-NOV
1944
DEC-FEB
MAR-MAY
JUN-AUG
SEP-NOV
45
DEC-FEB
MAR-MAY
2300
2800
3200
3200
MERCHANT SHIPS SUNK BY U-BOATS
MERCHANT SHIPS SUNK BY ALL CAUSES

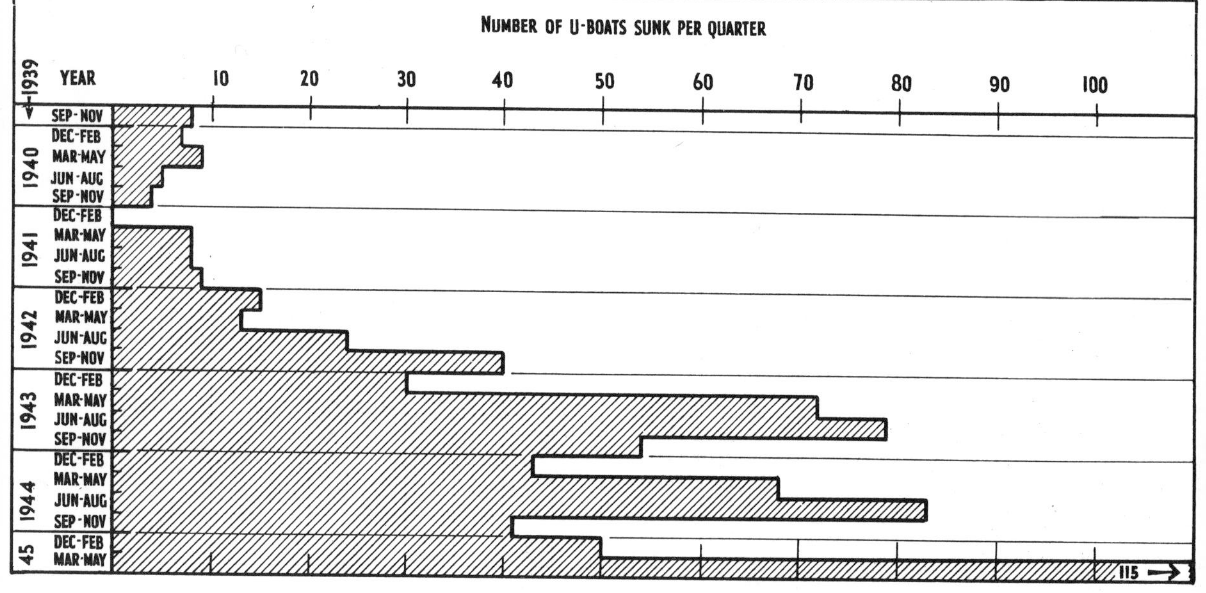
NUMBER OF U-BOATS SUNK PER QUARTER
YEAR
1939
10
20
30
40
50
60
70
80
90
100
SEP-NOV
1940
DEC-FEB
MAR-MAY
JUN-AUG
SEP-NOV
1941
DEC-FEB
MAR-MAY
JUN-AUG
SEP-NOV
1942
DEC-FEB
MAR-MAY
JUN-AUG
SEP-NOV
1943
DEC-FEB
MAR-MAY
JUN-AUG
SEP-NOV
1944
DEC-FEB
MAR-MAY
JUN-AUG
SEP-NOV
45
DEC-FEB
MAR-MAY
115

4

Away from the Convoy Routes

The Black Sea

By the summer of 1942 the German forces had spread so far east that they controlled parts of Russia and territory right up to the shores of the Black Sea. This inland sea was of little naval importance, as there were only a few insignificant ships, carrying small amounts of supplies from neutral Turkey to Russia. Strategically this was of no great threat to Germany, but a show of force was necessary to control the waterway and to make the local inhabitants believe that they were being ruled by a powerful military organisation—also to impress this on Turkey, in case she thought of joining the war against Germany. It was decided to move several surface ships and U-boats from Germany into the Black Sea. The U-boats were to be stationed at Constanca and Feodosia.

Such an undertaking was not as difficult as it might appear. It was possible to bring small Type II boats overland from their Baltic bases. They made their way, under their own power, through the Kiel Canal to Hamburg, from where they could continue along the river Elbe to Dresden. There the small 250-ton boats were lifted out of the water and taken on road transporters by autobahn to Regensburg, where they could be refloated in the river Danube to continue under their own power to the Black Sea. Three boats had arrived at Constanca by the autumn of 1942 and another three were shipped over as soon as the weather permitted the use of the inland routes during the following spring.

Between them these six boats, U 9, U 18, U 19, U 20, U 23, and U 24, sailed on about 55 operational tours, sinking nine small fighting ships and 25 merchant ships with a total of about 45000 tons. U 9 was eventually destroyed during a Russian air raid on Constanca. When the Russian army finally cut off their supply lines, the other five boats made their way to Turkey, where they were scuttled and the crews interned. This was, in the opinion of their commanders, infinitely preferable to allowing boats or men fall into Russian hands.

The Mediterranean Sea

Italy joined the war on June 10th, 1940 and fighting immediately broke out in North Africa between the Italian Army and British Forces. Some eight months later, Germany began to support the Italians by sending motorised, armoured troops (the Afrikakorps under the leadership of General Erwin Rommel). Provisions for these units were shipped across the Mediterranean where the Royal Navy, although badly shaken, was striking hard at the German supply lines. Eventually this struggle reached such a pitch that Britain was destroying about three-quarters of the German supplies. Thus it became clear that the war in the desert would come to a halt unless the German control of the shipping lanes could be reinstated. The *Oberkommando der Wehrmacht*, (*OKW* – Supreme Command of the Armed Forces) ordered the Navy to send U-boats into the Mediterranean. This was completely against Dönitz's plans. He argued that such action would only weaken the wolf packs in the Atlantic.

Up to the time that U-boats started to infiltrate through the Straits of Gibraltar, the Royal Navy in the Mediterranean had not developed any great submarine defensive methods, because, although the Italians had a large submarine fleet, their training had been so poor and old-fashioned that they presented no real threat.

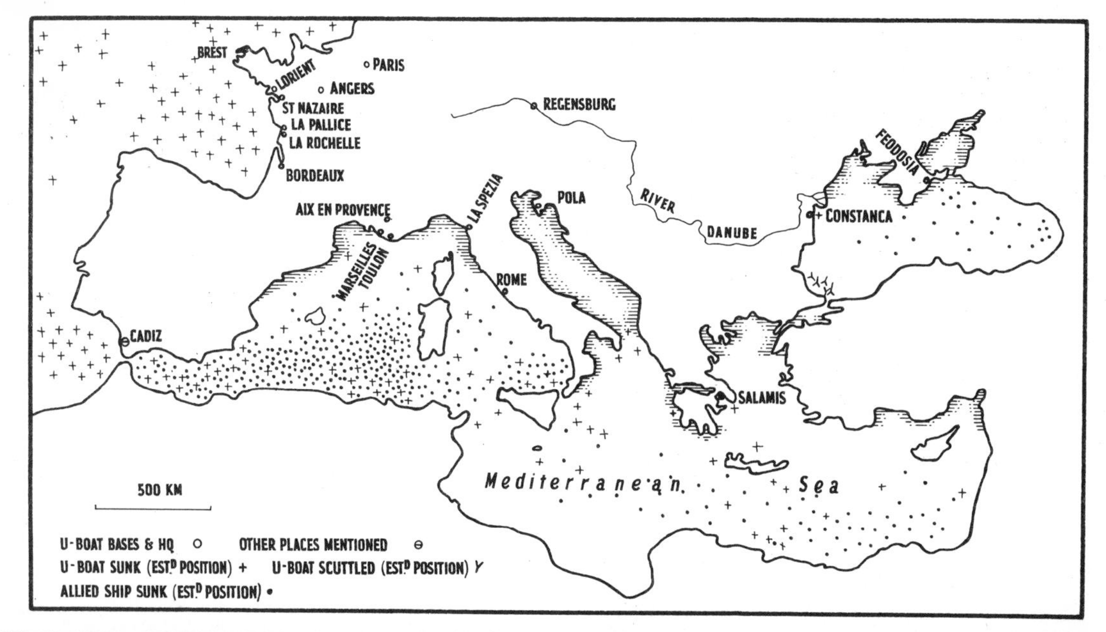

The electric motor control panel of HMS Graph *ex U 570 (Looking forward to the diesel engine room)*

The engine room of HMS Graph*, ex U 570. Note that the German name plates have not been removed.*

Entering the Mediterranean, however, was no easy matter since the Royal Navy maintained a heavy blockade across the narrow Straits of Gibraltar. U-boats trying to creep past the blockade did have a slight advantage in being able to benefit from a strong underwater current flowing in from the Atlantic. Furthermore, there was a startling difference in water temperature and/or salt content at a depth of 40 to 50 metres. This was well-known and as it reflected asdic impulses it was used to shield submarines from their attackers.

In spite of the heavy blockade six U-boats managed to slip past the British defence vessels. There was no hard and fast rule about how U-boats should attempt to beat the blockade and

U 570. One of the circular pressurised doors. This photo was taken during a re-fit in port. The pipes leading through the hatch are removed when the boat goes to sea. The wheel in the upper left corner operates number five vent.

commanders were left to decide the best method for themselves. U 81, commanded by Kapitänleutnant Guggenberger, made the journey on the surface at night taking maximum advantage of the incoming tide. The passage was quite nerve-wracking as not only did the boat pass two fishing vessels and two destroyers, but at one stage it was illuminated by a beam of light from a lighthouse at Tarifa (Spain). Once in the Mediterranean U 81 received a signal informing it to accompany U 205 to locate a fleet of British warships. Careful calculations and good guesswork was necessary to work out the route of this fleet, because the signal was several hours old by the time it was picked up. Just after 1400 hours on October 13th Guggenberger spotted warship mastheads through his periscope and closed in to attack. The initial attack of a salvo of four torpedoes produced no following depth charges. Then, just as the men thought that they had got away, an asdic 'ping' was heard. Well over 100 depth charges fell, all of which Guggenberger managed to dodge and eventually bring his boat safely back to port. As a result of this attack the battleship HMS *Malaya* and the pride of the Royal Navy, the aircraft carrier HMS *Ark Royal*, complete with its aircraft were damaged. The *Malaya* managed to limp into Gibraltar harbour. HMS *Ark Royal*, attempting to reach the same base, sank just a few miles short. The entire crew with one exception were taken off alive. Unfortunately all the *Ark Royal*'s aircraft went down with her because, as she started to take in water, the angle of the flight deck was too steep for them to take off.

HMS *Ark Royal* was not the only aircraft-carrier to go to the bottom of the Mediterranean. U 73, commanded by Korvettenkapitän Rosenbaum, scored four hits against the carrier HMS *Eagle*, which sank ten minutes later, taking some 230 men with her. U 73 also escaped a barrage of depth charges and hunted for a further year before being herself sunk by USS *Wolsey* and USS *Trippe*. Both Guggenberger and Kapitänleutnant H. Deckert (U 73's last commander) escaped and together with some of their crews were taken prisoners.

Another great success for the U-boats was the destruction of HMS *Barham*, the only British battleship to be sunk on the high seas. Torpedoes from U 331, commanded by Freiherr von Tiesenhausen, set off an explosion in her magazine, causing her to blow up with 962 men on board. U 331 had several narrow escapes in the Mediterranean. Once while surfacing Tiesenhausen opened the 'lid' as soon as his LI shouted 'Tower clear'. On looking up he saw an aeroplane pass directly overhead which did not spot them! On another occasion, closing in to attack a target, Tiesenhausen raised his periscope to take aim, only to find that he was so close that the target filled his entire field of vision. Eventually he steered into a suitable position and fired a salvo from periscope depth. This meant that the boat was suddenly several tons lighter and started to rise. The LI was working feverishly to get the boat down again. Tiesenhausen meanwhile was horrified to see through the periscope that the battleship HMS *Valiant* was steering straight at them. Luckily the *Valiant* changed course just before U 331 broke the surface, and when the helpless U-boat was seen it was too late to swing back on to the original collision course. She was also too close to the U-boat for her guns to bear down on to U 331. This tragic-

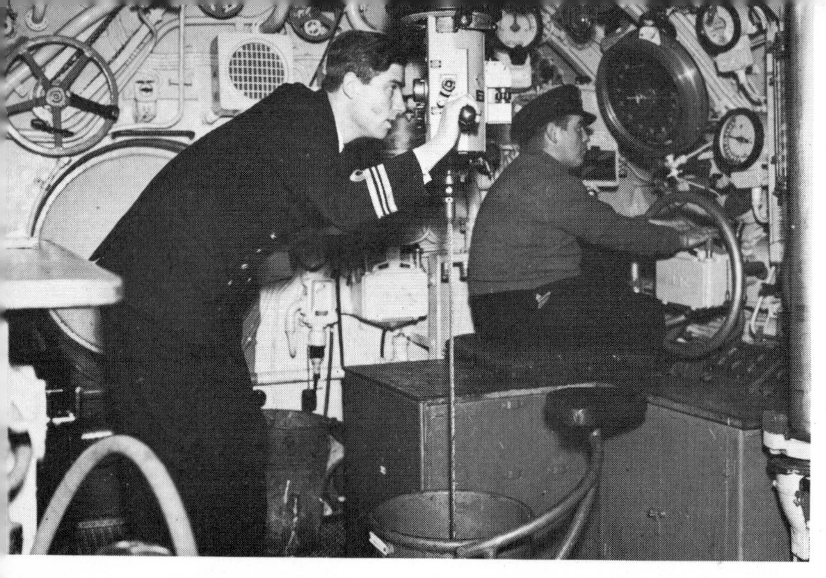

Above: *The trimming panel.*
....and some people have difficulty driving automatic cars....!

Above left: *The control room of HMS* Graph, *ex U 570, with a British officer at the sky/ navigation periscope. The man on the right is operating the hydroplane controls.*

Centre: *The control room was just one mass of dials, manometers, taps and switches.......... This photo shows the hydroplane controls.*

Bottom: *A British crew in the forward torpedo compartment of HMS* Graph. *Above their heads are chains and iron rails for hoisting torpedoes. The circular white covers of the upper two torpedo tubes are just visible in the background.*

comical situation resulted in many rounds being fired harmlessly above the submarine while she gratefully dived back to the relative safety of the depths and made off as quickly as her motors could drive her!

The Mediterranean was by no means a happy hunting ground for U-boats, because the natural elements and geographic location made operations rather difficult. Being fully enclosed by land the sea was under constant surveillance by the RAF and the cloudless days and nights and smooth water made it easy to spot a submarine, even when at periscope depth. The rough overcast weather of the Atlantic was far more suitable for the U-boats. Life in the Mediterranean became so difficult that daytime surfacing had to be completely abandoned. Some U-boats tried floating on the surface so that only the conning towers projected above the water, but although the boat could disappear in ten seconds, that was not really safe.

Another difficulty was that the inside of the boats became very hot, making life unbearable. Whereas in the Atlantic the crew might be ordered to rest so that they would be ready for action, in the Mediterranean the temperature on board made reactions very sluggish and this can be dangerous in a submarine. In the Atlantic U-boats were largely fighting comparatively defenceless convoys; in this theatre, however, they were up against the cream of the Royal Navy. Perhaps it was this fact which contributed to a relatively high number of escapes from sinking boats. The U-boat men knew that they were fighting under exceptional conditions, where at any time they might be spotted, so they were always prepared to 'get out quick'. The Royal Navy did not have to maintain constant speeds as with their Atlantic convoy duties and thus could allow more time to pick up survivors.

German submarines in the Mediterranean, including those operating in Italian waters, never came under Italian command. The *OKM* disliked the old-fashioned Italian training methods and refused to accept command of Italian boats operating from German bases in France, in order that the Italians would not have an excuse to ask, in return, for control of German boats in their areas. Some of the German U-boats did operate from Italian ports, but were always controlled by German personnel. A few German U-boats were commissioned into the Italian Navy, but these were built with Italian money for Italy and most of them were handed back to Germany a few months later.

Paukenschlag To America

The Japanese attack on Pearl Harbor, where they destroyed the United States Pacific Fleet on December 7th, 1941, encouraged the U-boat headquarters to also plan an attack against America. This plan was more or less complete by the time Germany declared war against the USA, but could not be carried out on the scale envisaged because there just were not sufficient boats available for immediate departure. Kapitänleutnant Hardegen, commander of U 123, returned from leave without being recalled and other large U-boats were hurriedly prepared in the bunkers. A flotilla of six boats was at sea, heading west, by Christmas Day. The plan was that boats should sail towards different American ports and that they would commence their attack at exactly the same time.

This first wave of boats left a world conditioned to total war. Lighthouses, navigation aids and even lights in dwellings had been extinguished at the outset. Towns were subject to air raids and were therefore blacked out. Radios on ships were only used in emergencies, so as not to reveal the sender's position. Every person had settled down to this frightful new way of life; even the once plentiful fishing vessels had largely disappeared and those remaining were treated with great caution by the U-boats in case they were disguised submarine traps.

After battling their way across the cold, stormy Atlantic, the U-boats cautiously crept towards the American coast, where, to their surprise, they found a completely different world. City lights and navigation aids were brightly illuminated and ships were sailing, as in peacetime, with all lights showing. The usual trade routes were being followed and even the ships' masters were freely discussing problems over the air. The expected strong U-boat defences were also non-existent, so that the sea wolves could pick and choose the best targets.

At zero hour the tanker *Norness* sank as a result of a torpedo hit, but sent an SOS stating that it had hit a mine. The following day all

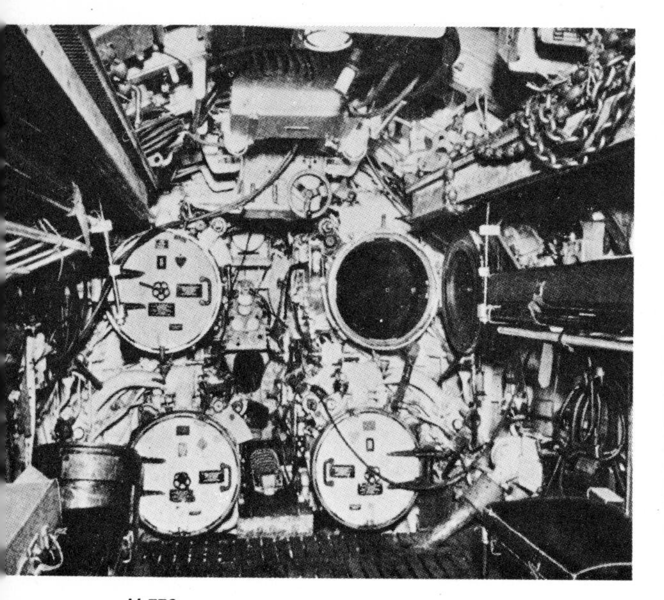

U 776.
Bow torpedo compartment with four torpedo tubes.

Stern torpedo compartment with one tube. On the left is a compressor.

shipping in that area was warned to take extra caution because of the danger of mines! The early American days proved restful for the U-boat crews and the nights produced rich hunting booty. It became evident very quickly that there were no anti-submarine patrols, so the look-outs had to merely take their choice of the ships passing near to them. It is no small wonder that this operation became known as the U-boats' 'Second Golden Period'. The fantastically high successes of 1940 were being repeated. News about the rich harvest reaped off the American coast spread like wildfire through the U-boat bases and everybody hoped that they would get a chance to cross the Atlantic. Later on in 1942 several supply U-boats were stationed at a secret rendezvous some 1000 kilometres west of New York, so that the smaller Type VII boats could also cross the Atlantic and operate in American waters.

At first the United States did not have many submarine chaser vessels available, specially as most of their Pacific Fleet was destroyed at Pearl Harbor. It was not long, however, before they started to alter the balance, especially in the area between Halifax and New York, where guarded convoys began to appear. The U-boats left these alone and moved further south where conditions were still easier. By the summer of 1942 they were operating as far south as the Caribbean. There they experienced conditions which they had not known since the early days of the war. Anti-submarine forces appeared to be completely absent and the numerous small islands offered no resistance, so that it was possible to sail past on the surface in broad daylight. The strict discipline necessary in the Atlantic could be relaxed. Even after spotting a target no great care was needed as resistance was rare. Such casual approaches were impossible in the Atlantic, where the air gap between east and west had narrowed down to about 3000 kilometres and both air and surface forces were inflicting heavy losses on the U-boats.

Attacking shipping in the Atlantic had become purely a night affair or a daytime submerged business, with little or no use found for the large gun in front of the conning tower. In the Caribbean, on the other hand, resistance was so minimal that the U-boats could even attack prominent land targets like fuel installations and storage tanks with this gun. It was during one of these shelling operations that Korvettenkapitän Hartenstein, commanding U 156, had

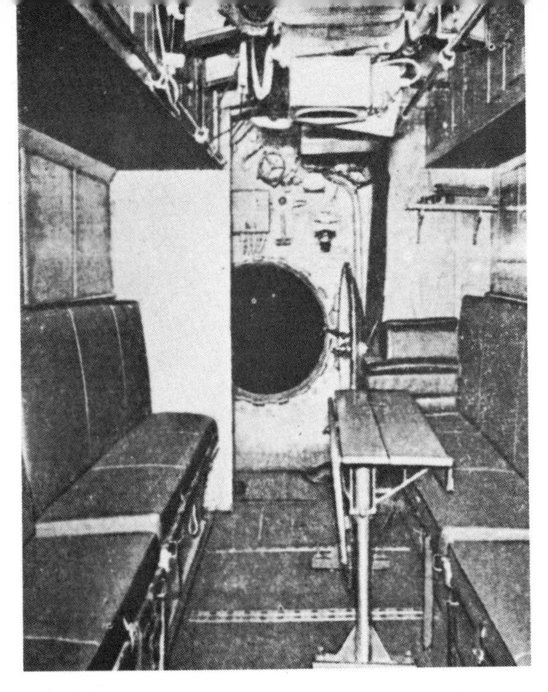

U 776.
The engineers' quarters.

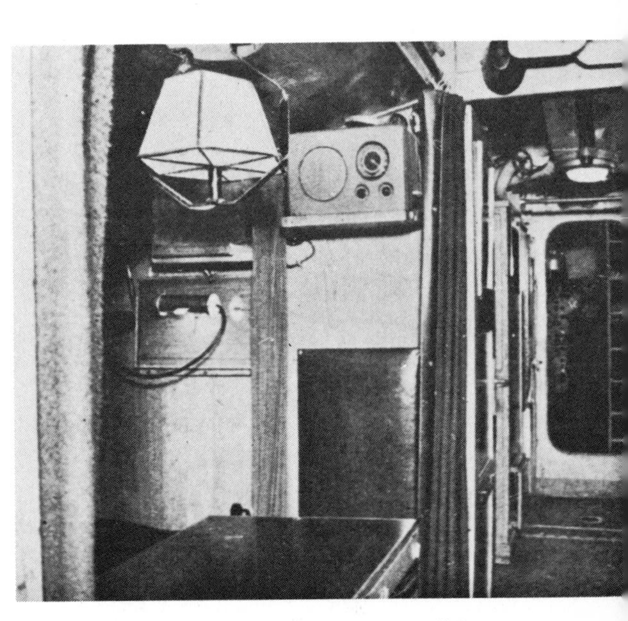

The commander's 'cabin'. This could be shut off from the rest of the boat by a heavy curtain.

to pay a heavy price for his men's benevolence. The boat had surfaced near the Dutch island of Aruba during darkness and closed in to destroy the main petrol storage tanks. The gunnery officer, Leutnant zur See von dem Borne, had spotted people walking along a road in front of the tanks. Being Sunday morning he concluded that they were on their way to church so he held his fire until they passed. This interruption made him forget the watertight tampion in the end of the barrel. On firing the whole gun exploded, leaving the end of the barrel split and the gunnery officer with a seriously injured leg. Without a doctor on board amputating the leg was no easy matter in the confined space of the submarine and, in spite of all efforts, the officer's condition began to deteriorate. Eventually he was set ashore at Port de France on the island of Martinique to receive professional medical attention. U 156 continued with her cruise, the damaged gun was repaired by sawing off the end and at least one ship was later sunk with it before the boat returned to Lorient for a complete refit.

The South Atlantic

The period when the U-boats moved into the Caribbean, during the first half of 1942, also saw the commissioning of the new long-range Type IX D_2 boats with a range almost twice that of the previously largest boat. These boats were unsuitable for the bitter fighting on the North Atlantic convoy routes, because of their limited manoeuvrability. The *Seekriegsleitung* wanted to use the larger vessels to increase the area of operations. This was very much against Dönitz's ideas. He claimed that all effort must be put into attacking the Atlantic convoy routes to cut off Britain's supplies. The decisive battle to win the war for Germany, he asserted, would be fought in the North Atlantic, where U-boats could be effective in starving the British population into submission; taking U-boats to other areas would only weaken the blockade. The *Seekriegsleitung*, however, insisted on sending the boats further afield; and so various Type IX boats, together with their supply boats, moved to operate in the southern waters around Cape Town, with some boats even making their way into the Indian Ocean as far as the Mozambique Channel and Mauritius. The boats in the South Atlantic experienced exceptionally favourable conditions and set many new records relating to endurance and of merchant ships being sunk.

There were no U-boat losses during the early

months. There was even a small, but successful *Paukenschlag* around South Africa, during which U 172, commanded by Korvettenkapitän Emmermann, who had been recalled from his wedding dinner, attacked shipping inside the mined defences of Cape Town. Aeroplanes and vicious U-boat hunters had not found their way into this area and during 1942 it was possible for two U-boats to meet on the surface so that the crew could drink coffee together.

Many South Atlantic operation areas were so far from base that these long patrols were not possible without refuelling at sea. This is where the first major disaster occurred. A supply U-boat failed to break through the 'Black Pit' of Biscay and had to return to base for repairs. Another 'Milkcow' (as the Type XIV were nicknamed) was directed to supply the southern flotilla, but this boat was sunk on the way. Luckily there were two large boats on their way out and they were ordered to break off their patrol and supply the stricken U-boats with fuel and provisions.

A request from U 126 for more fuel sparked off a whole chain of unfortunate events for the *Kriegsmarine*. It was arranged that *Ship* 16, the mysterious raider *Atlantis*, should supply the U-boat with fuel. The *Atlantis* had been at sea for 622 days by the time she met U126 and had refuelled numerous submarines. The procedure had therefore been well rehearsed and after the customary recognition signal U 126 cruised into her wake and a pipe line was passed over. The pipe line also carried a telephone cable which helped to break the monotony of the long patrol, because some of the U-boat's crew soon discovered that they had friends aboard the *Atlantis*. It was not long before a rubber dinghy was made ready so that U 126's commander, Kapitänleutnant Bauer, his LI and several others could paddle over to the larger ship.

The raider was, of course, completely different to the U-boat; it was clean with men in white uniforms pretending to be crewing a harmless merchant ship. Bauer was a little uneasy about the apparently general casualness of the entire operation, but Kapitän zur See Rogge assured him that they were in a lonely part of the ocean and that he had refuelled numerous U-boats without trouble. As a tribute to their guests, fresh bread had been baked on the *Atlantis*, their 'farm' had produced some green food and a pig had been slaughtered–luxury that submariners could only dream about! The peaceful atmosphere was suddenly broken by the clamour of the *Atlantis*' alarm bells. Bauer raced to the rail only to see his boat disappearing below the waves and the ugly silhouette of a warship looming up on the horizon. By pure chance the *Atlantis* was lying in the path of the cruiser HMS *Devonshire*, which was informed by a signal from Rogge that the *Atlantis* was an American merchant ship. This incident took place before America joined in the war, but a secret identification signal, which the *Atlantis* could not know, had already been agreed upon between Britain and the United States. Messages were exchanged for about one hour before the *Devonshire's* guns opened fire at a range of about eighteen kilometres–well outside the range of the German weapons. Rogge had no choice but to surrender, abandon ship and scuttle. *Atlantis*' guns were silent and the men took to the boats, but shells were still being punched into the burning wreck. Meanwhile U 126 had dived, but the important brains of the commander and LI were missing and without their skill the men could not hope to sink the *Devonshire*. Torpedoes were fired, but they missed their mark. After the *Atlantis* had gone down, the survivors spent the rest of the day under the scorching sun in lifeboats. The U-boat had probably been spotted and *Devonshire* did not dare approach any closer for fear of being torpedoed.

U 126 surfaced towards evening, after the survivors had spent some six hours in the lifeboats. Bauer immediately returned to his post to work out how he might accommodate his visitors. An SOS, in secret code, was sent back to HQ, while some 200 men were accommodated on and in U 126. Several U-boats together with another raider, the *Python*, raced to the scene and later survivors were taken aboard this ship. U 68, commanded by Kapitän zur See Merten, also appeared on the scene and was rewarded with more fuel and stores from the *Python*. After this refuelling another U-boat came to be refuelled. Shortly afterwards the group was joined by the Royal Navy's cruiser *Dorsetshire*. The officers aboard the *Python* reacted very quickly by putting their ship between the cruiser and the U-boats, thus giving them time to

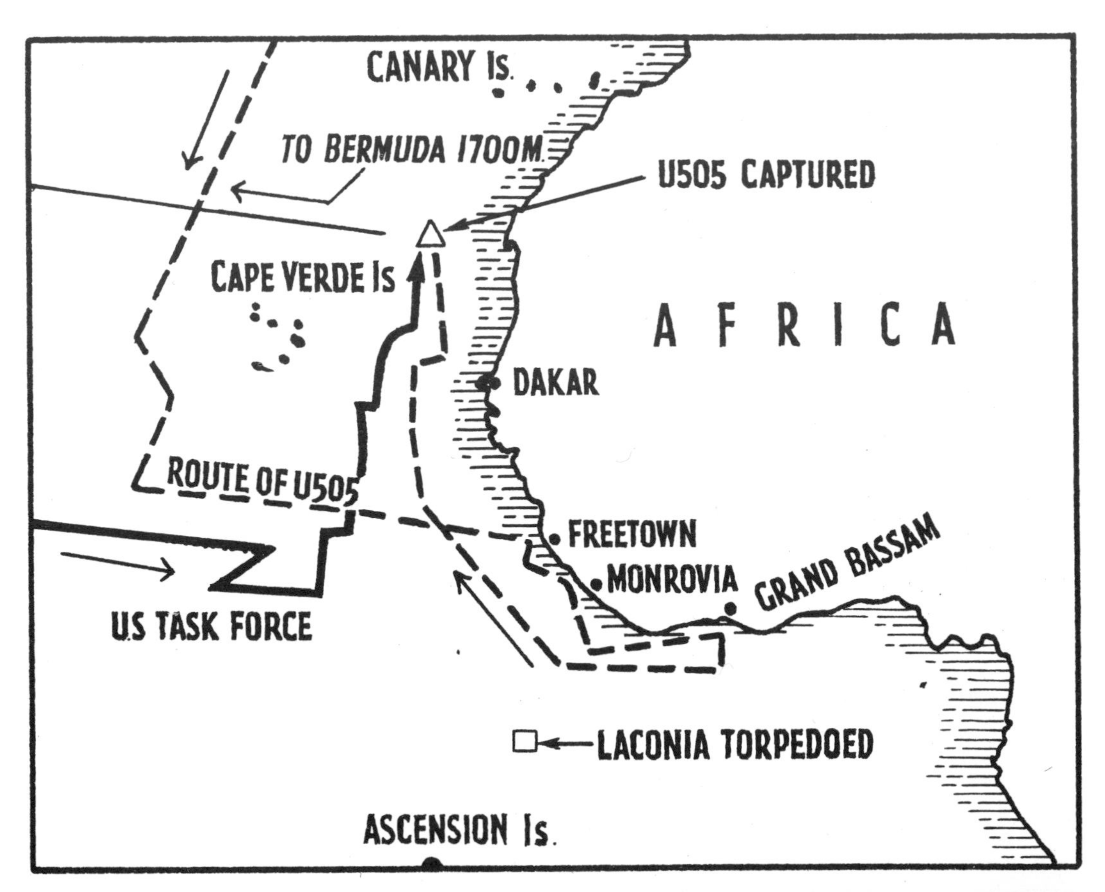

The African Coast

□ *The position where U 156 torpedoed the liner* Laconia, *on 12th September 1942 at 20.07 hrs. The exact position is 4° 52′ S 11° 26′W.*
△ *The position where U 505 was captured on Sunday, 4th June 1944 at 11.09 hrs. The exact position is 21° 30′N 19° 20′W.*
—— *U 505 was towed this way to Bermuda, some 1700 miles from the point of capture.*
(The time of capture given is as the United States Ship Chatelain *first made asdic contact with U 505.)*

U 776's vertical pump for main ballast. Towards the right is one of the circular pressure and watertight doors.

close the hatches and dive.

Then the *Atlantis* drama was repeated. There was no chance of the U-boats attacking because the stores put the boats out of trim and they were very unstable. The only way to keep U 68 submerged was to 'make her go up and down like a yoyo.' Occasionally, as the periscope came out of the water, Merten could see that the *Python* was being reduced to a burning wreck. Merten, unable to help in any way, suddenly had an idea. He ordered the tanks to be blown and once on the surface headed straight for the *Dorsetshire*. This trick worked; the cruiser, frightened of being torpedoed, turned away. The survivors from the two raiders were accommodated on U-boats and together the group made its way back to France.

In Arctic Waters

In the Arctic the U-boats' main enemy were not the Allied Forces, but the natural elements: continuous daylight during the summer months; darkness for twenty-four hours a day during the winter. Icy fog, rough seas and extreme cold all added to the problems. Both men and boats suffered in these, the most difficult conditions experienced during the whole war. Normal U-boat life was impossible at times and the crews had to devote all their energies to keeping their boats afloat.

At first standard boats, fitted with a few additional heaters, were used. This meant that from the men's point of view, merely sleeping in one's bunk required two or three sets of extra clothing. Even when the duty watch returned from their four-hour spell on the bridge, with underclothes frozen stiff against the body, there was no warm place for them to thaw out. Under such cold conditions the exterior of the boat would become completely encrusted with solid ice, so that normal combat was impossible. Even hacking it off did not help, because ice found its way into the interior of all vents, making it impossible to shut them. The only way to dive was to descend slowly while speeding through the slightly warmer water and hope that the pumps would pump out the sea water faster than it poured in. Later, special heaters were installed in vital places to prevent the vents from freezing up.

Eternal darkness in winter was one of the biggest morale breakers. Normally submariners did not miss the sun as they operated at night, but it was discomforting to know that the sun was not there at all, not even for navigation. After the long winter the sun would appear on the horizon for a few minutes each day. In some cases sleeping commanders were actually woken up, as in an emergency, so that they could dash up to the bridge to look at this ball of fire. Instead of queuing up for a smoke on the bridge, the men were known to have lined up to wait for their turn to look at the sun. Each day the sun would appear for a longer period, until eventually it would not set at all. This meant that the Arctic summer had arrived and that it would remain light until the following autumn.

The long daylight was another great hazard to U-boats because there was no darkness to cover the re-charging of batteries or an escape from submarine hunters. Once detected by the enemy it was difficult to escape, since only bad weather could offer cover on the surface. However, under such conditions U-boats were assisted by the fact that the water near the surface contained less salt than the lower depths. There was a remarkable difference in salinity (and probably temperature) at a depth of about 100 metres, which reflected asdic impulses making it possible to use this as a blanket to cover escape.

Icebergs posed a peculiar problem. On the one hand they had to be avoided because a collision could damage the boat, but on the other hand, large ice floes provided good cover, where destroyers could not follow. They also helped U-boats because once iced up a boat resembled a small iceberg–a valuable disguise. It is surprising how many icebergs look like ships; in fact quite a number of them were actually attacked by U-boats! One example of how icebergs sometimes aided the U-boats was when one boat tied up to a floating piece of ice and then crept up on a landed seaplane, using the ice as a shield. This was possible because the electric motors could run silently without leaving a wake or tell-tale exhaust smoke. Once in range the boat turned and destroyed the plane with gunfire.

There were several reasons for sending U-boats into the barren wastes of the Arctic. Some

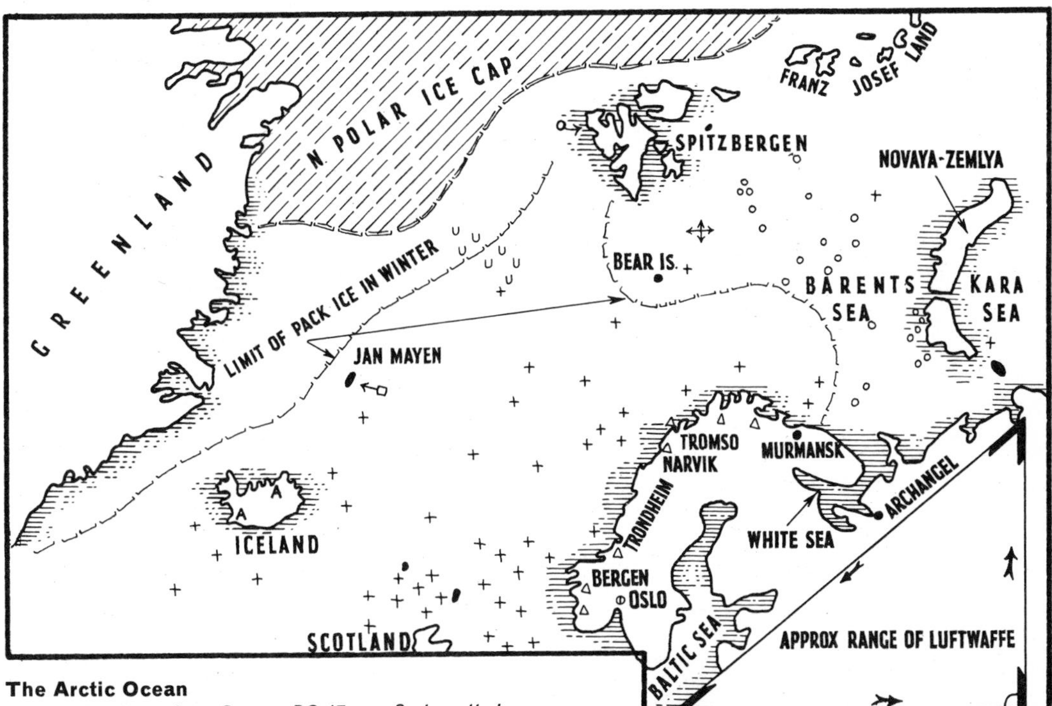

The Arctic Ocean

◄□ *Position where Convoy PQ 17 was first spotted by U 255 (Kptlt. R. Reche).*

\+ *Position where a U-boat sank. (There were more sinkings in the area south west of Iceland, but this area was not covered by the Arctic flotillas.)*

Δ *Luftwaffe bases during the battle for PQ 17. (Those bases that have been named were also radio receiving stations for messages from the secret Arctic weather stations.)*

O→ *Position of Cape Mitra.*

A *Allied Air Force bases.*

UU *Area covered by U-boats that were waiting to intercept Convoy PQ 17.*

o *Position where a ship from Convoy PQ 17 sank.*

✣ *Position where PQ 17 was ordered to scatter.*

Φ *Radio station for receiving messages from the secret Arctic weather stations.*

boats operated in wolf packs against convoys making their way to or from the north Russian ports. A few boats were engaged with secret weather stations and others were sent out individually to explore the Arctic Seas. These boats scoured the ice deserts to find possible convoy routes near the permanent ice cap and they also had the order to sink any shipping that they might meet.

Exploration Sorties in the Arctic

Today there are regular commercial flights over the North Pole, but in 1940 technical resources were still fairly primitive and little was known about general conditions in the Arctic. This led U-boats to explore the Greenland coast as far north as the ice permitted. U-boats also searched the North Polar ice cap itself to seek possible convoy routes close to the ice and also to see whether it was possible to dive underneath it. Such voyages were extremely hazardous as passages were often blocked by huge ice floes, which could only be negotiated by diving underneath. Several U-boats operated in the Kara Sea and sailed along the Siberian Sea Passage to Severnaya Zemlya at about 100°E. One German surface vessel sailed, with help from Russian ice-breakers, all the way along this north-eastern sea route and reached the Pacific through the Bering Strait.

Arctic Battles

The low total of shipping sunk in the Arctic, by comparison with other oceans, was not due to the negligence of the U-boat men, but to the lack of targets. The Arctic convoys from Britain and America to the north Russian ports sailed so infrequently that many U-boats never saw enemy

The Men and Their Uniforms

Above: *Admiral Dönitz was Commander-in-Chief of the U-boat Arm and he became Head of the whole Kriegsmarine after Erich Raeder's resignation in January 1943.*

The Grundausbildung *(Initial Training). This training was given to all men, no matter what fighting force they joined.*

Top right: *Men wearing Naval Infantry uniform.*

Right: *The White Naval Uniform. (Both photos taken at Wilhelmshaven during the summer of 1933.)*

The main gate at the 14th Schiffsstammabteilung *at Breda in Holland, where many U-boat men went through their* Grundausbildung *(Initial Training)*

Naval Infantry uniform being worn at Breda, during 1942.

Men wearing white 'drill clothes' during exercises at Breda.

shipping. Even once a convoy was known to be on its way, with its position reported, it had often 'vanished' into the mists by the time boats or aircraft reached the reported position. The long hours of daylight of course made surface attacks impossible for the U-boats and in winter darkness made aerial reconnaissance by the *Luftwaffe*, operating from Norwegian bases, difficult. Large parts of the Arctic Seas were within range of these bases, hence this area saw a high proportion of aerial reconnaissance and planes played an important role in the convoy battles of this region.

Probably the most famous of all convoy battles, that of PQ 17, one of the greatest disasters for the Allies, was fought north of the Arctic Circle. Convoy PQ 17 assembled near Reykjavik (Iceland) to sail on a north-easterly course, past Jan Mayen to Russia. The convoy was well organised and well protected, but a report was received that the German battleships *Tirpitz*, *Scheer* and the heavy cruiser *Hipper* had left Norway and the convoy was ordered to disperse immediately. The scattered ships became targets for heavy aircraft attacks and many ran into U-boats from the *Icedevil* group. Of the 35 ships which left Iceland, two turned back at the threat of danger; 24 were sunk – ten by U - boats – and the remainder managed to limp to Russia after the ordeal.

Another convoy, probably PQ 16, was spotted at more or less the same position where U 255, commanded by Reinhard Reche, first spotted PQ 17. This convoy might have suffered the same losses had it not been for a humanitarian U-boat commander, who disregarded his instructions to save another U-boat from destruction. Korvettenkapitän Otto Köhler commanding U 377 located this convoy east of Jan Mayen and started to trail it. As a shadowing U-boat, U 377 was not permitted to attack. It had to keep the convoy in sight and report its position at regular intervals.

Later U 592, commanded by Kapitänleutnant Borm, appeared. After rejecting Köhler's request to take over shadowing, U 592 moved into a suitable position for a submerged attack. It was just disappearing below the waves when U 337's lookouts noticed a destroyer change course. Additional smoke pouring from its rear funnel indicated that the second boiler had been fired for extra speed and that the attacker would soon reach U-Borm's position.

Köhler ordered full speed ahead, showed his boat's side view to the destroyer and sailed off. The destroyer immediately left its search for U 592 and headed towards U 377. The chief diesel engineer appeared at the top of the conning tower wanting to know why his *Bumsies* (Most engines on U-boats had pet names) suddenly had to 'tear their guts out'. Peering over the protective wall towards the convoy he was greeted with a barrage of artillery fire. "I think we're better off in the cellar," said Köhler. The engineer did not need any persuasion and quickly followed the duty watch as they tumbled through the hatch. A few depth charges exploded a safe distance away. Another terrific explosion was heard, making the men in U 377 think that Borm had hit an ammunition ship. Eventually U-Köhler returned to the surface only to find the U-boat hunters waiting and another pattern of depth charges exploded around them. Eventually, however, U 377 managed to crawl away. The convoy had been lost by that time and the movements of U 592 are not known, but the boat was not sunk and it returned safely to its Norwegian base.

Secret Arctic Weather Stations

It must be realised that knowledge of the climate in the Arctic is essential, as without it the weather for the Middle Atlantic or for the European land mass cannot be forecast. Before the war numerous meteorological stations frequently transmitted climatic data. When the war started these bases were either abandoned or they continued to broadcast in code, so that the information was of no use to the Germans. Germany immediately converted a number of deep-sea trawlers into floating weather stations and despatched them to the Arctic. U-boats were also frequently asked to report the weather in their area and at least two U-boats were stationed off the American coast with the sole objective of reporting climatic conditions. However, weather reports from operational boats had the disadvantage that rarely did two consecutive reports come from the same area, so that for a meteorologist the information was rather inconsistent. Stationary U-boats could not record or transmit details as required because of enemy activity and when the

Above: *An example of the Blue Naval Uniform. Taken during the 'Swearing in Ceremony' at Breda during the summer of 1942. (Fritz Köhl).*

Above: *Every soldier had to take an oath! After 1938 the men had to swear this oath to obey Hitler, not the German government, the Constitution or the people, but Adolf Hitler himself. The wording was as follows:–*

"Ich schwöre bei Gott diesen heiligen Eid, dass ich dem Führer des deutschen Reiches und Volkes Adolf Hitler dem obersten Befehlshaber der Wehrmacht unbedingten Gehorsam leiste und als tapferer Soldat bereit bin, in jeder Zeit für diesen Eid mein Leben einzusetzen..."

(I swear this holy oath by God, that I shall obey the Führer of the German Reich and People, Adolf Hitler, the Highest Commander of the Armed Forces and that I am prepared to give my life as a brave soldier at any time for this oath...)

Below: *The white naval uniform.*

Grand Admiral Erich Raeder inspects the men. (He is looking left. One broad and three thin stripes on the sleeve.)

May 29th, 1939. A version of the blue naval uniform.

United States joined in the war the first U-boat they sank was one of these weather stations.

Trawlers also suffered very heavy losses so that most of them had disappeared by the end of 1942. This, together with the unsuitability of U-boats, gave Germany no alternative but to abandon the idea or to adopt new methods. One new idea was the automatic weather buoy, consisting basically of a floating radio transmitter with a thermometer, hydrometer and later also with an anemometer. A clock would switch the apparatus on twice a day. It could automatically broadcast letters representing values on the various scales. All this equipment was built into a buoy of the same shape as a normal torpedo. It could be carried to its destination by a U-boat and discharged through a torpedo tube. Once expelled the buoy would float vertically to the surface with the nose out of the water. A weight in the tail would drop out unwinding about one kilometre (the original report says 10,000 metres of wire, but this seems unlikely) of thin steel wire as it fell. Simultaneously an aerial, some two metres long and containing the instruments, would rise from the nose. The buoy was highly successful. With the exception of the hydrometer, it could transmit accurate readings for about six months. In view of this it was decided to erect similar stations on land.

The first of these automatic land stations was installed during the early summer of 1942 on Spitzbergen, near Ny Alesund, by U 377. Basically the apparatus was similar to the weather buoy, but it could also report the direction of the wind. The first installation was quite straightforward. U 377 approached Spitzbergen, undertook a quick reconnaissance, and unloaded the equipment in an isolated spot. It consisted of a tripod with weather equipment on the top and heavy batteries at the bottom. Unfortunately the apparatus froze solid shortly after the boat left and it ceased to function!

Hans Robert Knöspel, an ornithologist who had been involved with floating weather stations, suggested creating permanent manned meteorological stations in the Arctic. Drawing on experience gained on a lengthy pre-war expedition to Greenland, he stated that it would be possible for units to pass the winter without being detected on the lonely Arctic islands. Training facilities for such a venture already existed as Knöspel had also founded a Polar Experimental Centre with the University of Breslau in the Riesengebirge (now in the DDR – Czechoslovakia – Poland borders). The risk involved was negligible compared with the value of such a venture and Knöspel was encouraged to go ahead with its development. He became the

Jak Mallmann wearing a Non-Commissioned Officer's walking out uniform.

Top: *Author's parents on May 1st, 1940, showing a Non-Commissioned Officer's coat with dagger.*

Above: *The author's father wearing a white mess jacket. These were not worn on U-boats, only ashore.*

leader of the first station, which successfully operated on Spitzbergen during the winter of 1941/42. In view of Knöspel's success, plans went ahead for more weather stations in Greenland and Bear Island.

Initially these weather stations were installed by fishing boats which were taken to the area by the "Weather Corps" and then scuttled after being unloaded. But one unit had an unlucky start. As its fishing boat transport reached the east coast of Greenland it was spotted by a patrolling aircraft. After failing to give the recognition signal it was bombed and sunk. The leader of the expedition, Leutnant Sonderführer Ritter, made his way over the ice to Greenland and some of the men were later picked up by the *Luftwaffe* and taken back to Germany.

Such experiences made it quite clear that surface vessels were completely unsuited for this task and that they would have to be replaced by aircraft or U-boats. Aircraft were ideal for supplying established stations, but a vast number would be required to carry all the equipment and personnel needed to execute the initial construction task. U-boats had several advantages over aircraft. They could approach unseen and there was sufficient space to carry all the cargo; moreover, the crew could help the Weather Corps with the initial erection work. The problem in

Officer's dress.
(U 377's L.I., Karl-Heinz Nitschke (right) and W.O., Leutnant zur See Pietschmann, (?) who later became commander of U 712 and U 762.)

using U-boats for this purpose was that they were completely unsuited for operating in the frozen water; they carried no crane and all the packages to be stowed inside the boat had to be less than half a metre in diameter, otherwise they could not be squeezed through the hatches. There were no side doors on submarines and the only way in and out was through the hatch in the 'ceiling'. This made unloading a special problem.

Secrecy and good location of the site was vital because the Weather Corps could only carry light arms, designed more for hunting than fighting. The camp would have to be well hidden from enemy eyes, because in the event of an attack there would be no military support. The men could only evacuate their station. In view of this several escape routes were planned, with special pick-up points equipped with food, weapons, rubber dinghies, emergency accommodation, radio etc. Experience showed that the winter camp was easily recognisable once daylight came the following spring, so a tented summer camp at a different location had also to be established.

Knöspel's party was withdrawn from Spitzbergen during the spring of 1942 and another party was established that summer, under the leadership of Dr Nusser. All the necessary equipment was taken on board U 377 in Norway. Building timber, coal, sledges and similar gear was stowed in the space between the pressure hull and the deck planking. The journey across the Arctic Sea was encountered without difficulty, although the boat had to dive several times to avoid aircraft or surface vessels, but traffic became less the further north the men sailed. Eventually the mountainous landscape of Spitzbergen came into sight. The lookouts had not reported any significant movements for hundreds of miles, making the men confident that they could proceed unobserved.

U 377 had been in that part of Spitzbergen before, but this time they were heading for unexplored waters around the northwest coast at Cape Mitra. Little was known about the depth of water, so the old-fashioned method of using a sounding lead was adopted. The lookouts scoured the horizon as the boat cautiously made its way up the almost three kilometre-wide Lilliehöök Bay towards the vast glacier at the end. Eventually the boat was anchored in good firm ground with about ten metres of water below the keel. Korvettenkapitän Köhler's first problem was that once unloading had started, the hatches would all be open and the boat would not be fit for immediate diving. The high hills of Cape Mitra gave good cover, but also limited the lookouts' field of vision. The lookouts were therefore despatched, with signalling equipment, to the summit of a nearby hill. The plan was that on spotting an aeroplane the hatches would be shut and the officer on duty would flood the tanks to settle the boat on the sea bed. The men on land would have to find cover as best they could. Cape Mitra, however, was not under regular air reconnaissance and the men worked undisturbed.

At first the sections of the wooden hut which would form the station headquarters were unloaded and, with the aid of rubber dinghies, floated to the shore. This proved to be a slow and unpleasant process because of the low water temperature. Later the entire bay froze over, with ice thick enough to enable the men to carry all equipment over it. This gave Otto Köhler sufficient experience of submarines freezing up in ice and on his second trip he attempted to do away with the rubber dinghy stage. This time U 377 arrived at a fair speed and stopped by ramming the soft pack ice, which left the boat firmly wedged so that unloading over the ice could start at once.

The Far East

Hitler issued a secret directive (directives were really 'orders') to military leaders about co-operation with Japan as early as March 1941. In this he outlined the importance of engaging Britain in the Pacific. He ordered that German military and technical experience should be made available to the Japanese, so that in the event of war Japan's contribution would have the maximum effect. This led the *Kriegsmarine* to consider sending German units to fight in the Pacific in conjunction with Japanese Forces. However, there were several problems which prevented further fermentation of this idea. First, the large Type IX D_2 U-boats had not been launched and the other long-distance boats, together with their supply ships, were needed in the Atlantic, so there were no suitable boats which could be sent to such far distant waters. Secondly, Dönitz held firm to his old belief that the only way to win the war was to put every available boat into the North Atlantic shipping lanes. Thirdly, the language barrier was thought to make a real close fighting liaison impossible, since the instant understanding of orders often meant the difference between success and failure.

This idea of fighting with the Japanese was revived on several occasions, but did not receive widespread support until the late autumn of 1942, by which time there had been a drastic change in sea strategy. Up to this time Germany operated an efficient, small surface fleet of raiders and blockade-breakers, which brought vital raw materials from various parts of the world back to German bases. However, these ships were no longer getting through the British blockade and that meant hardship in certain essential industries. Germany did manage to provide substitutes for a large amount of its usual imports by a variety of special home-made products, but some items such as rubber and opium were just not available on the Continent, and it was thought that U-boats might take over the role of blockade-breakers. The idea was that large, long-distance boats would fight their way to Japanese-controlled bases, refit, replenish stores and then return as cargo boats. Unfortunately, however, even the large type IXD_2 boats were not really suited for this task as their limited capacity would only allow for about 120 tons of zinc, 80 tons of raw rubber and some 15 to 20 tons of other cargo. This total is, of course, very small compared with the load of even the smallest of the cargo ships which made these journeys before the war.

The first eleven U-boats to be used for Far Eastern operations, christened *Monsoon Group*, did leave French and Norwegian ports during July 1943. Five of them reached their destination, the other six were sunk. The 2nd Monsoon Group was only one boat strong by the time it reached its destination. The crews also suffered from the lack of European food and to add to their problems a quarter of them went down with malaria. The commanding officer for U-boats in the Far East, Wilhelm Dommes, managed to sort out most of these problems, including the excessive red tape insisted upon by the Japanese. He was the only person in the whole area, apart from the men in the U-boats, with submarine experience, so a large proportion of his time was given to advisory work at a most elementary level.

At first Dommes only had two old aeroplanes at his disposal for transport between the widely dispersed ports. These two planes were at one time stationed on surface raiders and they had made their way to the Far East after their ships had been sunk. The Japanese curiosity for anything mechanical helped him to obtain another fairly good plane, by exchanging it for a *Bachstelze*, the gliding helicopter carried by the Far Eastern U-boats. Dommes worked very hard to do his best for the U-boat crews. He obtained seeds from Europe to grow vegetables and he arranged for medical facilities, which in the end proved to be better than those in Europe.

The lack of maintainance crews in the Far East was one of the biggest problems. The local labour forces were not skilled enough to cope with delicate submarines and the Japanese engineers, being used to coolie labour, refused such 'dirty' jobs. So there was only one choice left – the crews had to repair their own boats. In most cases however, the men were in far more need of repair than their boats and they were not pleased at the thought of the work involved. Another complication was that spare parts were not readily available and tools were of inferior Far Eastern quality. The general working conditions did not help to make the job any easier, particularly the temperature inside the boats, which was near that of a moderate baking oven, or some 60°C. Communications were quite good. All the bases had a radio link with the German Admiral in Tokyo, and depending on the time of day and season of the year there were also fairly good radio connections with Europe.

Loading the boats for the return journey was quite a feat of skill. Every available space had to be filled and everything utilised in the best possible way. Even containers for vegetables were made from pure zinc, so that once empty they could be flattened out and still be used as valuable raw material. Torpedoes were only carried for emergencies on the way home, so that the normal storage places for these could be used to hold additional cargo.

Inferior or non-existent spare parts and tools handicapped boats on their return voyage. Some boats even ran out of fuel and had to wait helplessly on the surface for help to arrive. Some did not get back at all; others, such as U 178 commanded by Wilhelm Spahr, returned with part of their rubber cargo being used to hold the engines together.

Korvettenkapitän Oesten, commanding U 861, returned to Norway by creeping up America's east coast to avoid detection by radar. He continued along the Greenland coast, past Spitzbergen and then the boat sailed south down the Norwegian coast to Trondheim.

The boats for the Far East were equipped with a new novelty – the Focke-Achgelis (FA 300), a gliding helicopter nicknamed *Bachstelze* (Wagtail). These, although quite ingenious, were only cheap subsitutes for the non-existent naval air arm, but they did help to increase the field of vision from about ten kilometres at boat level to about 45 kilometres at the cruising altitude of 120 metres. The individual parts of the *Bachstelze* were stored inside the boat and assembled on the gun platform, where the helicopter was launched from a small platform attached to the rails. There was no motor and it remained airborne by being pulled through the air. In the case of an emergency one could jettison the rotors in order to descend more quickly. The pilot could also carry a parachute to soften his landing. An example of this craft can be seen in the Aviation Gallery of the Science Museum in London.

5
Captured U-boats

Right from the start of World War II, as the Royal Navy went on anti-submarine duty, commanders were thinking of capturing enemy vessels and some of them trained and maintained small boarding parties that could be dispatched at an instant's notice. The Admiralty in London encouraged such action by stressing the importance of capturing U-boats. It was suggested that during favourable conditions commanders might try to force a U-boat to the surface by bombarding it with shallow set depth charges, and then encourage the crew to depart, without scuttling, by signalling that survivors would not be picked up if the U-boat sank. However, it was stressed that all survivors should be picked up, whether the U-boat sank or not. This suggestion was not an invitation for the Royal Navy to concentrate on captures as it was stated quite firmly that the escort commander's primary duty lay in ensuring the safe arrival of the convoy and that U-boats were to be destroyed as quickly as possible. Only in exceptional circumstances should captures be considered.

On the German side, on the other hand, it had been a strong tradition in the *Kriegsmarine* that the enemy only set foot on their vessels as prisoners. This was made exceptionally clear when the High Seas Fleet scuttled in Scapa Flow at the end of World War I. Numerous Royal Navy vessels were in positions to capture U-boats, but in almost all cases the last man out 'pulled the plug'. In fact many men went down with their boats because they returned from the relatively safe position of the bridge to the control or engine room to flood the tanks and then found that the boat went down too fast for them to get out again.

The importance of capturing an enemy vessel depends on the circumstances under which the crew is forced to surrender. During difficult operations capture was foreseen and the interior of the boat was prepared for instant destruction, so that nothing of importance should fall into enemy hands. If the actual time between forcing the boat to the surface and removing the crew was too long, then there was ample opportunity for the destruction of secret documents and interior fittings. So a really valuable capture

U-boat overalls.

Blue naval uniforms and U-boat overalls outside the Headquarters of the 9th U-boat Flotilla in Brest during 1943. Some of the men have just been awarded the Iron Cross 2nd Class.

Close-up of Iron Cross 2nd Class.

could only be made if the U-boat was surprised and then swiftly abandoned. In such a case a vast variety of valuable information might be obtained from the boat itself – for example the secret of the radio key, wavebands used and the nature of secret charts. It might even be possible to learn about enemy movements, so that a convoy could be re-routed around waiting wolf packs. The secret ship's manual would give information about performance, which would help surface ships in hunting similar U-boats because speed, diving time, diving depth, endurance under water would be known.

The first submarine to be captured during World War II was a British boat, HMS *Seal*, commanded by Lt-Cr R. P. Lonsdale. She had been sent on a mission from the Humber to lay mines in the Kattegat. Already before her departure this task was considered too dangerous for such a large submarine, because the operation area was shallow and heavily patrolled. The commander of the *Seal*'s flotilla even made a special trip to London to ask Admiral Max Horton, Flag Officer for Submarines, to cancel the mission; but that appeal was turned down.

Eventually HMS *Seal* left and crossed the North Sea without difficulty. She even negotiated the heavily mined waters of the Baltic Approaches without incident, but on May 4th, 1940 she was spotted by a German aeroplane and bombed. The damage was only slight and the mission continued.

Sometime after depositing her mines she was detected by the acoustic detectors of an anti-submarine patrol. Lonsdale stopped engines and waited, but the surface vessels dropped several accurate depth charges, which sent the *Seal* down to the sea bed. The engineers worked for six hours, carrying out vital repairs, to bring the boat to the surface. After several unsuccessful attempts most of the men came to the conclusion that their last hour had come. Lonsdale and several other men stood in the control room and prayed, then he ordered the diesel fuel to be pumped out of the bunkers. Slowly the boat began to rise. Once on the surface the men knew that they had a good chance to live, although their strategic predicament had not improved as both their electric motors were flooded and only one diesel engine would work in reverse. There was no chance of returning to Britain and Lonsdale could only see to the safety of his crew by cruising backwards into Swedish waters, where he hoped to get the men ashore and to

Raincoat and sou'wester. Oilskins were not issued to the man personally, but to the boat. Only a few sets were taken to sea and had to be shared.

Bootsmann (Boatswain) Albert Jungclaus of U 377 wearing 'large rain gear'.

scuttle the boat. There was no power except a few dimly-lit light bulbs inside the boat and the crew worked hard to destroy everything they could lay their hands on. With the lack of power it was impossible to jettison the six remaining torpedoes, although all other vital gear was thrown overboard.

At daybreak a seaplane, perhaps with Swedish markings, circled the *Seal* and landed by the boat. The crew were German and took Lonsdale and PO Nolte as prisoners. After this a pre-war trawler, the *Franken*, which had been commissioned into the German Navy as Submarine Hunter UJ 128 (*Unterseebootsjäger*), appeared in order to land a boarding party. Meanwhile the crew had been seeing to the final destruction of the internal machinery by smashing as much as possible with hammers and heavy spanners.

The *Seal* was first towed to Denmark and then after some emergency repairs she was taken to Kiel for a complete re-fit. During 1941 she joined the 3rd U-Flotilla as U B. Her most important asset was no doubt her propaganda value, as she was put to little use. The six remaining torpedoes, however, did supply the Germans with some information on firing mechanisms, which was built into German

Men relaxing on the bridge of U 377. Note the powerful U-boat binoculars. The flag is the Ensign of the Kriegsmarine.

Brest during the autumn of 1943 – U 377 is just back from patrol. Heinrich Lehmann-Willenbrock is talking to the men.

U 377's first commander, Korvettenkapitän Otto Köhler. His first speech to the crew, during the commissioning ceremony, was concluded with, '. . . . and above all I promise to bring you all back alive'——and he had the good fortune of being able to do so! On his right hand pocket is the Iron Cross 1st Class and below it is the U-boat Medal U-Bootsabzeichen. *This was awarded after the men had been on several operational patrols.*

designs after their tragic torpedo failure crisis.

The most dramatic and probably the most important capture of a U-boat during the whole war was when the 3rd Escort Group, made up of HM Destroyers *Bulldog* and *Broadway* and HM Corvette *Aubretia* commanded by Capt A. D. Baker-Cresswell, captured U 110 which was commanded by Kptlt Fritz Julius Lemp. The whole operation was carried out so quickly that none of U 110's crew knew that their boat had been captured. The secret was so well kept that only a handful of people at the Admiralty were informed. In fact the details of this brilliant capture only came to light after Capt S. W. Roskill had stated in his official history of the Navy that U 110 had been sunk. For thus it was recorded in all naval documents, except one small file relating to the capture – and that was well hidden away. On reading of U 110's sinking after the war Captain Baker-Cresswell wrote to Roskill informing him about the capture, and this was probably the first time the event came into the open. It led Captain Roskill to write his book *The Secret Capture* (German title *Das Geheimnis um U 110*), which still appears to be the only reliable source of information on this incident.

Kptlt Lemp is most famous for sinking the liner *Athenia* on the first day of the war, while he was commanding U 30. His good character and fine ability led him to become commander of U 110 and also to be awarded the Knight's Cross of the Iron Cross. U 110 was launched at Deschimag AG Weser in Bremen and it went through its initial trials in the Baltic during the winter of 1940/41. During the April of 1941 U 110 made its way into the North Atlantic, where lookouts spotted a convoy; but the night was too bright and Lemp decided to postpone his attack. The details of the convoy were radioed

Im Namen des Führers
und Obersten Befehlshabers
der Wehrmacht

verleihe ich

dem

Obermaschinisten

Jakob Mallmann

das

Eiserne Kreuz 1. Klasse.

....Befehlsstelle.,den 22.....März.....19..43

Kapitän zur See
und Führer der Unterseeboote West
(Dienstgrad und Dienststellung)

Close up of Iron Cross 1st Class and its certificate. The 2nd Class certificate looked similar, except that it had a '2' instead of the '1' in front of the word Klasse.

back to base and this message was intercepted by U 201, commanded by Oblt z S Adalbert Schnee, who immediately headed towards the position. At about dawn, on May 9th, the two U-boats sighted each other and after exchanging the customary recognition signals came together so that the commanders could shout to each other. Lemp's officers had suggested that they should wait a day or so before attacking, because the Royal Navy escorts were at their westerly limit and would soon have to turn back. However Lemp was not keen on going further west as that would waste time and precious fuel. During this conversation with Schnee it was decided that both boats should try a daylight submerged attack, with Lemp attacking first and U 201 following about thirty minutes later. During the next $3\frac{1}{2}$ hours both boats manoeuvred into a favourable attacking position. It was just one minute before midday as the first torpedo left U 110. Two ships were hit during the first attack, but Lemp's periscope was spotted by the nearest escort HMS *Aubretia*, which raced over to the spot. U 110 managed to survive the first depth charge attack, but HMS *Broadway* and HMS *Bulldog* joined in the hunt, making it possible for them to locate U 110 on their asdics and pass the location over to HMS *Aubretia*, which then dropped more depth charges. After about half an hour the U-boat appeared on the surface and instantly HMS *Bulldog* went on a ramming course, while HMS *Aubretia* stood by to pick up survivors. Then, when at a short distance from U 110, it occurred to Capt Baker-Cresswell that a capture might come off. He changed course, ordered *Bulldog* to stop and every available gun to open fire. U 110's crew came pouring out of her hatch and jumped straight from the tower into the sea. Lemp was last seen in the water asking various people about several crew members, hoping that they had escaped. Unfortunately he was not among the survivors.

HMS *Bulldog* lowered her whaler and a small boarding party, led by Sub-Lt David Balme, rowed over to the boat. Once inside they found it empty and quickly set about picking up as many odds and ends as they could lay their hands on. Their fear of being trapped inside subsided as time went on and everything that could be moved was taken out. The whaler

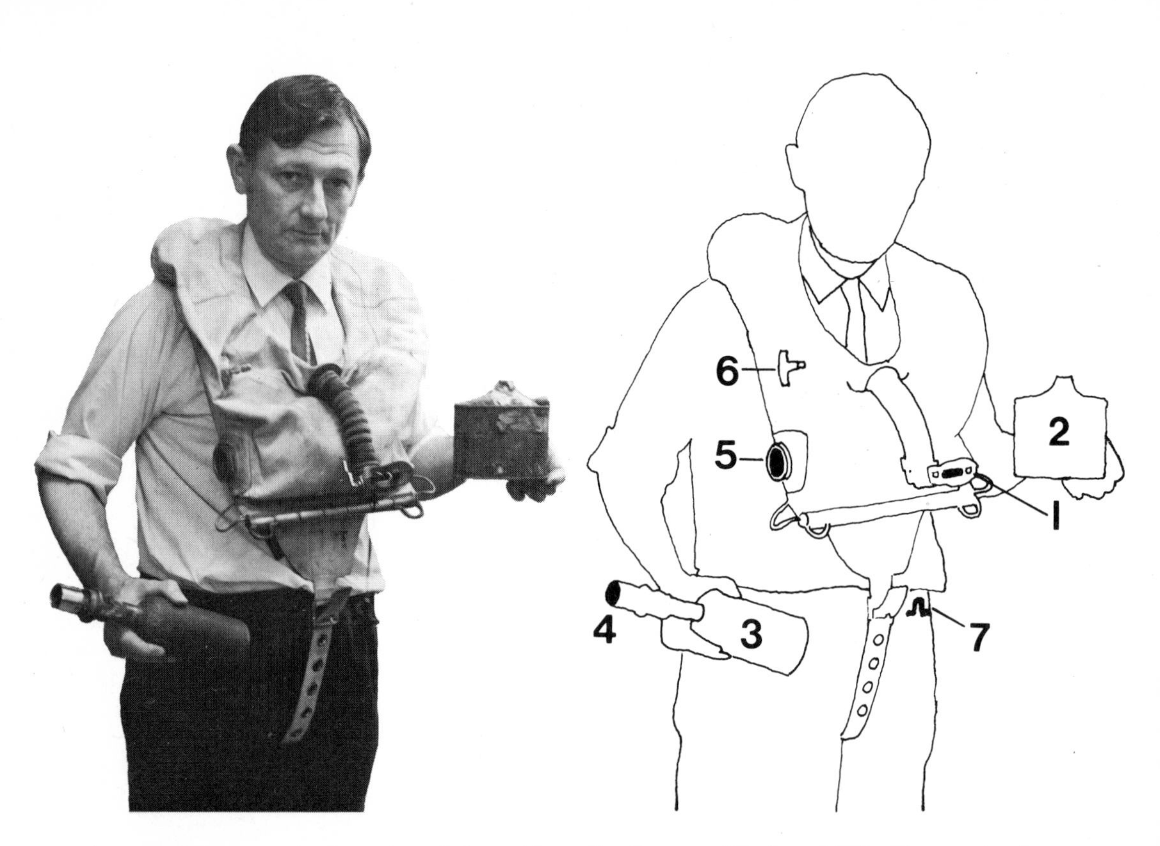

made several journeys backwards and forwards, each time carrying a heavy load of valuable material. Nobody on the British side knew anything about submarines, so that nothing could be done about U 110's buoyancy as Cresswell did not wish to sink the boat by accident. Later, after everything that could be moved had been taken aboard HMS *Bulldog*, a line was fixed to the U-boat and Cresswell attempted to tow his prize back to Iceland; but U 110 sank the following day The rest of the material was taken back to Britain. It is not known what had actually fallen into British hands, but one can assume that everything must have been captured. It is probable that the many U-boats which were destroyed on secret refuelling rendezvous were located partly through the information found inside U 110.

The second U-boat to be captured by the British Forces was U 570 and only three months after the secret U 110 incident. This was a completely different affair because only the shell of a Type VII C boat fell into British hands and in the first instance it surrendered to an aeroplane.

Ray Freeman of the Imperial War Museum, London, demonstrating a Dräger Tauchretter *(U-boat escape apparatus). The mouthpiece (1) should be in his mouth, but on this occasion, as the equipment was not exactly in prime condition, Mr Freeman was rather reluctant to give a full demonstration! The goggles are missing and the nose clip (7) is hardly visible.*
2 A tin containing a chemical which absorbs carbon dioxide. This would normally fit inside the air bag, under the breathing pipe.
3 Oxygen cylinder. (Also fits inside air bag.)
4 Tap for oxygen cylinder. This normally sticks out through the hole (5).
5 Hole for oxygen cylinder's tap.
6 Outlet valve.
The valve on the mouthpiece could be shut and the air bag could be inflated with oxygen to act as a life jacket once surfaced.

Kptlt Hans Rahmlow had commanded the small Type II U 58 and then became the first commander of the new U 570, which was launched in Hamburg during March 1941. After being commissioned U 570 made its way to Horten in Norway, where the initial trials, for both boat and crew, were carried out. During this period it was already evident that Germany was

Hans Staus wearing an inflated life jacket. Note the whistle.

producing U-boats faster than the highly specialised men needed to operate them, because it is believed that U 570's crew did not reach a satisfactory standard of fighting efficiency. If this is true then the boat should not have been declared operational, as the margin between life and death, even on an efficient U-boat, was too narrow to make allowances for inexperienced men.

Eventually U 570 left Trondheim on August 23rd, 1941 to operate in the North Atlantic and then to run into its new base at La Pallice. This journey must have been near hell for all in the U-boat. Tempers flared up on numerous occasions and many men suffered from sea sickness, so that the boat could hardly have been capable of fighting. On that fateful August 27th it was lying at 60 metres, out of reach of the turbulent waves, as Rahmlow decided to return to the surface at about 11.00 hours. The boat was hardly moving at the time and slowly it rose to periscope depth. A quick look revealed nothing and Rahmlow ordered the boat to surface.

Right above the boat, in the periscope's 'blind spot' was Sqn Ldr J. H. Thompson, flying Hudson 'S' on anti-submarine patrol from Iceland. The target that appeared was something that every Coastal Command pilot prayed for – a helpless U-boat coming more or less stationary out of the water with its anti-aircraft guns not yet manned. Thompson lost no time and attacked instantly, straddling U 570 with several well-placed depth charges. Shortly after the spray had subsided, a white flag was waved from the conning tower. Thompson, having no clue as to what he should do next, reported his capture to base and continued to circle the stricken U-boat as he himself could not claim his prize.

Meanwhile the Admiralty in London was informed and the nearest ships were ordered to the spot. There were no Royal Navy units in the immediate vicinity so Hudson 'S' continued to circle U 570. During the afternoon Catalina 'J' piloted by Flying Officer E. A. Jewiss arrived to relieve Thompson. Jewiss had been instructed to watch the U-boat and if the Royal Navy did not show up by nightfall then he was to warn the Germans and sink the U-boat. This did not become necessary as the trawler *Northern Chief* showed up at 23.00 hours, some twelve hours after U 570 had surrendered. The sea was still rough as a near gale had been blowing all day, making it impossible to launch a small boat, so Lt N. L. Knight, commander of the trawler, sent over a message that he would not wait to pick up survivors if the U-boat sank during the night. Rahmlow replied that he could neither dive nor scuttle and requested to be rescued the following day. Navy reinforcements arrived during the hours of darkness, the first being another trawler, the *Kingston Agate*, followed by the destroyer *Burwell* and two more trawlers *Wastwater* and *Windermere*. Finally the group was joined by the Canadian destroyer *Niagara*.

There was an anxious moment, just after dawn, as an aeroplane appeared on the scene to drop two depth charges, which luckily missed their target. Since daybreak the sea had been too rough to launch a boat and in the end the First Lt of the trawler *Kingston Agate* suggested that he might cross over in a life raft rather than a boat. A line was shot over to U 570 and three men attempted the crossing, although the waves were still like mountains. By the time Temporary Lt H. B. Campbell reached the U-boat there had been ample time to destroy secret documents and to break up internal machinery.

In the end U 570 was towed to Iceland, where she was beached and made seaworthy for a trip to Britain under her own steam and under the new name of HMS *Graph*. After extensive trials she joined the British submarine fleet and even shot a torpedo at U 333, but failed to sink it. Eventually HMS *Graph* was wrecked on the Island of Islay off the coast of Scotland.

Rahmlow and his men were taken to Britain where, after the usual interrogation, they were sent to prison camps. The officers went to POW Camp No. 1 at Grizdale Hall, where the ace Otto Kretschmer was already the senior German prisoner. At first the Germans did not speak to the survivors from U 570 and it was not until after an illegal court of honour, headed by Kretschmer, that the officers were accepted as innocent, except for the First Lt, who it was held should either have arrested Rahmlow to avoid surrender or have scuttled the boat. As the result the IWO was isolated from the rest of the prisoners and not permitted to take part in the usual prisoners' activities.

Later, when it was learned that HMS *Graph*, was moored at Barrow-in-Furness, not all that far away, it was suggested that the IWO might regain his honour by escaping and sinking the boat. The escape worked well, but the IWO was caught the following day by the home guard and shot while trying to escape. Rahmlow arrived at the camp just after this incident, by which time the British authorities had gathered what was going on and moved him to another camp, which housed mainly Luftwaffe personnel, who would not be aware of the fuss over U 570. Even today, when one talks to some ex-U-boat men one gets the impression that Rahmlow is still an 'outcast'.

The other major U-boat capture during the war was when a United States Hunter-Killer Group, Task Force 22.3, managed to take possession of U 505 near the African coast and successfully tow it across the Atlantic to Bermuda. U 505 had been an unlucky boat in many ways. Not only did it have to break off several promising cruises to return for repairs, but it was also caught several times in the 'Black Pit of Biscay' and did not succeed in breaking into the Atlantic. Then for its last voyage the boat left Brest on March 16th 1944 and made its way as far as the Ivory Coast. All went well until 11.00 hours on Sunday June 4th when it became necessary to surface so that the batteries could be charged. At this critical stage they ran into the American Hunter-Killer Group.

Oblt z S Lange had to attack with the very little power left, hoping that he could sink his hunters. Not only were two destroyers visible but also the U-boats' most dreaded enemy–an aircraft-carrier. At least one torpedo left U 505, but it had no effect and it was not long before she was at the receiving end, being bombarded with shallow set depth charges. The U-boat went out of control, leaving Lange no choice except that of plummetting to the bottom or blowing the ballast tanks to surface.

The United States Task Force was made up of the aircraft carrier *Guadalcanal* and five destroyers *Pillsbury*, *Pope*, *Flaherty*, *Jenks* and *Chatelain*, which had sailed from Norfolk in Virginia, under the command of Capt Daniel V. Gallery, to destroy U-boats in the Atlantic. Gallery, like his Royal Navy counterparts, had thought that it must be possible to capture a U-boat, by keeping it under water until its power was exhausted and then to encourage the crew to abandon ship very quickly so that a boarding party could get on board.

The *Chatelain* was first to make asdic contact with U 505 and while it went into attack, two fighter planes were sent up from the carrier. Seeing the U-boat lurking in the depths they marked the spot by shooting their machine guns at it. Several more depth charges produced large patches of oil followed by the submarine itself. As the men came out of the hatch the Americans opened fire with anti-personnel shells to discourage manning of the anti-aircraft guns, but not to damage the boat. Several U-boat men were injured, but only one person was killed. At this stage, when the men had left U 505, a whaler came alongside and a boarding party under the leadership of Lt Albert David tried to get on board. This was no easy task as U 505 was still going round in circles at a speed of about seven knots. Once inside the control room it was discovered that the only scuttling action that had been taken was to

Korvettenkapitän Heinrich Bleichrodt wearing the Ritterkreuz mit Eichenlaub *(Oakleaves to the Knight's Cross). He commanded U 48, the most successful U-boat during the war, also U 67 and U 109. With these three boats he sank a sloop and 24 merchant ships totalling 151. 319 tons and he damaged a merchant ship of 6. 548 tons.*

Admiral Hans-Georg von Friedeburg wearing a leather coat. He was chief of the Organisation Department of the U-boat Arm and in 1941 he became Admiral for U-boats. During April 1945 he was promoted to Ob.d.M. (Commander-in-Chief of the Navy).

remove one small cap, which was emitting sea water. This was quickly replaced and a hosepipe lowered from a destroyer to pump out the water.

Gallery did not risk taking the U-boat to the nearby African coast because he felt certain there would be German sympathisers who would inform Germany of his secret capture (U 505 had not used its radio) or even attempt to sink the boat; so U 505 was towed over the Atlantic to Bermuda. It was used first for extensive tests and now is a memorial to the Battle of the Atlantic at the Science and Industry Museum in Chicago.

A few more U-boats can be added to the 'captured' list, although they did not remain afloat long enough to be of much use to their captors. Some secret information might have been removed from them.

U 501 was forced to surface by HMCS *Chambly* and HMCS *Moose Jaw* on September 10th, 1941, which was not very long after the capture of U 570. Once on the surface, the U-boat became entangled with one of the destroyers and her commander Korv Kpt Hugo Förster jumped on to the *Moose Jaw*. This was considered by the Germans as a serious case of abandoning command and when he arrived at POW Camp No. 1 (Grizedale Hall) Förster was ordered to stand trial at the illegal Court of Honour, which had passed sentence on U 570's officers. However Förster was moved to another POW Camp after the British authorities gathered what was afoot. Later on he was exchanged for British prisoners, whereupon he committed suicide.

Another hunt lasting one and a half days by British and Canadian ships resulted in some men from HMCS *Chilliwack* getting aboard U 744 to hoist the white ensign and to collect a few documents. However this took place on March 6th, 1944, by which time such secret information was probably largely known by the British.

U 1024 was captured by HMS *Loch Glendhu* on April 12th, 1945 and taken in tow, but it sank a few hours later while being towed by HMS *Loch Moore*. U 175 was boarded by Lt Ross Bullard, from US Coast Guard Cutter *Spencer*, with the aim of throwing a hand grenade down the hatch to kill the occupants in order to capture the boat. After jumping on to the conning tower Bullard saw a blood-covered control room, the result of an earlier artillery action. He found that the boat was already sinking and that there was nothing that he could do to save it.

6

Administration of the U-boat Arm

Before the War

The establishing of a Submarine Defence School in Kiel on October 1st, 1933 was the unofficial foundation of Germany's new U-boat Arm. The purpose of this school was not so much to train the men to fight against submarines but to prepare them to become the future U-boat personnel. Some of these hand-picked students gained practical experience aboard the various submarines constructed by the Submarine Development Bureau, but on the whole their training was very much land-based on specially constructed equipment, simulated to look like control panels of U-boats. So, by the time U 1 was commissioned, there was already a core of well-trained men to man these new boats.

The first boats to be launched in 1935 became training vessels and even those classed as *operational* were really training boats during the first years. On September 27th, 1935 Kpt z S Karl Dönitz became chief of this first small operational or advanced training flotilla. At that time the U-boat arm was made up of the following submarines:

1st U-boat Flotilla (Flotilla Weddigen)

BASE: Kiel
CHIEF: Kpt z S Karl Dönitz
U-BOATS: U 7 Kptlt Freiwald
U 8 Kptlt Grosse
U 9 Kptlt Looff
U 10 Oblt z S Scheringer
U 11 Kptlt Rösing
U 12 Oblt z S von Schmidt

U-boat School with Flotilla

BASE: Kiel
Head of school and chief of flotilla: Freg Kpt Slevogt
U-BOATS: U 1 Kptlt Ewert
U 2 Oblt z S Michahelles
U 3 Oblt z S Meckel
U 4 Oblt z S Weingärtner
U 5 Oblt z S Dau
U 6 Oblt z S Mathes

In addition there was a mine and torpedo inspection unit and a committee that examined and tested new U-boat designs. The following surface vessels were also attached to the U-boat arm: T 23, T 156 and T 158 as well as the depot ship *Saar*. These ships were used as general purpose boats, flagships, tenders and also to help train new recruits.

The development which followed 1935 was not directed on building up a strong U-boat fighting force, but to creating a system which provided the best and most rapid training facilities. This meant that the Weddigen Flotilla was kept small and a further flotilla was added, with a new base at Wilhelmshaven, thus greatly increasing the number of key jobs and the machinery needed to maintain the fleet. As the 2nd Flotilla (Flotilla Salzwedel) was added, there was also some additional reorganisation; Dönitz became overall commander of U-boats and two new flotilla chiefs were promoted to head the operational flotillas. This development pattern of creating the largest number of key positions continued until the start of the war. Sometimes flotillas were even reduced in strength so that sufficient boats could be scraped together to form a new flotilla. The U-boat arm changed rapidly, so that at the beginning of August, 1939 it was as follows:

In Port – Early Days

Building U-boats at Germaniawerft in Kiel. Note the camouflage nets and that the second boat from the right has been covered with metal sheets. On the left are two mine-layers of Type X B.

U 34 (Type VII A)
The insignia shows Winston Churchill being squashed by an elephant. The black and white squares are a tactical sign from the U-boat school.

Type VII C boats in Danzig. Possibly U 377, showing the conning tower and 88mm quick firing gun.

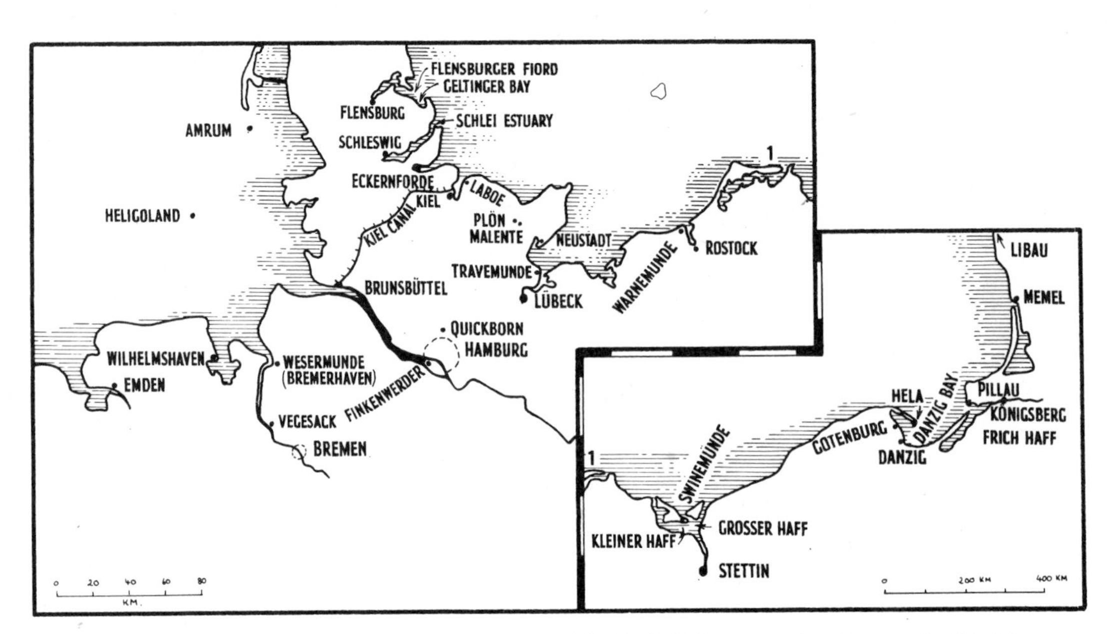

North Germany
Showing U-boats bases, headquarters, teaching establishments and other places mentioned. Note the different scale: (1) indicates the same spit of land on both maps.

Right: *U 377's commander, Korvettenkapitän Otto Köhler and watch officer. The W.O. is resting his hand on the torpedo aiming device. which would have special water and pressure resistant binoculars clipped onto the top when in use.*

General U-boat Headquarters

Based at Kiel.
Führer (Commander) of U-boats: Kpt z S Karl Dönitz.

Assisted by a large staff of administrative, mechanical, medical, meteorological etc., officers and by legal advisors.

Attached to headquarters was the U-boat escort vessel *Erwin Wassner* and the flagship for the FdU was the convoy tender *Hai.*

1st U-boat Flotilla (Flotilla Weddigen)

BASE: Kiel
CHIEF: Kptlt Looff
U-BOATS: U 9, U 13, U 15, U 17, U 19, U 21, U 23, U 59.
OTHER UNITS: U-boat escort vessels *Donau* & *Memel.*

2nd U-boat Flotilla (Flotilla Salzwedel)

BASE: Wilhelmshaven
CHIEF: Korv Kpt Ibbeken
U-BOATS: U 26, U 27, U 28, U 29, U 30, U 31, U 32, U 33, U 34, U 35.
OTHER UNIT: Depot ship *Saar*

3rd U-boat Flotilla (Flotilla Lohs)

BASE: Kiel
CHIEF: Kptlt Eckermann
U-BOATS: U 12, U 14, U 16, U 18, U 20, U 22, U 24.
OTHER UNIT: U-boat tender *Weichsel*

4th U-boat Flotilla

This flotilla existed only on paper during August 1939. There were several commanders attached to the flotilla at one time, but no boats.

5th U-boat Flotilla (Flotilla Emsmann)

BASE: Kiel
CHIEF: Kptlt Rösing
U-BOATS: U 56, U 57, U 58, U 60.
OTHER UNIT: U-boat escort vessel *Lech*

6th U-boat Flotilla (Flotilla Hundius)

BASE: Wilhelmshaven
CHIEF: Korv Kpt Hartmann
U-BOATS: U 37, U 38, U 39, U 40, U 41, U 42 (?), U 43 (?).
OTHER UNIT: U-boat escort vessel *Isar*

7th U-boat Flotilla (Flotilla Wegener)

BASE: Kiel
CHIEF: Kptlt Sobe
U-BOATS: U 45, U 46, U 47, U 48, U 51, U 52, U 53.
OTHER UNIT: (?)

U-boat School

BASE: Neustadt
HEAD OF SCHOOL: Kpt z S Scheer.
CHIEF OF THE SCHOOL'S FLOTILLA: Kptlt Beduhn.
SCHOOL'S FLOTILLA: U 1, U 2, U 3, U 4, U 5, U 6, U 7, U 8, U 10, U 11, U 25, U36.

In addition there were several supporting committees, such as those mentioned earlier.

N.B: The flotillas were named after first World War U-boat heroes. The organisation pattern for the beginning of August 1939 accounts for 55 U-boats. U 49 and U 61 were commissioned on August 12th, 1939, so that there was a total of 57 U-boats by the time war started. 58 boats had actually been commissioned, but this includes U 18, which sank after a collision with T 156 on November 22nd, 1936, and was salvaged to be commissioned a second time. It may appear strange that U 44, U 49, U 50, U 54 and U 55 are not included in the list, but these boats were commissioned after the war started. Commissionings and launchings did not take place in numerical order.

Up to August, 1939 there had been little difference in the organisation and activities of the operational and school boats, with the latter often working in the same area as the former. In addition to this recruits were not always thoroughly trained in school boats, because there were ample opportunities to finish training in the operational flotillas. With the coming of war all this had to change; school boats had to restrict their movements to the Baltic, out of reach of the RAF, and it became impossible for the operational boats to carry too many inexperienced men. Even the administrative organisation was unsuitable for war and rapid changes had to be made. Some temporary reorganisation was carried out during the autumn, 1939 to meet the immediate demands of war. It was not until the end of that year that a major reshuffle took place. This new set-up lasted until the decline in 1944.

The existing six flotillas were merged into three larger units and later new flotillas were added, as more boats became available. These new flotillas were by no means equal in strength; since those serving the Atlantic had to carry the main burden of the fighting, they also had the largest number of boats. Boats did not always remain under the command of one flotilla leader, but sometimes were swapped around. The strongest of these flotillas was, without doubt, the 5th U-boat Flotilla (*Flotilla Emsmann*), which from its foundation until the end had some 340 U-boats among its ranks.

The Main War Years

Dönitz was promoted to Admiral during October 1939, with the new title of *Befehlshaber der Unterseeboote* or *BdU* (Commander-in-Chief for U-boats). His title before this had been *Führer der Unterseeboote* or *FdU* (Commander/leader for U-boats). Four new *FdU*s were appointed, each to be responsible for an *Operation Area*. Three areas, the Black Sea, the Baltic Sea and the Far East were covered by so few boats that they did not warrant a special leader. These areas were controlled by a flotilla chief.

Operation Area: West

FdU headquarters: Paris/Angers.
1st U-boat Flotilla—bases: Kiel/Brest
2nd U-boat Flotilla—bases: Wilhelmshaven/La Rochelle
3rd U-boat Flotilla—bases: Kiel/La Pallice/La Rochelle
6th U-boat Flotilla—bases: Danzig/St Nazaire
7th U-boat Flotilla—base: Brest or St Nazaire
9th U-boat Flotilla—base: Brest
10th U-boat Flotilla—base: Lorient
12th U-boat Flotilla—base: Bordeaux

The 2nd, 3rd and 7th Flotillas later moved to Norway.

Operation Area: Norway and Arctic

FdU headquarters: Narvik

11th U-boat Flotilla—base: Bergen
13th U-boat Flotilla—base: Trondheim

Operation Area: Central

This group was founded sometime during the early summer of 1944 with about 45 boats to prepare as a special invasion defence force.

Operation Area: Mediterranean

FdU headquarters: Rome/Toulon/Aix de Provence

23rd U-boat Flotilla—base: Salamis
29th U-boat Flotilla—bases: La Spezia/Toulon/Pola/Marseille/Salamis.

Action Area: Black Sea

30th U-boat Flotilla—bases: Constanca/Feodosia.

Action Area: Baltic Sea

22nd U-boat Flotilla—base: Gotenhafen.

Action Area: Far East

No special flotilla operated in this area. Long distance U-boats made the journeys from France and Norway. There was a German maintenance administrative force in Penang and later in other Far Eastern ports.

Admiral Erich Raeder resigned as Commander-in-Chief of the Navy on January 30th, 1943 and was succeeded by Karl Dönitz, who for the time being also carried on as *BdU*. Later the two tasks in combination proved to be too difficult and Admiral Hans Georg von Friedeburg, second in command of the U-boat arm, took on the job of *BdU*, so that Dönitz could turn his attention to the other parts of the navy.

During 1944 the U-boat Arm's role changed drastically from the offensive to the defensive. The situation became so difficult that the normal operation of U-boats became impossible. During the fall of France there were several small isolated groups, all trying to survive in the best way they could. The administrative pattern of the period was just as chaotic as the war and was often in need of revision to keep pace with the ever-changing front. The following, therefore, only attempts to show the rough pattern during the last six months of the war:

Bases in France

The higher officers departed from their French headquarters to safer places in Germany or Norway, leaving flotilla chiefs and boat commanders to organise whatever forces remained. A number of U-boats became non-operational due to mechanical breakdowns, and in some cases the crews were transferred to the land forces in order to help defend bases against the advancing Allied armies.

Flotillas in France:

2nd U-boat Flotilla—base: Lorient
chief: Kpt z S Kals
(Later some boats and personnel managed to escape to Norway.)

7th U-boat Flotilla—base: St Nazaire
chief: Korv Kpt Diening

Other forces in France had been disbanded, with the remaining boats moved to other flotillas; some were amalgamated, and a few managed to make their way to Norway.

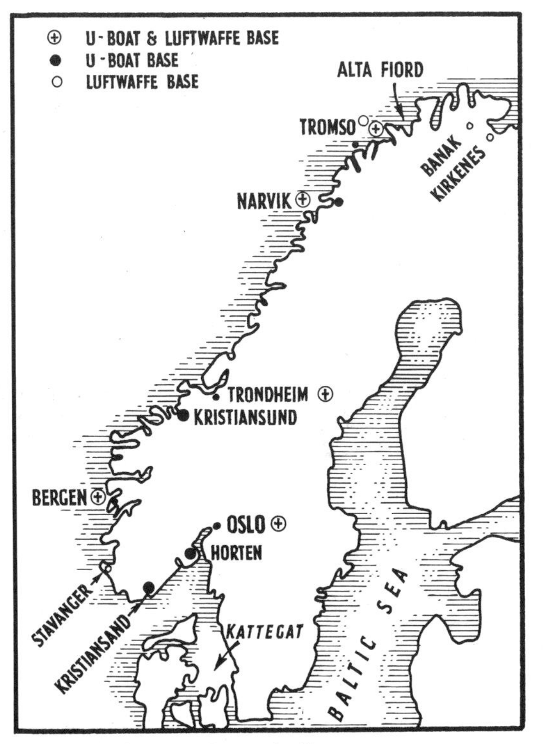

The Main German Bases in Norway

Kristiansand is often followed with "S" or "Süd' (South) so as not to confuse it with Kristiansund. The first mentioned is the larger of the two towns and this was the U-boat base, but Kristiansund is also a sea port and it features in some U-boat documents.

Top right: *Lookouts on the bridge of U 377. The compass attached to the 'stand' of the attack periscope is clearly visible in the middle of the photo. The metal rods at the top are part of the torpedo loading device.*

Right: *Jak Mallmann and Karl-Heinz Nitschke wearing "Machine overalls" on the gun platform of U 377. Thick gloves were necessary for handling machinery. The flag is the* Kriegsmarine's *Ensign.*

A Focke-Wulf-Kurier, the type of plane used for reconnaissance in the Atlantic.

Above and Right: *U 377 patrols a Norwegian fiord.*
Far right: *U 377 tied up in Narvik.*

Operation Area: West

FdU headquarters: Bergen

11th U-boat Flotilla—base: Bergen
chief: Freg Kpt Lehmann-Willenbrock

15th U-boat Flotilla—base: Kristiansand(Süd)
chief: (?)

(This flotilla was planned to become operational during spring 1945, but the lack of boats and trained men prevented this.)

33rd U-boat Flotilla—base: Flensburg later Penang and Djakarta
chief: Korv Kpt Kuhnke

Operation Area: Arctic

FdU headquarters: Narvik

13th U-boat Flotilla—base: Trondheim
chief: Freg Kpt Rüggeberg

14th U-boat Flotilla—base: Narvik
chief: Korv Kpt Möhlmann

Operation Area: East (Baltic)

FdU headquarters: Danzig

4th U-boat Flotilla—base: Stettin
chief: Freg Kpt Fischer

5th U-boat Flotilla—base: Kiel
chief: Korv Kpt Moehle

8th U-boat Flotilla—base: Königsberg/Danzig
chief: Freg Kpt Pauckstadt

31st U-boat Flotilla—base: Hamburg/Wilhelmshaven/Wesermünde
chief: Kpt z S Mahn, later Korv Kpt Emermann

32nd U-boat Flotilla—base: Königsberg, later Hamburg
chief: Freg Kpt Rigele, later Freg Kpt Heyse

Operation Area: Far East (Asia)

There was a German Admiral in Japan.

U-boat chief: Freg Kpt Dommes
Main base: Penang
Other bases: Shonan, Singapore, Djakarta, Batavia, Surabaja, Kobe.

Educational Units

1st U-boat Training Division

Operational period: June 1940 to March 1945.
Base: Neustadt, Holstein, later Hamburg and Pillau.

(This was the same school as the U-boat school of Neustadt which was commanded by Kpt

z S Scheer. (See earlier pages). It was renamed *1st U-boat Training Division – Pillau*, and it was also known as *1st U-boat Training Division – Finkenwerder (Hamburg)*. Some post-war publications state that although the Division was renamed *Pillau*, the base remained at Neustadt. A change of base certainly took place very rapidly: the author's father was a student at Neustadt during this period. He went on weekend leave from Neustadt and on returning was suddenly informed that everybody had to move to Pillau more or less straight away.

21st U-boat Flotilla

Attached to the 1st Training Division.
(The same flotilla which was once commanded by Kptlt Beduhn. See earlier pages.)

2nd U-boat Training Division

Operational period: November 1940 to January 1945
Base: Gotenhafen

22nd U-boat Flotilla

Attached to the 2nd Training Division. The flotilla moved from Gotenhafen to Wilhelmshaven and continued to be operational after the disbanding of the Training Division.

3rd U-boat Training Division

Operational period: Late 1943 to May 1945
Base: Neustadt

4th U-boat Training Division

Operational period: For about 10 months during 1944
Base: Memel

1st U-boat Instruction Department

Operational period: February 1940 to May1945
Base: Plön

2nd U-boat Instruction Department

Operational period: May 1941 to May 1945
Base: Neustadt/Zeven (Hannover)

3rd U-boat Instruction Department

Operational period: Spring 1941 to May 1945
Base: Pillau, later Schleswig.

(*U-boat Training Division* is *U-Bootslehrdivision* in German and *U-boat Instruction Department* is *U-Bootsausbildungsabteilung* in German.)

Educational Flotillas

FdU for Educational Flotillas: Kpt z S Viktor Schütze.
FdU headquarters: Gotenhafen.

Christmas 1942 being celebrated inside the forward torpedo compartment of U 377, while the boat was stationed in Norway. The torpedo tubes have been hidden by the flag.

18th U-boat Flotilla

Operational period:	First three months of 1945
Base:	Hela

19th U-boat Flotilla

Operational period:	October 1943 to May 1945
Base:	Pillau/Kiel

20th U-boat Flotilla

Operational period:	June 1943 to February 1945
Base:	Pillau

23rd U-boat Flotilla

Operational period:	August 1943 to March 1945
Base:	Danzig

24th U-boat Flotilla

Operational period:	November 1939 to March (?) 1945
Bases:	Danzig/Memel/Trondheim/Gotenhafen/Eckernförde

(In 1940 this was called the *1st U-boat Training Flotilla.*)

25th U-boat Flotilla

Operational period:	April 1940 to May 1945
Bases:	Danzig/Trondheim/Memel/Libau/Gotenhafen/Travemünde

(This was called *2nd U-boat Training Flotilla* in 1940.)

26th U-boat Flotilla

Operational period:	April 1941 to May 1945
Base:	Pillau/Warnemünde

27th U-boat Flotilla

Operational period:	January 1940 to March 1945
Base:	Gotenhafen

(This was called *taktische U-Bootsfrontausbildungsflotille* in 1940.)

Technical Training Group for Operational U-boats (*AGRU Front*)

Operational period:	September 1941 to May 1945
Bases:	Hela/Bornholm/Echernförde

In addition there were various experimental units and a number of general supporting committees.

The U-boat Flotillas

Flotilla Number and Name	*Total† number of boats in flotilla.*	*Main base(s) and remarks*
1st (Flotilla Weddigen)	140	*Kiel.* After June 1941- *Brest.* Disbanded in September 1944.
2nd (Flotilla Saltzwedel)	90	*Wilhelmshaven.* After June 1941- *Lorient.*
3rd (Flotilla Lohs)	110	*Kiel.* After October 1941 *La Pallice.* Later also *La Rochelle.*
4th (Training Flotilla)	281	*Stettin* after 1941.
5th (Flotilla Emsmann)	340	*Kiel.*

6th (Flotilla Hundius)	93	*Wilhelmshaven.* After August 1941 in *Danzig.* Moved to *St Nazaire* during February 1942. Disbanded during August 1944.
7th (Flotilla Wegener)	114	*Kiel.* After June 1941 at *St Nazaire.* Moved to Norway during August 1944.
8th (Training Flotilla)	256	*Königsberg.* Moved to *Danzig* during February 1942.
9th	85	*Brest.* Founded during November 1941 and disbanded during August 1944.
10th	81	*Lorient.* Founded during January 1942 and disbanded during October 1944.
11th	189	*Bergen.* Founded during May 1942.
12th	48	*Bordeaux.* Founded during October 1942 and disbanded in August 1944.
13th	55	*Trondheim.* Founded during June 1943.
14th	6	*Narvik.* Founded during December 1944.
15th	0	Base (?). This flotilla was planned, but never made operational.
16th	0	Never operational. No details.
17th	0	Never operational. No details.
18th	4	Operational for first 3 months of 1945.
19th (Training Flotilla)	4	Founded during October 1943. Base after February 1945 at *Pillau* (?). Before this date. *Kiel*(?)
20th (Training Flotilla)	(?)	*Pillau* (?) Founded during June 1943 and disbanded in February 1945. No further details May not have been operational.
21st (Training Flotilla)	50	*Pillau.* Founded during June 1940 and disbanded in March 1945.
22nd (Training Flotilla)	45	*Gotenhafen.* Towards the end of the war at *Wilhelmshaven.* Founded in January 1941.
23rd (Training Flotilla)	30	*Danzig.* Founded in August 1943 and disbanded during March 1945.
24th (Training Flotilla)	52	*Danzig,* then *Memel,* then *Trondheim.* After this back to *Memel* and towards the end of the war at *Gotenhafen* and *Eckernförde.*
25th (Training Flotilla)	(?)	Bases in following order: *Danzig, Trondheim, Memel, Libau, Gotenhafen* and in the end *Travemünde.*
26th (Training Flotilla)	7	*Pillau* and towards the end at *Warnemünde.* Founded during April 1941.
27th (Training Flotilla)	1	*Gotenhafen.* Did it ever function as flotilla?
28th	0	Not operational. No details.
29th	54	*La Spezia, Toulon, Pola, Marseille* and later *Salamis.* Operational between December 1941 and September 1944.
30th	6	*Constanca* (*Black Sea*) Founded during October 1942 and disbanded in October 1944.
31st (Training Flotilla)	153	*Hamburg, Wilhelmshaven* and *Wesermünde.* Founded during September 1943.
32nd (Training Flotilla)	43	*Königsberg* and after January 1945 in Hamburg. Founded during August 1944.
33rd	75	*Flensburg,* with some boats in the Far East. Founded in September 1944.

Christmas 1942
Each man received a small present from the Flotilla Chief: A copy of the book Prien greift an *by Wolfgang Frank. This label, showing the insignia of the 11th U-boat Flotilla, was glued onto the first page. (Both the book and Dr Frank are still going strong!).*

†This is the total number during the whole 1935-1945 period. Please note that there is a list of which boats belonged to each Flotilla in Bodo Herzog's *U-Boats in Action*, published by Ian Allan, 1971.

7
Radar

No other invention contributed more to Germany's downfall than radar. It certainly had the greatest influence on the general appearance of conning towers and was responsible for the development of completely new types of U-boats, and for causing the greatest catastrophe in the history of the German Navy.

The name radar evolved from *Radio Detection and Ranging*, which was how the system was first known. Although many readers are no doubt familiar with this now commonplace equipment, at the beginning of World War II this method of being able to detect targets, by measuring the time taken (i.e. distance) for a radio signal to be reflected back from a solid object, was completely new. By using radar, targets could be 'seen' in conditions which had previously been impossible for optical rangefinders eg at night, in heavy rain or in fog.

The story of U-boats and radar really started about the time that Hitler came to power and not, as it is often stated, during the war. It is not true that the Allies surprised Germany with it. The first serious experiments with radio ranging methods were carried out by the Germans on March 20th, 1934 in Kiel. This was some 1½ years before the Admiralty in London officially approved the start of British radar development. The basic difference between these two initial projects was that Britain was thinking of a detecting and ranging device and Germany was more concerned with a radio rangefinder, to be used after the target had been located. The reason for these two ideas was that radar waves can easily be picked up by casual observers thus revealing the user's position and the *Kriegsmarine*, being so weak against the Royal Navy, could not afford to reveal its presence on the high seas. In fact the only way Germany could score against Britain was in the Royal Navy not knowing where the German ships were.

Radio rangefinders, known as *Drehturm Gerät* or just *DT* or *DeTe Gerät* (revolving turret apparatus), were in effective use long before the start of the war. During those early days only the *Kriegsmarine* experimented with radio rangefinders. The *Luftwaffe* and U-boat Arm had not yet been formed and the army showed no interest. This meant that the weight and size of the equipment was not a critical factor as it was intended for use aboard large battleships. After success with the initial equipment it was thought that better results might be obtained from a smaller device which would work on a shorter waveband than the 1½ metre used by the *DT Apparatus*. This would for technical reasons, produce an overall smaller and lighter set, which could perhaps be installed in aircraft. Research was carried out into the possibilities of smaller wavebands, but the responsible brains concluded that any wavelength under ½ metre would not work. Indeed they even produced spectacular graphs to convince their superiors that the effectiveness of the invention declined as the wavelength shortened and that the waves disappeared completely at about 50 centimetres; centimetre waveband radio ranging was 'utterly impossible'.

This research did, however, result in a smaller radar device than the *DT Apparatus* which went into production during the winter of 1938/39. Not more than a dozen or so sets were produced during this period. Two sets were installed aboard U-boats during the early summer of 1939. Both boats considered the performance of the radar to be only satisfactory. The aerials had to be specially reduced in size, so that they could be housed on the conning tower. Modifications enabling the antennae to resist high water

Establishing a Secret Weather Station
Dr Nusser and his men of the secret Weather Corps on the bows of U 377 while on their way to Spitzbergen. In the foreground is the 88mm gun.

U 377 moored in a fiord at Cape Mitra, Spitzbergen. The stores were unloaded with rubber dinghies until......

....the water froze over completely.

At first the men were anxious in case the ice crushed the boat......

....later it was found that men could walk on the ice and the stores were unloaded with sledges instead of rubber dinghies.

U 377 silhouetted against the midnight sun.

pressure were also necessary. Altogether the equipment was rather complicated and space inside U-boats was too limited for this still cumbersome device to be accepted. It was decided therefore, less than one month before the start of the war, that U-boats should not be supplied with radar sets and that they would be fitted with underwater detection devices instead. This decision contributed to the cancelling of research in the field of radio ranging.

As the war started there were still numerous fears, particularly among the U-boat personnel, that Britain would have some secret device for locating submarines. As the war progressed it became apparent that this was not true. It was possible to approach close to Royal Navy vessels without being detected. There were even reports of British destroyers passing less than 100 metres from a U-boat without spotting it. Günther Prien in U 47 made submarine history by penetrating the heavily defended waters of Scapa Flow. These experiences contributed to the idea that radar would never play an important role in the war. Later as the war pulled a tight cord around Germany's resources and numerous projects had to be curtailed, Hitler ordered that all research which could not be concluded within one year should be cancelled. As a result large areas of German radar research was abandoned.

The first radar assisted attack against a U-boat took place on November 19th, 1940, but the U-boat escaped.

According to British records the first U-boat actually sunk after being located by radar was one attacked by a Whitley on February 10th, 1941, although there is no record on the German side of a U-boat having been lost during that month. These were important events for Britain, but radar was not sufficiently used to arouse serious thoughts in Germany, where these incidents were written off as ordinary attacks. U-boat Headquarters began to receive reports from commanders who claimed that they were attacked under conditions when they could not have been located by visual sightings. The reports often stated that aircraft dropped out of low clouds or that they suddenly appeared on a pitch-black night and that they must have spotted the U-boat first, before moving into the best attacking positions. The shore-based officers, who evaluated such reports, always came back to the same conclusion that 'lookouts were not awake'. It was not until 1942 that someone in high authority mentioned 'radio ranging'.

After several experiments, Germany came to the conclusion that Britain was using a similar device to the *DT Apparatus* and that this could be rendered useless by producing a radio set which could detect such radar signals. There was nothing available immediately since research and development had been stopped earlier in the war and at least some six months were needed to develop a suitable radar warning device.

Information about a primitive aerial for picking up Very High Frequency radio waves was, however, passed to all U-boats in order that the men could construct their own. The aerial consisted of a rough wooden cross with wires strung around the outside. Construction was so simple that only a few nails, screws and pieces of wood were needed in addition to the wire. It worked on 1.4 metre to 1.8 metre wavelengths and could detect a radar set up to a distance of about 30 kilometres.

This first cross-like aerial was nicknamed the *Biscay Cross*, because it was first used in the Bay of Biscay. The receiver was called *Metox* or *FuMB 1.* In operation the cross was held in a fitting on the conning tower, where it had to be turned by hand. On receiving a signal it had to be thrown down the hatch (it was too fragile to remain on the tower with water washing around it) often with the duty watch landing in the control room on top of it, so that it had to be repaired before further use. The Biscay Cross was succeeded by a more sophisticated Metox aerial, which was also fixed on the conning tower and could detect radar impulses at ranges exceeding 100 kilometres. At this early stage both the clumsy Biscay Cross and the circular dipole aerial were being used at the same time. The crew were put on the alert once an aerial contact was picked up on the 100 kilometre range antennae, but the boat would not dive until these signals were also received on the Biscay Cross, indicating that the plane was merely 30 kilometres away.

The main problem with the Metox receiver was that it did not always respond in the same way. Sometimes it would buzz and at other times it would give out hair-raising whistles. This

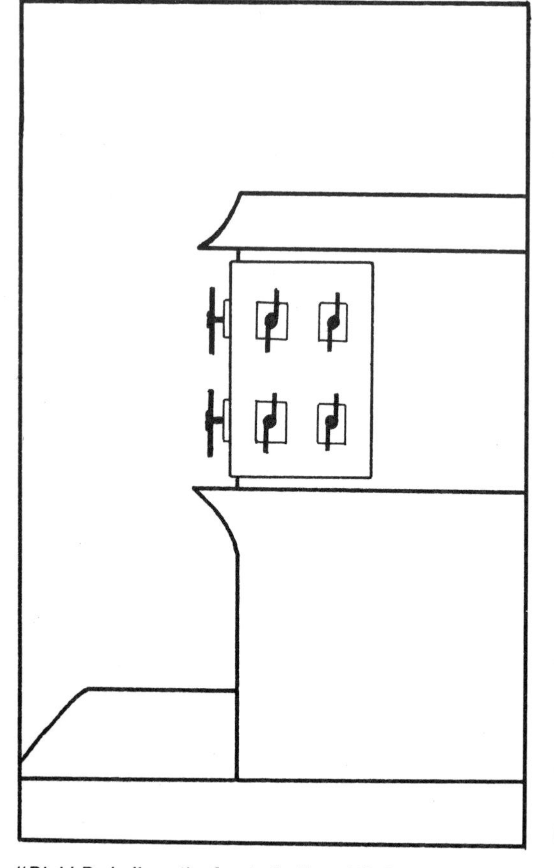

"Rigid Radar" on the front of a Type VII C conning tower. This apparatus was based on the same principle as the D. T. Gerät. *It was fixed in position and the only way it could do a 360° sweep was for the boat to sail in a complete circle. This radar was only fixed to a few boats.*

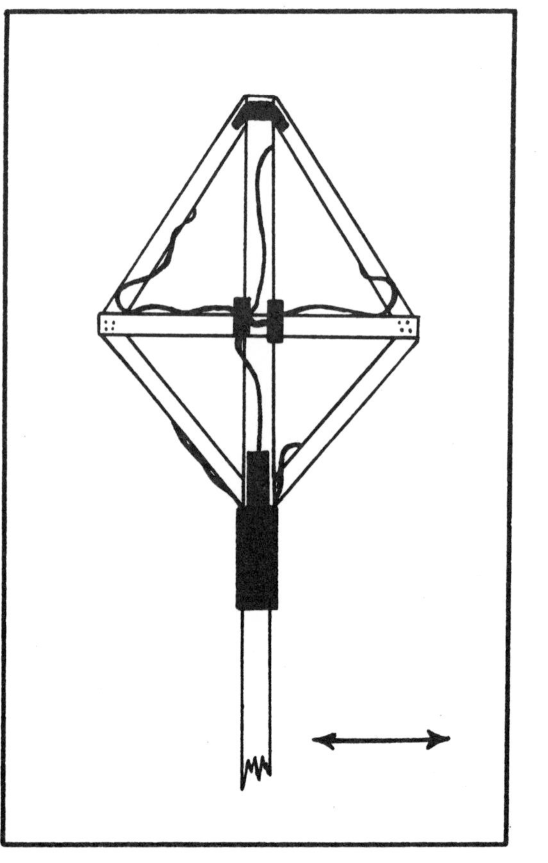

The first Metox Radar Aerial – The "Biscay Cross". Some of these were made from old planks obtained from packing cases. The wood around the outside of the cross was sometimes missing and the wires were just crudely wrapped around the structure.
The arrow indicates the approx. width of a man's head.

played so much on the crews' nerves that commanders often switched the 'blasted thing off in order to remain sane'.

This radar set, which the Allies were using, was known as *Air to Surface Vessel Apparatus* or *ASV Radar*, and it functioned on a wavelength similar to the German *DT Apparatus.* It was not rendered completely useless, as the German crews had hoped, after the U-boats were capable of receiving its impulses. The RAF merely adopted a different attacking technique. Attacking planes would cruise at a high altitude with ASV switched on. On making contact, the radar was switched off and the pilot informed of the approximate position. He would then manoeuvre into a favourable attacking position, while losing height for the last 'run up'. If the visibility was good, he would attack without further use of the radar. At night, however, the ASV might be switched on several times for a single sweep to ensure that the plane was still following the correct path. If it was so dark as to be impossible to see anything, then the Leigh Light (Powerful searchlight) would be switched on for final location. At this stage the operation became rather nerve-wracking for the pilot, because two out of three times he could be faced with a tall merchant ship and not a low U-boat. There were numerous reports from the Merchant Navy of aeroplanes just managing to clear the mastheads. RAF pilots soon learned that it is very difficult to judge distances in the dark and that the U-boat gunners would start shooting as soon as the Leigh Light was switched on, even though the plane was still beyond their range. The pilot would then home on to the flashes from the anti-aircraft gun and pray that the gun would be vacated, with the boat diving, by the time he came within range. (This was at a time when U-boats were still equipped with only one single AA gun.)

Radar was not the sole weapon introduced by Britain. The *Leigh Light*, fitted under the aircraft's wing, was a very effective searchlight with a beam which could pick out a U-boat on the surface on a dark night, at over one kilometre's range. This greatly contributed towards night time 'kills'. Another successful invention was the *High Frequency Direction Finder*, abbreviated H/F D/F and known as 'Huff Duff'. This was a revolutionary method of determining the source of radio signals. (Dönitz often broadcast to his commanders and many messages were passed from one boat to another. These were usually too short for conventional triangulation direction finders to get a bearing on and so this free conversation was regarded as safe). Huff Duff could quickly pin-point the source of even a brief radio call and was of great use to the Allies because U-boats made frequent use of their radios. Huff Duff receivers were installed from October, 1941 onwards, both on ships and in coastal stations. Only a relatively few sets were required; for example–a whole convoy required merely one set in order to be able to learn when U-boats were near them.

In addition to these new tools Britain also introduced new anti-U-boat techniques, turning her role in the battle from the defensive to the offensive. Improved fighter aircraft launching rails were fitted to some merchant ships while others, especially tankers, were converted to aircraft carriers. This meant that a convoy could launch its own planes to hunt U-boats.

Meanwhile back in Germany, the hierarchy of the *Kriegsmarine* did not admit defeat with the introduction of radar. Instead they stated that this would help U-boats and it was even suggested that U-boat commanders might use radar signals to locate convoys! The commanders were not told, however, that they would be virtually committing suicide if they attacked when the enemy knew their exact position. It is not known how many commanders tried this method of locating their targets; many of them probably died in the attempt, taking their crews with them. Still it was accepted practice and at least one commander who tried this method of seeking out a convoy did live long enough to tell the tale.

Oblt z S Gerhard Kluth, who had succeeded Otto Köhler, left Brest in U 377 for the boat's 12th sortie against the enemy and managed to cross the 'Black Pit' of the Bay of Biscay without incident. Once in the Atlantic, the boat was directed against a west-bound convoy, which the lookouts had spotted during the early hours of the night. The convoy was so well protected that Kluth was forced to attack a nearby destroyer with a salvo of torpedoes fired from the surface. The following necessary dive manoeuvre made it impossible to observe results, but a large explosion and the sudden absence of propeller noise made them think that they had been successful. (Diving is always a time-consuming manoeuvre and the convoy had disappeared by the time U 377 resurfaced).

A thick fog developed shortly before radar impulses were picked up again. This gave the enemy more than the normal advantage because they could detect the U-boat, but Kluth had no way of knowing where the destroyers would be. In spite of this Kluth was determined to have another 'kill' and slowly closed in on the convoy using the radar impulses as a guide and relying on his iron nerve to keep him moving forward. Everything went well, with the boat running on the surface, until one of the lookouts spotted a destroyer heading straight towards them. The men were already tumbling down the hatch as the alarm sounded and U 377 dropped rapidly into 'the cellar'. Sometime during this confusion the boat gave a violent shudder, but the machinery continued to function, so no notice was taken of it. For some unknown reason, there were no further attacks from the destroyer. Had it run into the U-boat by accident? No depth charges followed. Noises from several propellers were heard. Kluth carefully took the boat up to periscope depth, but did not spot anything.

Eventually after resurfacing the fog had lifted and the men examined the boat to discover the

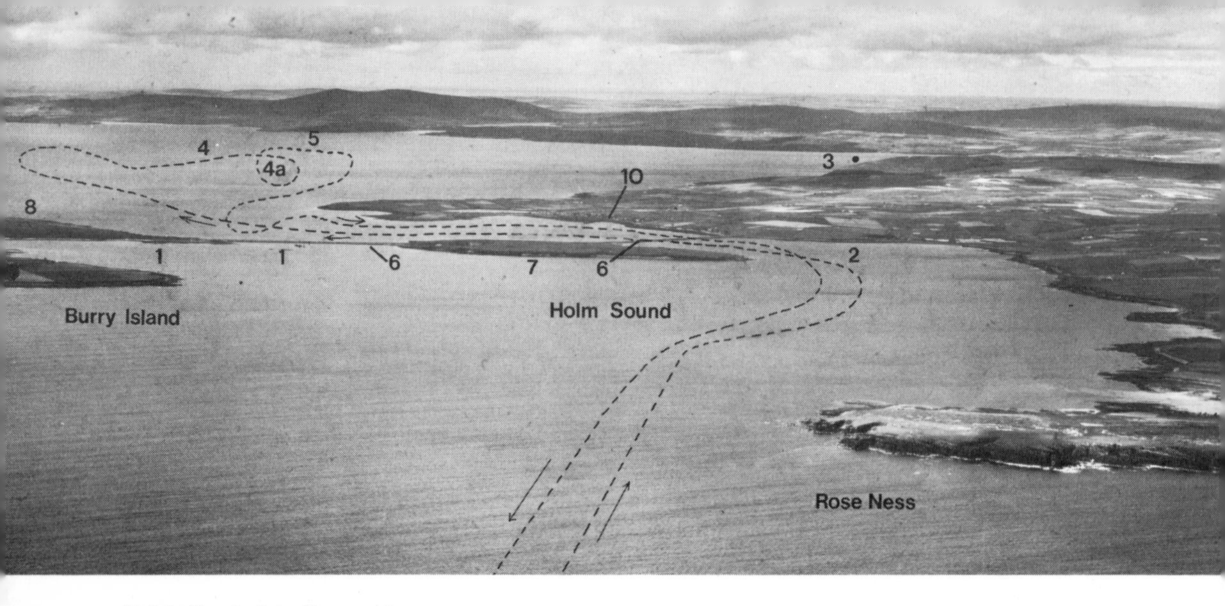

U 47's Route into Scapa Flow

1. These channels were blocked with underwater obstructions. 2. Around this spot were some underwater obstructions. 3. Approximate position of HMS Royal Oak. *4. Approximate position from where U 47 fired its first salvo. 4A. Approximate position from where the rear torpedo was fired. 5. Approximate position from where the U-boat shot the second salvo. 6. The Churchill Barrier, erected after Prien's visit. 7. Island of Lamb Holm. 8. Island of Glims Holm. 10. St. Mary's village with small pier.*
The photo was taken over the North Sea looking into Scapa Flow in a north-west direction.

reason for the sudden shudder: they were appalled to discover that the bows had been torn open! This damage was fortunately not fatal as the diving tanks and pressure hull were untouched. Before any decision regarding further action could be made a Liberator aircraft appeared on the scene. At first it circled well out of range of the 20mm anti-aircraft guns, then it flew in to attack. Kluth managed to out-manoeuvre the depth charges, but cannon fire from the plane killed two lookouts and injured Kluth's arm. This situation decided the course of action – with the boat's commander out of action there was no alternative but to return to base, because he was the only person on the boat trained to take it to battle and had no capable deputy.

Metox radar detectors were in widespread use by the end of 1942 and the initial shock of Britain's introduction of radio ranging methods was over. In fact the months following August, 1942 saw a steady increase in U-boat successes, with November showing the highest total of Allied tonnage sunk of any month during the whole of the war. At the same time the number of U-boats sunk, or at least attacked, steadily declined until December, when not a single boat was lost to radar. This led the *Kriegsmarine* to think that the 'radar stage' of the battle had been won by Germany because the detection aid had been rendered useless. A few sceptical people still argued that more research was necessary in this field, especially in the exploration of new wavebands. On the whole, this was considered unnecessary because earlier the 'experts' had stated that such radar could not possibly work.

Strange new reports started coming in from U-boat commanders, just as the *Oberkommando der Marine* (Naval High Command) was resting on its laurels of success. Commanders claimed that they were attacked under conditions in which visual sightings would have been impossible and the Metox gave no warning. The shore-based officers of the U-boat Headquarters knew that the Metox emitted hair-raising whistles, buzzes and shrieks and they thought that commanders had, against orders, switched the receiver off and were thus caught by surprise. The U-boat HQ officers even went so far as to study detailed weather reports, to see whether visibility was in fact as bad as the commanders had made out! Eventually they managed to convince themselves that these attacks were due to the men's negligence.

Several factors helped them to reach this conclusion. First there were the overall successes already mentioned. Secondly, a shot-down member of the RAF managed to convince the Germans that planes were homing in on the heat from the boats' exhausts (this is possible using infra-red light). Another British airman told a convincing story of how the Metox set also sent out radio waves which could be picked up by British aircraft. Thirdly, the radar 'experts' had been called in again and had quite definitely stated, as they had done at the beginning of the war: 'Radar with smaller wavebands is impossible!' All this convinced the *Seekriegsleitung* (Directorate for the war at sea) that further experiments were unnecessary. Germany tried an idea of coating U-boats with a type of foam rubber to absorb radar impulses, but this only reduced the performance of the boat and salt water and wave action soon removed the foam layer. This method was never universally adopted and was only used to coat small areas, such as schnorkel head valves.

The next chapter of radar and U-boats opened on February 12th, 1943, as German anti-aircraft fire shot down a British bomber near Rotterdam in Holland. Following usual standing orders *Luftwaffe* personnel located the wreck and carried out a routine examination. This search revealed something new – a badly battered and blood-encrusted box which had not been seen before. Superior technical staff were called at once for a closer examination. They discovered nothing noteworthy, except 'Experimental 6' written in pencil on the side. Telephone contact was made with the *Luftwaffe's* Supreme Command in Berlin, who asked for the box to be dismantled and brought as quickly as possible to their laboratories. The box was named 'Rotterdam Apparatus' for easy identification.

On arrival in Berlin the box was found to be badly damaged by the crash. However, experts found enough evidence to suggest that it was what Germany had long considered impossible – short-wave radar. Research into the reconstruction of the Rotterdam Apparatus started at once, but it was interrupted on March 9th as the Royal Air Force scored a direct hit (by accident) on the laboratory. The engineers considered the research so important that they climbed into the still-smouldering ruins to retrieve the apparatus. Hermann Göring, Commander-in-Chief of the Luftwaffe, also realised the importance of this little box. He made the most heavily-defended laboratories available and gave orders that the apparatus was to be reconstructed as quickly as possible. This research was suddenly given a boost as a similar set was found in a crashed bomber shot down over Berlin. The Rotterdam Apparatus in this plane was also heavily damaged, but those parts missing from the original set were still intact.

The reconstruction continued through the summer and it was August before the completed set was taken to the top of a tall radio tower and switched on. The result was much more than the engineers had anticipated. The screen showed a perfect map picture of some thirty kilometres around the tower, with every detail clearly visible. A direct telephone call was immediately made to Military Headquarters. The Naval Delegation took one look at the radar set and knew why there had been such dreadful U-boat losses during the past months. No matter what the visibility, this 'box' was capable of accurately detecting a U-boat on the surface over vast distances. They knew that the U-boats did not stand a chance of avoiding detection even on the foggiest day. This box could enable the enemy to seek them out in all conditions: and, more important, Germany had no device for detecting its presence.

This problem was so serious that Göring immediately gave orders for all technical firms in the field to start research: first to find a receiver which could detect these new 9cm radar waves; and secondly to build a similar device for Germany. About 10,000 men were released from the armed forces to return to their normal jobs to try to find an answer to the 'Rotterdam Problem'. Germany had stopped its research in this field at a time when it had been ahead, but now they were so hopelessly behind that there was very little chance of catching up. It was necessary for the German engineers to start at square one again and follow up all the possibilities which might lead to a successful result and this was when large towns were suffering the first 'thousand bomber' raids and the RAF was destroying most of the houses.

Telefunken was one of the firms which had not stopped all its research in 1940 and it was not long before they managed to produce a receiver which could pick up short-wave radar

The Convoy

The first indication of a convoy was the smoke........Is it a cloud or smoke? Will it mean success or death? Men on the bridge of U 377.

....then mast heads come into view and finally the whole convoy.. ......

Torpedo Damage....

The merchant vessel Brisbane Star *crawled into Malta Harbour after a torpedo damaged her bows.*

HMS Broadway *helped to capture U 110. At the back is an empty rack for holding depth charges. Note the torpedo tubes in front of the aft cabin. A life raft can be seen just behind the last funnel.*

signals. The receiver, named 'Naxos', was actually fitted to some U-boats, but not sufficiently large numbers to have any great effect upon the war in general. The first Naxos aerials and receivers were also rather primitive sets with a range of less than twelve kilometres. In other words, a plane flying at about 250mph (400km hr) would be over the U-boat in about one minute after the Naxos first picked up its radar impulses. As the quickest diving time for a large U-boat was 30 to 40 seconds, the margin between life and death was only about twenty seconds!

Naxos was refined a little before the end of the war, but this did not effect the tide of battle greatly. Now, with the introduction of centimetre radar, it was necessary to add another aerial to the already overcrowded conning tower, because long-wave radar was still in use and the Metox aerial could not be removed. A new device which needed only a single aerial and automatically searched through the various radar wavebands was introduced just before the end of the war.

Germany also experimented with several successful radar 'foxers'. The *Thetis* was a three dimensional cross, with wires strung between the wooden supports. It would float on the surface of the water and reflect radar signals. The *Aphrodite* consisted of a lighter-than-air balloon which was attached, with a sixty metre wire, to a float, which the balloon could not lift clear of the water. Three strips of metal foil were tied under the balloon and these also reflected radar impulses. Success of these was confirmed as German monitored Allied radio reported that U-boats had been noted in the areas where the 'foxers' had been placed. Germany had also developed an asdic 'foxer' which could be ejected from U-boats. On making contact with sea water the canister would start to discharge bubbles which reflected asdic 'pings'. These devices were used to deflect the asdic of hunting destroyers.

The author is indebted to Kpt z S a.D. Helmuth Giessler for reading through the proofs and raising the following points.

Today German submariners still consider radar to have been their main enemy, probably because it helps to distract from their own mistakes. High Frequency Direction Finders played an even greater role in the destruction of U-boats. Even by the end of the war Germany had not understood the significance of this apparatus.

It should be made clear that although Dönitz often received messages from his boat commanders, these broadcasts were always in code and could not have been understood by monitoring stations, but the HF/DF direction finder could instantly pin point the source of radio signals. Thus the boat could be quickly engaged.

8
Tables of Technical Data

Type	Description	Date First launched	Complement[1]	Displacement[2] Official	Surfaced[3]
IA	Ocean going/Conventional	1936	4/39	712t	862t
IIA	Coastal/Conventional	1935	3/22	250t	254t
IIB	Coastal/Conventional	1935	3/22	250t	279t
IIC	Coastal/Conventional	1938	3/22	250t	291t
IID	Coastal/Conventional	1940	3/22	—	314t
VIIA	Sea/Ocean going/Conventional	1936	4/40 to 56	500t	626t
VIIB	Sea/Ocean going/Conventional	1938	44 to 56	517t	753t
VIIC	XSea/Ocean going/Conventional	1940	44 to 56	—	c. 769t
VIID	As Type *VIIC* + Additional mine shafts	1941	4/40	—	965t
VIIF	As Type *VIIC* only with Additional section to carry freight	1943	4/42	—	1084t
IXA	Long distance Ocean going Conventional	1938	4/44	740t	1032t
IXB	Long distance Ocean going/Conventional	1939	4/44	—	1051t
IXC		1940	4/44	—	1120t
IXC/40		1942	4/44	—	1144t
*IXD*1	Ocean going/Conventional transporter	1941	4/51 inc MO	—	1610t
*IXD*2	Ocean going/Conventional/long distance	1941	4/51 to 61 inc MO	—	1616t
XB	Ocean going minelayer/ Could be used as supply boat	1941	5/47 inc MO	—	1763t
XIV	Ocean going Transporter 'Milkcow'	1941	6/47	—	1688t
XXI	Planned to replace Type *VIIC*	1944	5/52	—	1621t
XXIII	Similar to Type *XXI* only smaller coastal boat	1944	2/12	—	234t
V80	Experimental	1940	4	—	71t
XVIIA (*WA201*)	Experimental boats	1943	25	—	236t
XVIIA (*WK202*)	Experimental boats	1943	3/9	—	236t
XVIIB	Double hulled experimental	1944	3/16	—	312t
XVIIK (*U798*)	Experimental/Not completed	1945	3/16	—	308t
XIA	Double hulled U-cruiser	Not built	110 to 120	—	3140t
XVIIA	V300 (U 791) Experimental	Project cancelled	25	—	610t
XVIIG	Experimental	Project cancelled	3/16	—	314t
XVIII	Appearance similar to Type XXI	Project cancelled	4/47	—	1485t
XX	Long distance transporter	Project not developed	c. 55–60	—	c. 2710t
XXII	Coastal	Project not developed	2/10	—	155t
UA	Ocean going	1938	45	—	1128t
UB	Ex *HMS Seal*	1938	c. 47	—	1770t
UC1 & *UC2*	Ex Dutch Norwegian *B5* & *B6*	1929	21–25	—	427t
UD1	Ex Dutch *O8*		c. 25	—	360t
UD2	Ex Dutch *O12*	1930(?)	34	—	555t
UD3, *UD4*, *UD5*	Ex Dutch *O25*, *O26* and *O27*	1940	45	—	1054t
UF2	Ex French *La Favorite*	1940(?)	40	—	928t
UIT17	Ex Italian *CM1*	1943	8	—	92t
UIT21	Ex Italian *Giuseppe Finzi*	1935	72	—	1550t
UIT22 & *UIT23*	Ex Italian *Alpino Bagnolini*, *Reginaldo Giuliani*	1939	57	—	1166t
UIT24	Ex Italian *Commandante Cappelini*	1939	57	—	1060t
UIT25	Ex Italian *Luigi Torelli*	1940	57	—	1191t

Original German building plans give dimensions correct to the nearest millimetre and in this table they have been rounded off to the nearest centimetre. Similarly other data has been simplified for easier reading.

	Length	Beam		Maximum speed		Radius of action		
ubmerged	Overall	Maximum	Depth	Surfaced	Submerged	High speed	Cruising	Diesel electric run
00t	72·4m	6·2m	4·3m	17·8kt	8·0(+)kt	17kt/3300sm	12kt/6700sm	10kt/8100sm
0 (+) t	40·9m	4·1m	3·8m	13·0kt	6·9kt	12kt/1050sm	8kt/1600sm	8kt/2000sm
4t	42·7m	4·1m	3·9m	13·0 (—) kt	7·0kt	12kt/1800sm	8kt/3100sm	8kt/3900sm
5t	43·9m	4·1m	3·8m	12·0kt	7·0kt	12kt/1900sm	8kt/3800sm	8kt/4200sm
0t	44m	4·9m	3·9m	12·7kt	7·4kt	12kt/3450sm	8kt/5650sm	8kt/5650sm
5 (—) t	64·5	5·9	4·4	16·0 (+) kt	8·0kt	16kt/2900sm	10kt/6200sm	10kt/6800sm
40t	66·5m	6·2m	4·7m	17·0 (+) kt	8·0kt	17kt/3850sm	10kt/8700sm	10kt/c. 9500sm
1070t	66·5m	6·2m	4·7m	17·0 (+) kt	7.6kt	17kt/3250sm	10kt/8500sm	10kt/c. 9500sm
85t	76·9m	6·4m	5·0m	16·0kt	7·3kt	16kt/5050sm	10kt/11200sm	10kt/13000sm
45t	76·9m	7·3m	5·0m	17·0 (+) kt	7·9kt	16kt/5350sm	10kt/14700sm	10kt/13950sm
08t	76·5m	6·5m	4·7m	18·0 (+) kt	7·7kt	18kt/3800sm	10kt/10500sm	10kt/11350sm
30t	76·5m	6·8m	4·7m	18·5 (—) kt	7·3kt	18kt/3800 sm	10kt/12000sm	10kt/12400sm
40t	76·4m	6·8m	4·7m	18·3kt	7·3kt	18kt/5000sm	10kt/13450sm	10kt/16300sm
45t	76·8m	6·9m	4·7m	18·3kt	7·3kt	18kt/5100sm	10kt/13850sm	10kt/16800sm
50t	87·6m	7·5m	5·4m	17·0 (—) kt	7·0kt	15kt/5600sm	10kt/12750sm	10kt/13000sm
50t	87·6m	7·5m	5·4m	19·0 (+) kt	6·9kt	19kt/8500sm	10kt/31500sm	10kt/32300sm
10t	89·8m	9·2m	4·7m	17·0kt	7·0kt	16kt/6750sm	10kt/18450sm	10kt/21000sm
00t	67·1m	9·4m	6·5m	15·0kt	6·5kt	14kt/5500sm	10kt/12350sm	10kt/12000sm
00t	76·7m	8·0m	6·3m	15·6kt	16·8kt	15kt/5100sm	10kt/15500sm	—
5t	34·5m	3·0m	3·7m	9·7kt	12·5kt	8kt/2600sm	6kt/4450sm	—
t	22·0m	2·1m	3·2m	4kt	28kt	—	—	—
0t	34·1m	3·4m	4·6m	9·0kt	5·0kt	9kt/1840sm	—	—
0t(?)	34·0m	3·4m	4·5m	9·0kt	26·0kt	9kt/1140sm	—	—
5t	41·5m	4·5m	4·3m	8·8kt	25·0kt	8kt/3000sm	—	—
5t	40·7m	4·5m	c. 4·9m	14·0kt	16·0kt	14kt/1100sm	10kt/2600sm	—
50t	115·0m	9·5m	6·2m	23·0kt	7·0kt	22kt/4000sm	10kt/20600sm	10kt/2400sm
5t	52·1m	4·0m	5·5m	9·3kt	20·0 (—) kt	9kt/33sm	5kt/500sm	—
5t	39·5m	4·5m	4·7m	8·5 (+) kt	25·0kt(?)	8kt/3000sm	—	—
85t(?)	71·5m	8·0m	6·4m	18·5kt	24·0kt	17kt/3000sm	10kt/7000sm	—
3420t	c. 77·0m	c. 9·2m	c. 6·6m	12·0 (+) kt	6·0 (—) kt	12kt/11000sm	10kt/18900sm	—
5t	27·0 (+) m	?	?	7·0kt	20·0kt	6kt/1550sm	—	—
84t	86·7m	6·8m	4·1m	18·0kt	8·5kt	18kt/4900sm	10kt/13100sm	10kt/16400sm
13t	89·3m	7·7m	5·2m	16·0kt	8·5 (+) kt	14kt/4950sm	10kt/6500sm	—
4t	51·0m	3·7m(?)	3·5m	15·0 (—) kt	10·0 (+) kt	—	—	—
0t	44·7m	4·9m	3·9m	13·0kt	9·0 (—) kt	13kt/c. 1300sm	—	—
5t	60·5m	5·4m	3·6m	15·0kt	8·0kt		10kt/3500sm	
72t	77·5m	6·6m	4·0m	20·3kt	8·0kt	19kt/2500sm (n)	10kt/7100sm (n)	—
78t	68·2m	5·3m	4·6m	14·0 (+) kt	10·0kt			
4t	33·0m	2·9m		14·0kt	6·0kt		10kt/2000sm	
60t	84·3m	7·7m	5·2m	17·0 (+) kt	8·0 (−) kt	—	8kt/11400sm	—
85t	76·1m	7·1m		17·0 (+) kt	8·5kt	—	8kt/13000sm	—
13t	73·1m	8·2m		17·5kt	8·0kt	—	8kt/9500sm	—
89t	76·4m	7·9m	4·7m	18·0kt	8·0kt	—	8kt/10500sm	—

Type	Radius of action Submerged	Maximum Diving Depth	Diving Time[4] Stationary	Alarm moving	Approx. Reserve Buoyancy	Oil Fuel Carried	Diesel Engines Number	HP
IA	4kt/90sm	200m	60 (−) sec	30 sec	120t	96t	2	3000(+)
IIA	4kt/35sm	150m	45 sec	30 (−) sec	49t	12t	2	700
IIB	4kt/43sm	150m	35 sec	30 (−) sec	50t	21t	2	700
IIC	4kt/43sm	150m	25 sec	25 (−) sec	50t	23t	2	700
IID	4kt/56sm	150m	25sec	25 (−) sec	50t	38t	2	700
VIIA	4kt/95sm	200m	50 sec	30 sec	119t	67t	2	2300
VIIB	4kt/90sm	200m	50 sec	30 sec	104t	108t	2	2800 to 3200
VIIC	4kt/80sm	250m[5]	50 sec	30 sec	102t	114t	2	2800 to 3200
VIID	4kt/69sm	200m	50 (−) sec	30 (−) sec	115t	170t	2	2800 to 3200
VIIF	4kt/75sm	200m	60 (−) sec	30 sec	97t	199t	2	2800 to 3200
IXA	4kt/78sm	200m	?	35 sec	121	154t	2	4400
IXB	4kt/64sm	200m	?	35sec	127t	166	2	4400
IXC	4kt/63sm	200m	?	35 sec	112t	208t	2	4400
IXC/40	4kt/63sm	200m	?	35 sec	103t	214t	2	4400
IXD$_1$	4kt/115m	200m	50 sec	35 sec	189t	252t plus c.200t		
						as cargo	2	2800 to 3200
IXD$_2$	4kt/57sm	200m	50 sec	35 sec	188t	442t	2×9 cyl	5400
							2×6 cyl	
XB	4kt/95 (−) sm	200m	?	c. 40 (−) sec	414	368	2	4800
XIV	4kt/55 (−) sm	200m	?	?	368	203t + 432t		
						as cargo	2	3200
XXI	10kt/110sm							
	5kt/365sm	250 (+) m[7]	?	18 sec	?	250t	2	4000
XXIII	10kt/35sm							
	4kt/194sm	160m	?	10 (−) sec	?	20·7t	1×6 cyl	576 to 630
V80	28kt/50sm	?	?	?	?	20t of H_2O_2	One Walter turbine developing	
								2000 BHP
XVIIA						40t perhydrol		
(*WA201*)	2kt/76sm	?	?	?	?	or Aurol 18t oil	1×8 cyl	230 BHP
XVIIA						14t oil		
(*WK202*)	26kt/80sm	?	?	?	?	40t perhydrol	Diesel & Electric 210 BHP	
						or Aurol		
XVIIB	15kt/163sm						1×8 cyl Diesel with	
	25kt/123sm	150m	?	?			provision for two	
XVIIK						26t oil		
(*U798*)	6kt/30sm	150m	?	?		55t Ingolin	1×20 cyl	1500 BHP
XIA	4kt/50sm							
	2kt/140sm	200m	?	?				
XVIIA	19kt/205sm					24t Perhydrol		
(*U791*)	10kt/450sm	?	?	?	?	100t Aurol		300–330 BHP↑
XVIIG	25kt/123sm	150m	?	?			1×8 cyl	
							(2 were planned) ?	
XVIII	24kt/200sm						Diesel engines/Electric motor a	
	16kt/350sm	?	?	?			Walter turbine/4000 to 15000 BH	
XX	4kt/50sm	c. 200m	?	?	?	470t+ c. 700	2	2800
						as freight		
XXII	20kt/100sm	?	?	?	?		Diesel engine/Electric motor an	
							Brückner & Kanis/Walter turbin	
								210 to 1780 BHP
UA	3kt/130sm	200m			?	c. 200t.	2	4200 to 4600
UB		120m			?	140 (−) t	2	3300
UC1 &								
UC2		50m				20 (−) t	2	900
UD1		50m				20 (−) t	2	480
UD2	8kt/25sm	90 (−) m			?	?	2	1800
UD3, UD4								
UD5		c. 100m			?	?	2	c. 5500
UF2		c. 100m				100t	2	3000
UIT17	4kt/70sm						2	600
UIT21	4kt/80sm	200m			?	250 (−) t	2	4400
UIT22 &								
UIT23	4kt/108sm	100m			?	135t	2	3500
UIT24	4kt/80sm	100m			?	110t (?)	2	3000
UIT25	3kt/100 (+) sm	100m			?	200 (−) t	2	3600

NOTES

[1] Either Officers/Men or Total
[2] 'Official' figure as published before the war.
[3] As designed.
[4] Time to put 10 metres of water above the hull.
[5] Many boats went much deeper.
[6] Some boats only had 2 bow tubes and 1 stern tube
[7] Probably down to 500m
[8] U792–U793
[9] U794–U795

lectric Motors umber	HP	Torpedo tubes Bow	Stern	Approx T or M carried	Guns fitted
	1000	4	2	14T or 42M	1 × AA 20mm (2000rds)/1 × 105mm (150rds)
	360	3	0	5T or 18M	None or 1 to 2 × AA 20mm (850rds). After 1940 4 × AA 20mm
	360	3	0	5T or 18M	Same as Type *IIA*
	410	3	0	5T or 18M	Same as Type *IIA*
	410	3	0	5T or 18M	Same as Type *IIA*
	750	4	1	11T or 33M	1 × 88mm (250rds) 1 × AA 20mm (4380rds). Later modified – see page 118 & 119
	750	4	1	14T or 39M	Same as Type *VIIA*
	750	4 (usual)[6]	1	14T or 39M	Same as Type *VIIA*
	750	4	1	12T or 39M	1 × 88mm (250rds)/AA?
	750	4	1	14T and 21T (As freight)	1 × AA 37mm (c. 2000 rds)/2 × AA 20mm (c. 4400rds) 1 × 88mm (250rds)
	1000	4	2	22T or 66M	1 × 105mm (180rds)/1 × AA 37mm (2625rds)/ 4 × AA20mm (8500 rds)
	1000	4	2	22T or 66M	As Type *IXA*
	1000	4	2	22T or 66M	As Type *IXA*
	1000	4	2	22T or 66M	As Type *IXA*
	1000	None/After re-fit same as Type 1XD₂		—	1 × 105mm (c. 200rds)/1 × AA 37mm (575rds)/ 1 to 2 AA or Twin AA 20mm (8000 (+) rds)
double	1000	4	2	24T or 72M	As Type *IXD₁*
	1100	0	2	15T or 22M plus 66M in special mine shafts	1 × 105mm (200rds)/1 × AA 37mm (2500rds)/ 1 × AA 20mm (4000rds)
	750	0	0	—	1 to 2 × AA 37mm/2 to 4 × AA 20mm
double plus 2 double or slow speed	4200	6	0	24T or ?M	2 × Twin AA 20mm (16000rds) with provision for 2 × Twin AA 37mm (4188rds)
double for fast speed plus single for slow speed.	580	2	0	2T	None
?	?	None	None	—	This boat was only experimental and not planned to be put into operational service?
Plus 2Walter/Germania urbinesdeveloping5000BHP	?	None – Provision for 2 Bow tubes		About 6	None
Walter/Germania turbine 000 BHP		2	0	4	None
Electric motor and Brückner & Kanis/Walter urbine		None – Provision for 2 bow tubes		c. 4	None
	1500BHP	None	—	—	—
		4	2	?	4 × 127mm (940rds)/2 × AA 37mm (4000rds)/ 1 × AA 20mm (2000rds) 1 small aircraft.
	150–4360 BHP	Provision made for 2 Bow tubes		c. 6T	None
Plus Walter turbine	?	Provision made for 2 Bow tubes		c. 4T	None
		6	0	c. 24T	2 × AA 30 Twin (4180rds).
2	750	None	None	—	2 × AA 20mm Twin (8000rds)/1 × AA 37mm Twin (3000rds)
		2	0	c. 2	No Conning tower or gun platform.
2	1300	4	2	c. 24	1 × 105mm/2 × AA 20mm
2	1630	6	0	Over 100 mines	1 × 102mm
2	700 (+)	2	2	6T (?)	
2	300 (+)	4	?	8T (?)	
2	600	4	1	c. 10	2 × 40mm (c. 500rds). Later only 1 × AA 20mm (c. 1000 rds).
2	1000	4	2 + 2 on deck	c. 14	Variable
2	1400	4 bow, 2 stern plus deck tubes			1 × 88mm/1 × AA 20mm
2	60	2	0		None (?)
2	1800	4	4	c. 16T	2 × 120mm/4 × AA ?mm
2	1400	6	2	c. 21T	2 × 100mm
2	1300	6	2	c. 25 (+) T	2 × 100mm
2	1250	6	2	c. 21T	2 × 100mm

Abbreviations used in this table

+) More than. (–) Less than. ↑ On surface. ↓ Submerged. MO Medical officer. c. circa (about). sm Sea mile. kt Knots. H_2O_2 Hydrogen peroxide. (?) After statement means that the statement has not been verified. (?) In place of a statement means that the nformation is not known. t Tons. AA Anti-aircraft gun. m Metre. mm Millimetre. T Torpedo. M Mine. rds Rounds of ammuniion. HP Horse Power. Cyl Cylinder. BHP Brake Horse Power.

Type	XXVII A Hecht	XXVII B Seehund	Molch	Neger[1]	Biber
Description	Mainly used for training and testing		All electric/to operate mainly below surface		
Date and origin of design	1944/Official design from Type 'Molch'	1944/Official design from improved Type 'Hecht'	1944/45	1944/45	
Complement	2	2	1	1	1
Weight: empty	12·0(—)t	15·0(—)t	11t	c.5t	7·0t
Total	12·5(—)t	16·0(—)t	?	?	—
Length	10·5 m	12·0(—)m	10·8m	8.0m	9·0m
Beam	1·3m	1·7m	1·8m (inc Ts)	c.0·6m	1·1m
Depth	1·4m	1·7(+)m(?)	c.2·3m	c.1·0m	1·7m
Diameter of pressure hull			1·2m	c.0·6m	—
Maximum speed	6·0 kt	↑ 7·5 kt ↓ 6·0kt	↑ 4·3kt ↓ 5·0kt	?c·20kt(?) ?c·20kt(?)	↑ 10kt ↓ 6kt
Cruising speed	3·0kt	3 to 4kt		4kt	—
Radius of action	6 kt/20 to 40 sm 4kt/40 to 70sm 2kt/45 to 80sm	↑ 6kt/720sm ↓ 3kt/60sm	↑ 4kt/50sm ↓ 5kt/45sm	?	300km max (?) ↑ 9kt/c·150sm (?) ↓ 5kt/c·15sm (?)
Operational radius	?	?		?	?
Maximum diving depth (as designed/actually achieved)	2m	10m max. Diving time to leave surface 5(—)sec	25m	?	50m max/
Armament	1M or 1T	2T	2×G7T	1×G7T	2T
Type of engine	1 Electric	1 Diesel 1 Electric	1 Electric	1 Electric	1 Petrol 1 Electric
Performance	12 HP	60HP (Diesel) 11HP (Electric)	13hp	12hp(?)	32 PS (Petrol) 13 PS (110v) (Electric)
Special equipment					

Marder	'Delphin'	Hai	Seeteufel (Elefant)	Schwertwal I	Schwertwal II	Grundhai
	Experimental (Apparatus 205)		Could also move on land like a tank	Experimental for 'fighter' craft (Similar to fighter aircraft)		Deep sea rescue craft
	1944 Dr Ing K Haug		1944/Dip. Ing. A Lödige	Versuchskommando 456		1944/Versuchs-kommando 456
		1	2	2	1 pilot and 1 engineer	1 ?
	c·2·5t	c.5·0t	18·0t		7t	c. 1·5t
	c.5·5m		20·0t		18t	3·6m
	c.1·0m		13·5m		13·5m	2·0m
	c.1·0m		c.2·0m		2·8m	
			5·5m (With Schnorkel mast) 2·9m (Without Schnorkel mast)		2·0m	0·8m
			1·8m			
	17kt (Achieved during tests)	20 kt (Achieved during tests)	10kt (Petrol) 8kt (Electric)	30kt	32kt (Turbine) 38kt (Electric)	3kt
	14kt (Schnorkeling)		c.6kt	10kt	10kt (Turbine) c. 4kt (Electric)	
		5kt/30sm	10kt/300sm (Petrol) 8kt/80sm (Electric) 6kt/500sm (Petrol) 6kt/120sm (Electric) c. 1000sm (Diesel)	30kt/100sm 10kt/500sm	32kt/100sm (Turbine) 8kt/80sm (Electric) 10kt/c. 500sm (Turbine) 4kt/120sm (Electric)	20sm
			Top speed 30hr (Petrol) 10hr (Electric) Cruising speed 80hr (Petrol) 20hr (Electric)[5]	3½hr (Top speed) 50hr (Cruising speed)	Top speed 3½hr (Turbine) 10hr (Electric) Cruising speed 50hr (Turbine) 20hr (Electric)	?
	Trials not carried out		50m[6]	100m	100m	1000m
	None[3]	Tor M	2 T (or M)	T or Special underwater weapons such as rockets		None
	Prototype had torpedo motor[4]		Provision made for diesel engine[7]	Walter Turbine	Walter Turbine Electric Motor	2 Electric
			80 HP (Petrol) c. 200–300 HP (Diesel) 30 HP (Electric)	800 HP	800 HP (Turbine) 30 (—) HP (Electric)	30HP (Each motor)
			Fitted with Dräger ventilation and air purification system.	Dräger ventilation and air purification system, automatic pilot and automatic direction finder fitted.		Caterpillar tracks for moving on land or sea bed.

NOTES

All information has been estimated.

Various ideas such as torpedoes, mines or even towing a mine was suggested.

[4] OTTO Kreislaufanlage' and Electric motor were planned.

[5] On land 10km/hour (Petrol)
30km/hour (Diesel)

[6] Prototype went down to 20 metres.

[7] The prototype was fitted with a petrol engine instead. Also Electric motor.

9

The Boats

(U-boat types which have not been included in this chapter did not progress beyond the initial design stage and were not considered for construction.)

The Beginning

The term German Navy often conjures up visions of a large, ultra-modern and highly efficient submarine fleet. Such views are understandable because twice in about thirty years the U-boats almost defeated the most powerful navy afloat. However, the facts reveal a completely different picture. The U-boats were without doubt good examples of German craftsmanship, but their designs were neither revolutionary nor ultra-modern; in fact they were only marginally better than their World War I predecessors.

Before the war and during the early months of the war there was no person in high authority who anticipated Britain discovering an efficient anti-U-boat weapon. The gentlemen of the Navy High Command, who were responsible for formulating the construction policies, were content with conventional ideas. They showed little interest in the new U-boat designs, which had been proposed as early as 1934. Far more emphasis was laid on the mass production of conventional submarines than on exploring new fields. As a result of this short-sighted approach Germany suffered a severe setback in 1943 because the conventional submarine had become obsolete and there was nothing to replace it.

HMS Starling. *The most successful U-boat hunter, with 14 U-boats to her credit. For part of her life she was commanded by Captain F. Walker, who helped to sink 25 U-boats. Note the type 272 M radar aerial on the lattice mast aft, and an HF/DF antenna on top of the tripod foremast.*

It is of course true that the revolutionary electro boats (Types XXI and XXIII) were introduced—towards the end of 1944, but they became operational so late that they can be considered to have had no real effect on the final outcome of the war.

It is interesting to compare the vital fighting statistics of the boats which carried the burden of the fighting during World War II with their World War I predecessors. Three boats, Types II, VII and IX, were based on World War I boat designs and thus it is quite easy to compare them:

Type	*Displace-ment* ↑	*Displace-ment* ↓	*Top speed* ↑	*Top speed* ↓	*Range* ↑	*Range* ↓	*Deepest Diving Depth*	*Armament*
UB II (1915)	274t	303t	9.2kt	5.8kt	5kt/6450sm	4kt/45sm	50m	2 Torpedo tubes/ 1 × 88mm gun
UF (1918)	364t	381t	11kt	7kt	7kt/3500sm	4kt/35sm	75m	5 Torpedo tubes/ 1 × 88mm gun
IIA (1935)	254t	381t	13kt	6.9kt	8kt/1600sm	4kt/35sm	150m	3 Torpedo tubes 1 or 2 × 20mm AA Gun later increased to 4.
II D (1940)	314t	460t	12.7kt	7.4kt	8kt/5650sm	4kt/56sm	150m	As II A.
UB III (1915/1916) (Latest type)	c. 555t	c. 684t	13.5kt	7.5kt	6kt/7120sm	4kt/50sm	75m	5 Torpedo tubes/ 1 × 105mm
VII A (1936)	626t	915t	17.0kt	8.0kt	10kt/6200sm	4kt/94sm	200m	5 Torpedo tubes/ 1 × 88mm + AA guns
VII C (1940)	769t	1070t	17.0(+)kt	7.6kt	10kt/8500sm	4kt/80sm	200m	5 Torpedo tubes 1 × 88mm + AA guns.
U 81 (1915)	808t	946t	16.8kt	9.1kt	8kt/11220sm	5kt/56sm	50m	6 Torpedo tubes/ Guns variable
IX A (1935)	1032t	1408t	18.2kt	7.7kt	10kt/10500sm	4kt/78sm	200m	6 Torpedo tubes/ Guns variable
IX C (1940)	1120t	1540t	18.3kt	7.3kt	10kt/13450sm	4kt/63sm	200m	6 Torpedo tubes/ Guns variable

Two aircraft used on anti-U-boat duties: **Below left:** *A Catalina in flight. The hull of the aircraft formed the main float. There were two stabilizing floats which when raised (as shown on the photo) formed the tips of the wings.* **Below right:** *A long distance Liberator ready for take off.*

Further noteworthy modifications introduced in World War II vessels and not shown in these tables were as follows:

(a) The diesel engines and electric motors could operate with much less noise. This made life easier for the crew and it meant that the boat could not so easily be detected by acoustic methods.

(b) The batteries were far more efficient, therefore it was possible to remain submerged for longer periods.

(c) The torpedoes could be fired without expelling compressed air, so there were no tell-tale bubbles on the surface to give the position of the boat away.

(d) The World War II torpedo did not leave a wake of bubbles and exceptionally good conditions were needed to spot them travelling through the water.

Type I

I A (2,) 25 & 26

The information in brackets gives the total number of boats launched and then the particular U-boat numbers. The "U" has been omitted from all boat numbers.

Only two boats, U 25 and U 26, were built of this type. They were based on the Turkish *Gür*, which had been constructed at Cadiz by the German U-boat development bureau, Ingenieurskantoor voor Scheepsbouw. Both boats had the distinguishing feature of being almost uncontrollable in the mildest of seas and exceptionally careful handling was necessary. Great care had to be taken during alarm dives to make sure that the boat levelled off at the required depth, because both had the habit of wobbling sideways or going too deep. Keeping them at periscope depth was another special headache, as it was difficult to keep the bow or stern from angling up to break the surface. Even fully surfaced, they were objectionable because the conning tower design permitted exceptionally large quantities of water to wash over the top. Both boats were banished to the submarine school, with the view that ". . . if trainees can keep those things under control then they can also manage other boats". However, they were ocean-going submarines and later the shortage of boats necessitated their return to operational flotillas.

Type II (Nicknamed Dugout Canoes)

II A	(6)	Based on UB II (1915), UF (1918). Prototype: Finnish *Vesikko*. 1, 2, 3, 4, 5, 6
II B	(20)	Improved version of Type II A 7, 8, 9, 10, 11, 12, 13, 14, 15, 16, 17, 18, 19, 20, 21, 22, 23, 24, 120, 121
II C	(8)	Improved version of Types II A & B 56, 57, 58, 59, 60, 61, 62, 63
II D	(16)	Improved version of Types II A, B & C 137, 138, 139, 140, 141, 142, 143, 144, 145, 146, 147, 148, 149, 150, 151, 152

A number of this type had been pre-fabricated in Finland, Holland and Spain, and were transported secretly to Kiel before the Treaty of Versailles was officially repudiated by Hitler. The first boats launched proved to be exceptionally seaworthy and promised to be a good design, except for the fact that their range was limited to a mere 2000 sea miles. The Weddigen Flotilla's engineer, Korvettenkapitän (later Admiral) Thedsen, modified the interior and without any major structural changes managed to make space for about nine more tons of fuel oil within the existing hull, which almost doubled the maximum range. The engines were not enlarged to compensate for the extra weight, so there was a slight drop in top performance, but this was so little that it was hardly noticeable.

The resulting new Type IIB was further modified to produce Type IIC, and this in turn was later changed to become Type IID. The basic difference between the 'C' and 'D' series was the addition of external fuel bunkers. These increased the range to almost three times that of the original U 1. This increase in range did not, however, mean that the boats could remain at sea three times as long, or that they were three times as powerful a weapon. There had been no corresponding increase in torpedo armament and only a little more space was made available for drinking water and food storage. The boats were still therefore limited to a maximum of about four weeks at sea. When suitable targets were discovered and attacked early during a patrol, boats often had to return to port within a few days of leaving in order to take on more torpedoes.

The Type II boats were most profitably employed as minelayers because they could carry some eighteen mines in place of their five torpedoes, and their small size coupled with good

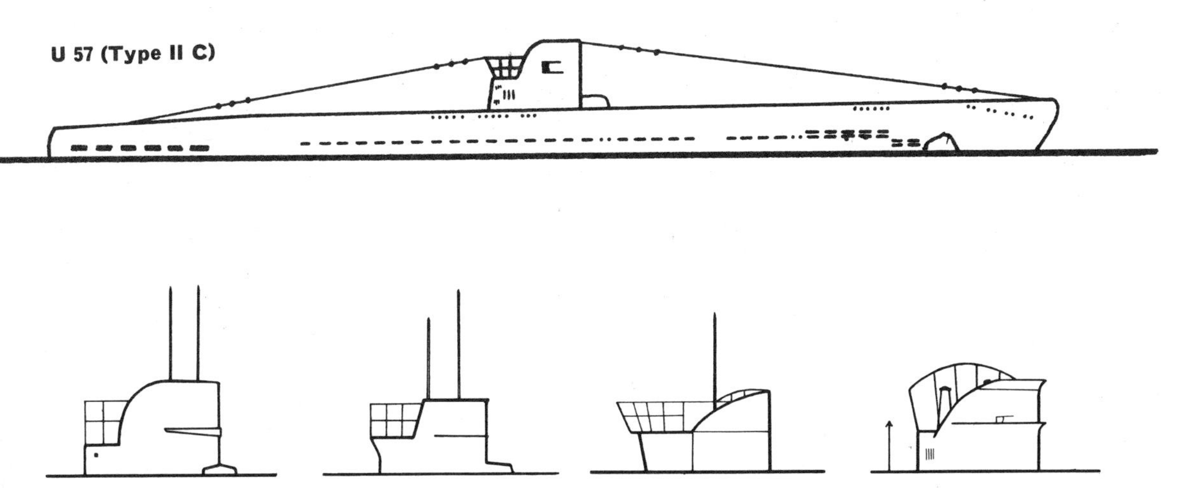

Type II Conning Towers:

Left: *U 120 and U 121, also called* China Boats *because they were originally built for China. The conning tower design proved to be useless and unpractical.*
Right: *Type II B.*

Two Different Type II D Conning Towers.

(Left U 142, right U 139)
The arrow behind U 139's tower indicates the approximate height of a man.

manoeuvrability made them particularly useful for approaching close to British harbours. Towards the end of 1939 these boats were withdrawn from operational flotillas and moved to the U-boats schools in the Baltic. Six Type II B boats were later moved to the Black Sea.

There were two *odd* Type II boats: U 120 and U 121, which were originally built for China. The war had started by the time they were launched and they were therefore not delivered. They both had basic Type IIB hulls, fitted with a different conning tower design which proved to be unseaworthy and was not further adopted.

Type VII

VII A	(10)	Based on UB III (1915). Prototype: Finnish *Vetehinen*. 27, 28, 29, 30, 31, 32, 33, 34, 35, 36
VII B	(24)	Improved version of Type VII A 45, 46, 47, 48, 49, 50, 51, 52, 53, 54, 55, 73, 74, 75, 76, 83, 84, 85, 86, 87, 99, 100, 101, 102
VII C	(Over 600)	Improved version of Types VII A & B 69 to 72 77 to 82 88 to 98 132 to 136 201 to 212 221 to 232 235 to 329 331 to 458 465 to 486 551 to 683 701 to 722 731 to 779 821 to 822 825 to 828 901 to 908 921 to 930 951 to 1032 1051 to 1058 1063 to 1065 1101 to 1110 1131 to 1132 1161 to 1172 1191 to 1210 1271 to 1279 1301 to 1308
VII C/41	Included with VII C	An improved version of Type VII C It had a stronger pressure hull for deeper diving to about 250 metres. The conning tower carried more armour and there were several other minor modifications. These, however, were so small that there was no major mechanical difference between this type and the ordinary VII C.
VII D	(6)	213, 214, 215, 216, 217, 218
VII F	(4)	1059, 1060, 1061, 1062.

Type VII formed the backbone of the German navy, with well over 600 boats having been built. The first, U 27, was launched during June 1936, about one year after U 1 appeared, and a further ten boats were completed during the remainder of that year. This group proved to be exceptionally seaworthy and easily manoeuvrable, even under the most difficult conditions. Various teething problems were sorted out and a completely modified version was launched some two

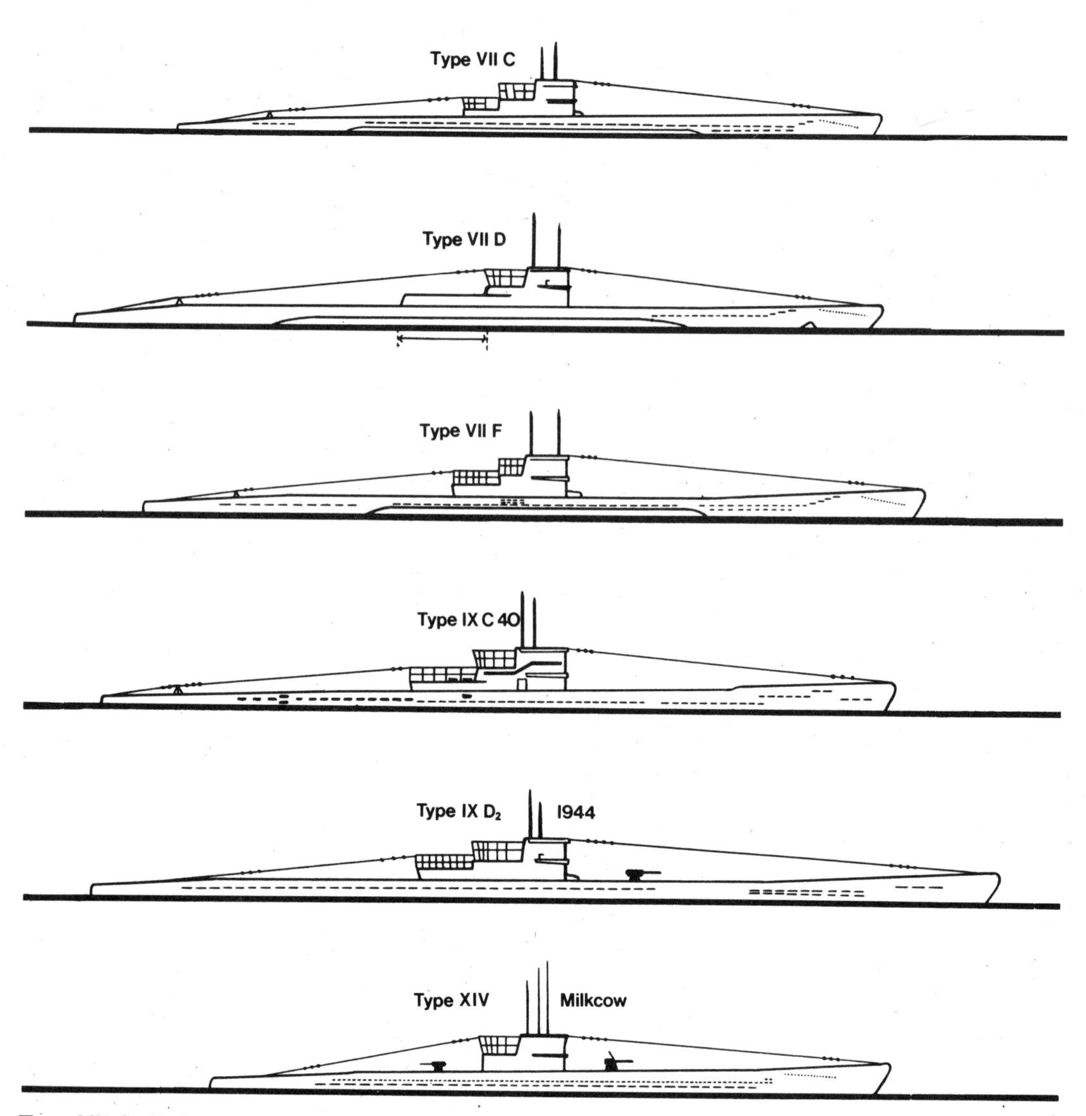

Type VII C. *1944 with additional AA gun platform behind the conning tower. Details of vents – see photos.*
Type VII D. *This type was similar to Type VII C, only there was an additional section to carry 15 mines just behind the conning tower.*
Type VII F. *Similar to VII C, only with additional section, to carry torpedoes or general cargo, in front of the conning tower.*
Type IX C 40. *1944.*
Type IX D2 (1944). *These were the large U-boats that made the voyages to the Far East.*
Type XIV or "Milkcow". *This was a large submarine tanker that could supply fighting U-boats with fuel, ammunition and provisions.*

years after the first Type VII A. These new Type VII B boats were thought at the time to be Germany's best design and it was believed that they would be responsible for bearing the brunt of the war at sea. Later, however, wartime conditions and the rate of general progress presented numerous unforeseen problems and in 1940 the design received further modifications to become a Type VII C. These boats proved to be outstanding as a class and their construction was continued throughout the war until the end of 1944. In fact the type continued to be produced long after it had become obsolete, when the new electro boats had already been laid down.

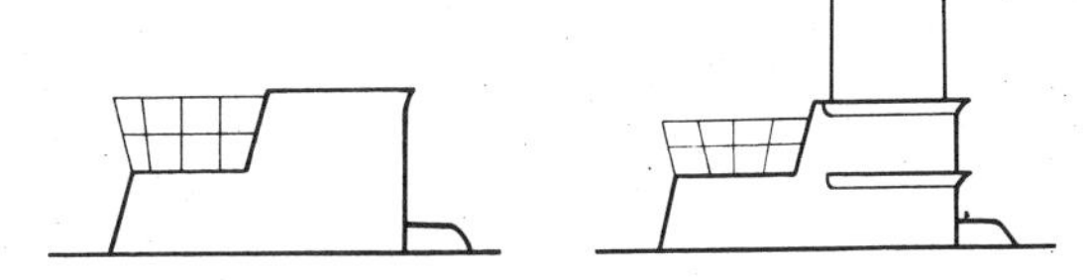

Type VII Conning Towers
Left: *VII A, 1936.*
Right: *VII B/C, 1941.*

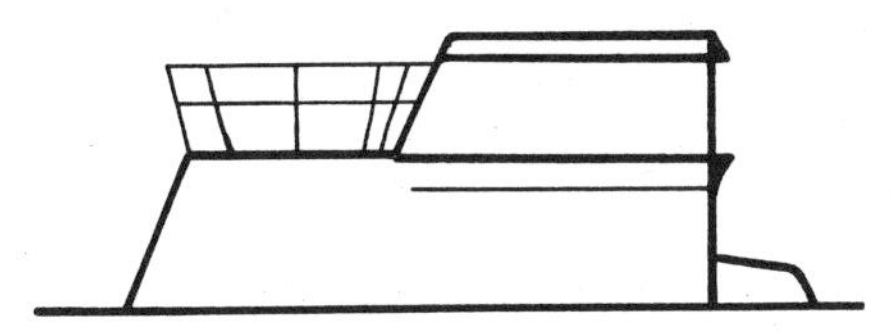

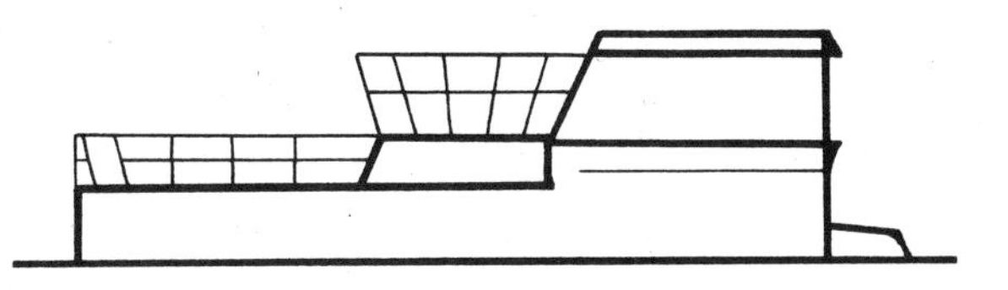

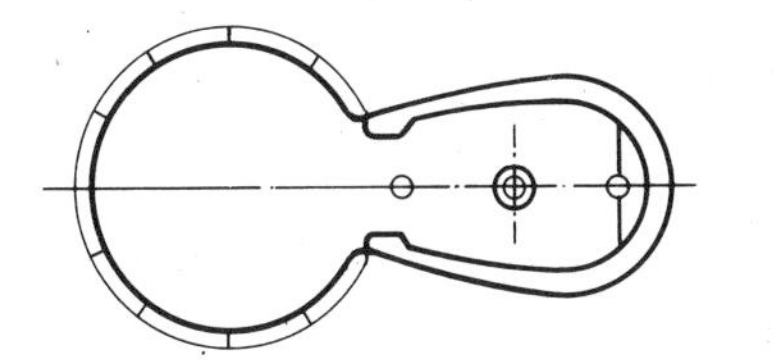

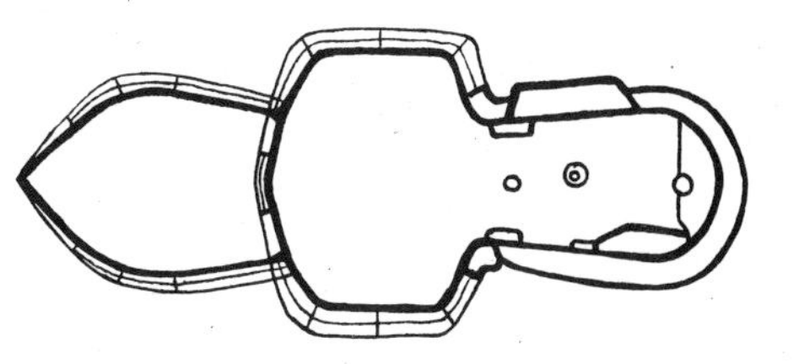

Side and Top View of Standard VII C Conning Towers

Above left: *The early type of tower. Usually with one 20mm AA gun on the platform and one 88mm gun on the deck in front of the tower.*
Above right: *The same type of tower modified to meet the threat of attacking aircraft. The 88mm gun was removed, the walls of the conning tower armoured to give lookouts extra protection and the AA gun platform was enlarged. The actual arrangement of AA guns differed from boat to boat. Two 20mm twin AA guns were common on the upper platform. The lower platform carried either one 37mm or one 20mm quadruple AA gun.*

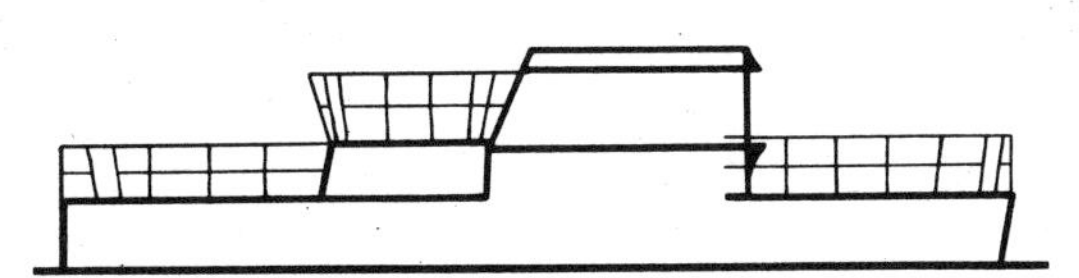

Type VII C modified as "Aircraft Trap"

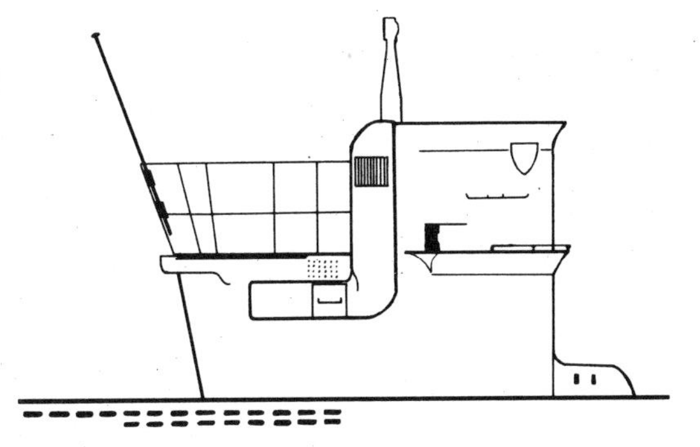

Conning Tower of U 73 (Type VII B)
April 1941.

Type VII C boats were used for a great variety of different missions and as a result they also received a great deal of individual modification, both for operational and experimental purposes. So, although these boats belonged to the same type, there was an enormous difference in their fittings. It is impossible to list all the differences, but noteworthy variations, which might be spotted on photographs, were as follows:

1 Schnorkels, with different types of head valves, were fitted from summer 1943 onwards.
2 Some VII C boats were without the rear torpedo tube and others only had two bow tubes.

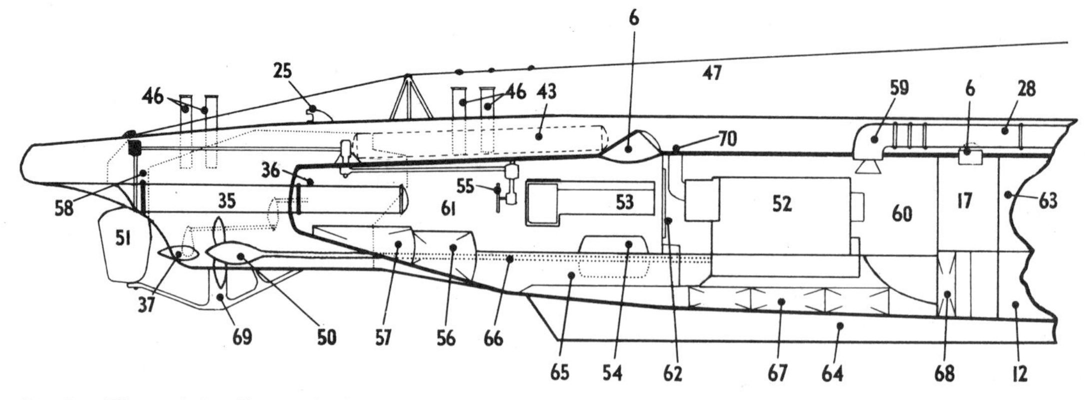

Section Through the Stern of a Type VII C

6. Hatch. 12. Battery room. 17. Galley (kitchen). 25. Light. 28. Air duct. 35. Torpedo tube. 36. Manual hydroplane control (only used in emergencies). 37. Hydroplane. 43. Storage space for torpedoes. 46. Bollard. 47. Jumping wire. 50. Propeller. 51. Rudder. 52. Diesel engine. 53. Control panel. 54. Electric motor. 55. Emergency steering wheel. 56. Torpedo tank. 57. Trim tank. 58. Position of diving tank I. 59. Air inlet into engine room. 60. Diesel engine room. 61. Rear torpedo and electro control room. 62. Door. 63. Accommodation. 64. Keel. 65. Storage space for torpedoes. 66. Propeller shaft (clutches not shown). 67. Various oil tanks. 68. Position of tanks for drinking water and used water tanks. 69. Propeller guard and bottom bracket for rudder. 70. Diesel exhaust.

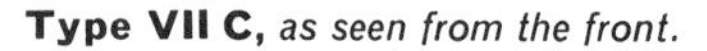

Type VII C, *as seen from the front.*

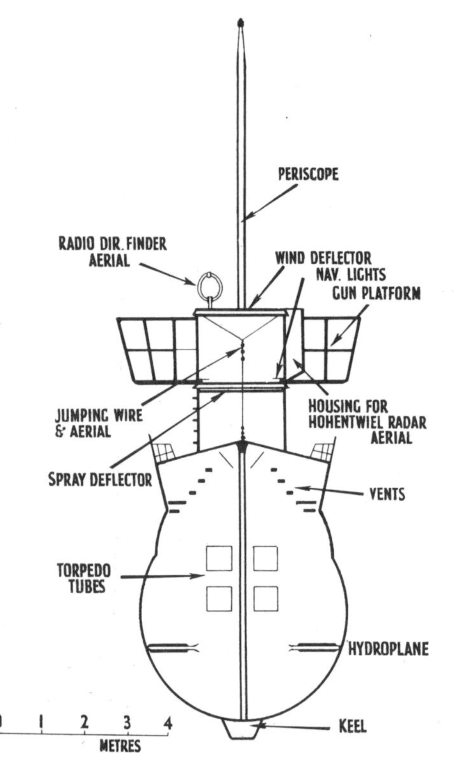

(Without rear tube: U 203, U 331, U 351 U 401, U 431, U 651. With two bow tubes and one rear tube: U 72, U 78, U 80, U 554, U 555).

3 Different *Atlantic bows* were fitted to some boats. See diagram on page 107.
4 A few boats were fitted with *balcony apparatus*. housing underwater sound detecting receivers. See diagram on page 107.
5 Conning towers and armament also differed a great deal. This will be explained in later pages.

Type VII D also had a basic VII C design, except it had an additional section, designed to hold fifteen mines, added immediately behind the conning tower. Type VII F was also similar, with the additional section, for holding torpedoes or general cargo, added aft of the forward torpedo room. Type VII C boats were single-hulled with part of the fuel and diving tanks on the outside of the pressure hull. (This is clearly visible on several photos). By increasing the length of the boat, the fuel tanks were also automatically enlarged, giving the VII D & F boats a much greater range.

Compared with British submarines of similar

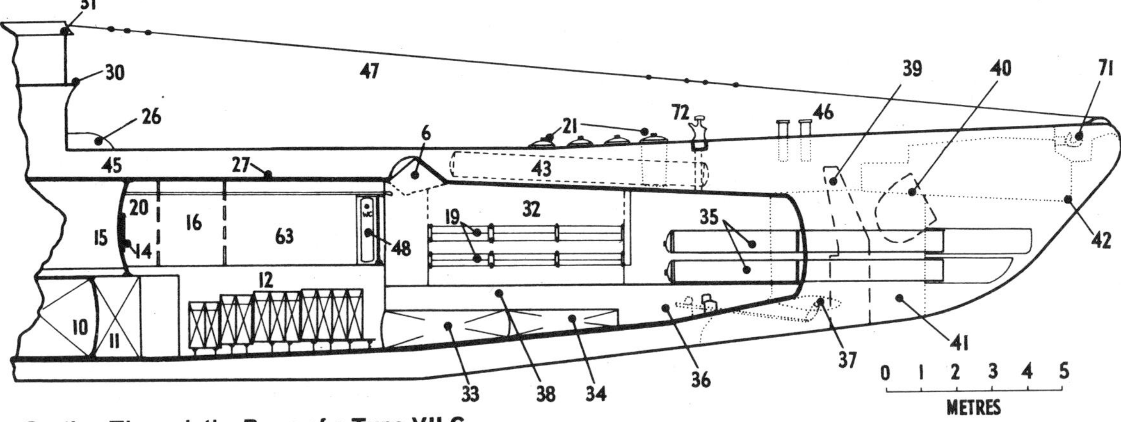

Section Through the Bows of a Type VII C With Atlantic Bows

6. Hatch. 10. Diving tank III. 11. Oil tank. 12. Battery room. 14. Circular pressurized door. 15. Control room. 16. Commander's "cabin". 19. Bunks. These could also be used for storing torpedoes. 20. Pressurized walls. 21. Pressurized containers for inflatable life rafts. 27. Pressure hull wall. 30. Wave or spray deflector. 31. Wind deflector. 32. Bow torpedo room with accommodation for crew. 33. Torpedo tank. 34. Trim tank. 35. Torpedo tube. 36. Manual hydroplane control (only used in emergencies). 37. Hydroplane. 38. Storage space for torpedoes. 39. Anchor chain locker. 40. Anchor hawse. 41. Position of diving tank II. 42. Stabilizing tank. 43. Storage space for torpedoes. 26. Magnetic compass. 45. Storage space for rigid schnorkel. 46. Bollard. 47. Jumping wire and aerial. (Prevents boat being caught in nets.) 48. Toilet. 63. Accommodation. 71. Hook and tow rope. 72. Winch.

size, the Type VIIs were of poor interior design, having little regard for crew comfort. Washing and recreation facilities, for example, were very bad or non-existent and both the control room and accommodation was very cramped.

Type IX

IX A (8) Developed from U 81 (1915).
37, 38, 39, 40, 41, 42, 43, 44.

IX B (14) Improved version of Type IX A
64, 65, 103, 104, 105, 106, 107, 108, 109, 110, 111, 122, 123, 124.

IX C (143) Improved version of Type IX A & B
66 to 68
125 to 131
153 to 176
183 to 194
501 to 550
801 to 806
841 to 846
853 to 858
865 to 870
877 to 881
889 to 891
1221 to 1235

IX C/40 Improved version of Type IX C.
The modifications were only very slight. See Table of Technical Data.
There appears to be some dispute about which boats belonged to this group and all boats have been listed with the ordinary Type IX C. The following boats were probably built with the C/40 modifications:
167 to 170
183 to 194
525 to 550
801 to 806
841 to 846
853 to 858
865 to 870
877 to 881
1221 to 1235

IX D_1 (2) Based on Types IX A, B & C.
180 & 195.

IX D_2 (30) Based on Types IX A, B & C.
177, 178, 179, 181, 182, 196, 197, 198, 199, 200, 847, 848, 849, 850, 851, 852, 859, 860, 861, 862, 863, 864, 871, 872, 873, 874, 875, 876, 883, 884.

Nicknamed *Seekuh* (Sea Cow) and Type IX D *Überseekuh* (Overseas Cow). This was Germany's attempt to produce large, long-distance submarines; however, the overall design was not as good as the Type VII C. At high speed, or during heavy seas, the conning tower became much wetter and the largest boats, Type IX D, were not so manoeuvrable. Accommodation was more spacious, but often extra provisions were packed into the boat to enable it to remain at sea for longer periods, so that the extra space did not benefit the crew at all – it was not unknown even for one of the two toilets to be used as a larder!

Type IX D_1 was originally designed as a cargo transporter and built without torpedo tubes. Only two of this type were built before construction

The Nerve Centre of a Type VII C.

1. Surface attack periscope. 2. Sky periscope. 3. Hohentwiel *radar aerial. 4. Radar detection aerial. 5. Radio direction finder for long wave radio waves. 6. Hatch. 7. Commander's seat at periscope. 8. Pressurized cabin in conning tower. (Commander's position for submerged attacks.) 9. Periscope well. 10. Diving tank III. 11. Oil tank. 12. Battery room. 13. Water tap. 14. Circular pressurized door. 15. Control room. 16. Commander's "cabin". 17. Galley (kitchen). 18. Lockers. 19. Bunks. 20. Pressurized walls. 21. Pressurized containers for ammunition. 22. Flag pole. 23. Upper gun platform. 24. Lower gun platform. 25. Light. 26. Magnetic compass. 27. Pressure hull wall. 28. Air duct to engine room. 29. Air intake. 30. Wave or spray deflector. 31. Wind deflector. 63. Accommodation. 64. Keel.*

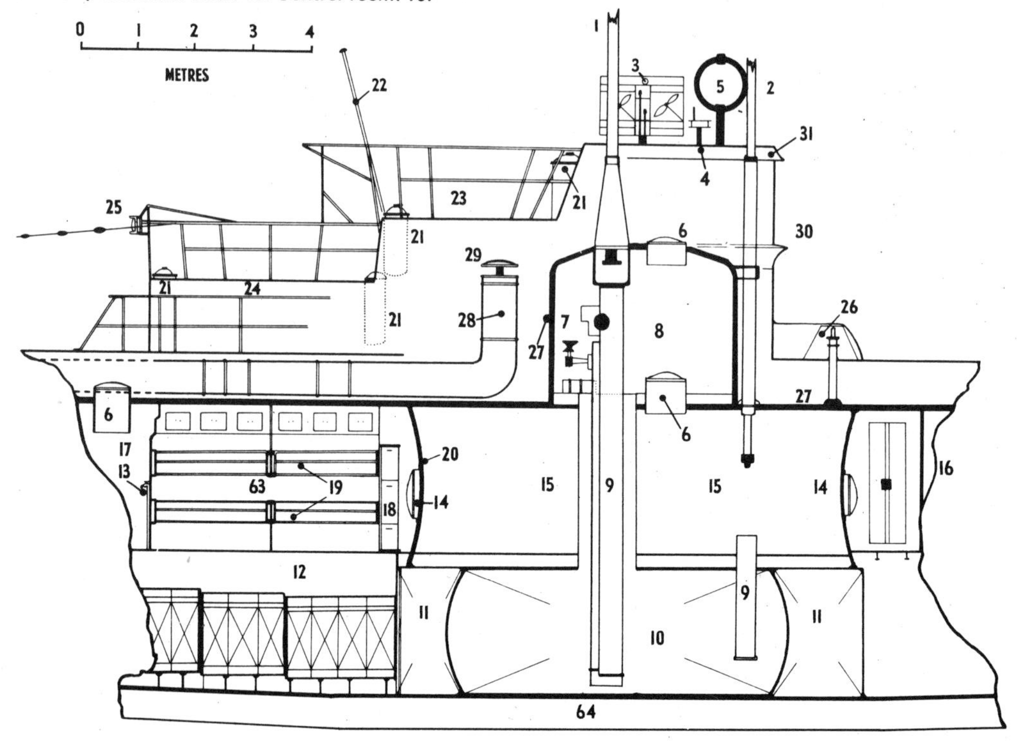

Type VII C Conning Tower

After 1943 with enlarged gun platform, as seen from the top.

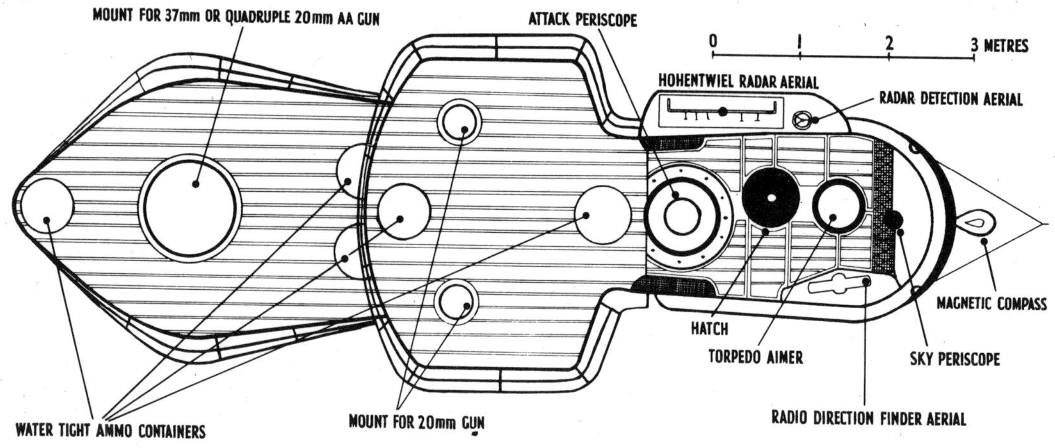

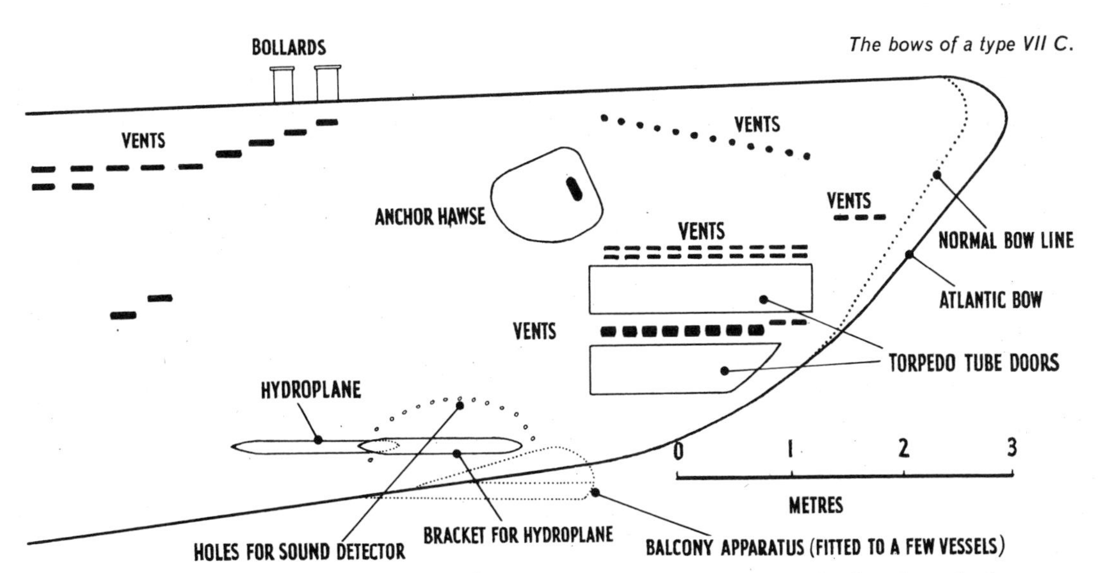

The bows of a type VII C.

was switched to Type IX D_2, which was a fighting version of the Type IX D_1. These large boats were specially built to operate in the Indian Ocean, Pacific and other distant waters. They were unsuitable for the convoy battles of the North Atlantic because their large size made them too clumsy.

Type XB

X B (8) Developed from Type I A (1936) and from the design of Type X A.
116, 117, 118, 119, 219, 220, 233, 234.

This large minelayer was completely unsuited for convoy battles. It was far too clumsy, took too long to leave the surface and only carried two stern torpedo tubes. Instead of torpedoes it carried a large number of mines: eighteen in six bow shafts and another 48 in side shafts. In addition to minelaying duties these boats were used as supply vessels.

Type XIV

XIV (10) 459, 460, 461, 462, 463, 464, 487, 488, 489, 490.

Nicknamed *Milchkuh* (Milk Cow). These boats were designed to supply fighting boats with the basic necessities, such as ammunition and provisions to enable them to operate further afield without having to constantly return to base. However, all ten *Milk Cows* were sunk in quick succession and they did not contribute a great deal to the overall war effort. The reason for their quick demise lay in their size. It took them too long to leave the surface, making them easy prey for radar-equipped aircraft.

Metamorphosis Starting 1943

The Gun Platforms

Nineteen-forty-three saw the start of a drastic change in the external appearance of U-boats. This change really started towards the end of 1942, by which time there had been a dramatic decrease in the numbers of merchant ships sunk by U-boats. Simultaneously there was a steady increase in the number of U-boats sunk, or at least attacked by aircraft. These losses rose to such an alarming level that Dönitz informed Hitler on May 24th, 1943 that U-boats would have to be withdrawn from the Atlantic for the time being. Hitler immediately replied that the Atlantic was Germany's most important battlefield and he ordered that the boats should remain in this theatre. Dönitz felt certain that in the long run planes could not harm submarines and urgent preparations were made to increase the anti-aircraft armament of the U-boats. This was done by enlarging the existing gun platform and adding another one to carry either one 37mm gun or, more often, one quadruple 20mm gun. The latter did not prove to be successful. Such guns were effective in attacking single aircraft, but the RAF was quickly able to devise a way of combatting this new weapon. Instead of attack-

Type IX D1. *1943, shown with rigid schnorkel.*

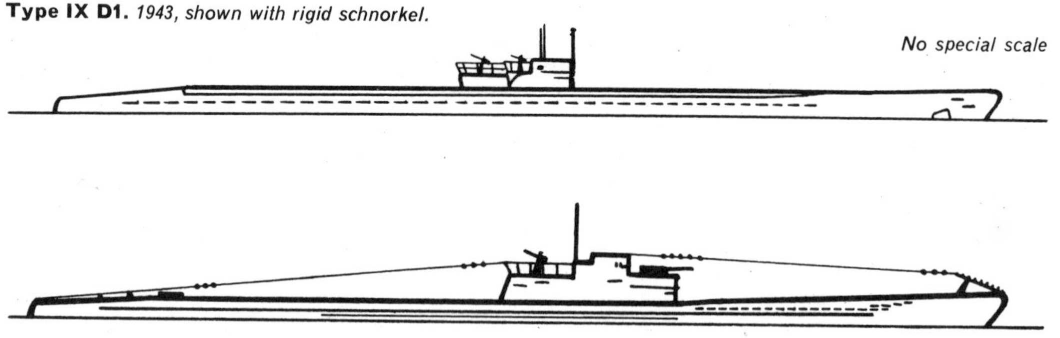

No special scale

UA

This was a conventional ocean going submarine originally build for Turkey as Batiray, *but never handed over. It was completed during March 1939 and then commissioned into the German Navy on 20th September 1939.*

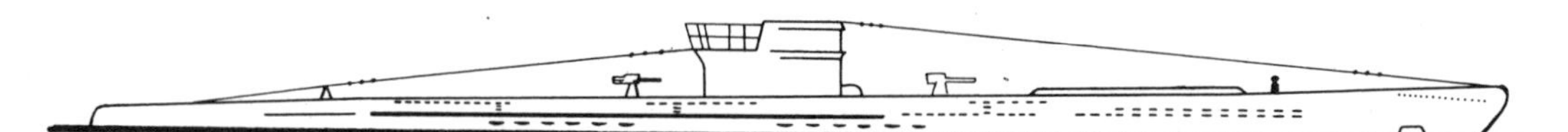

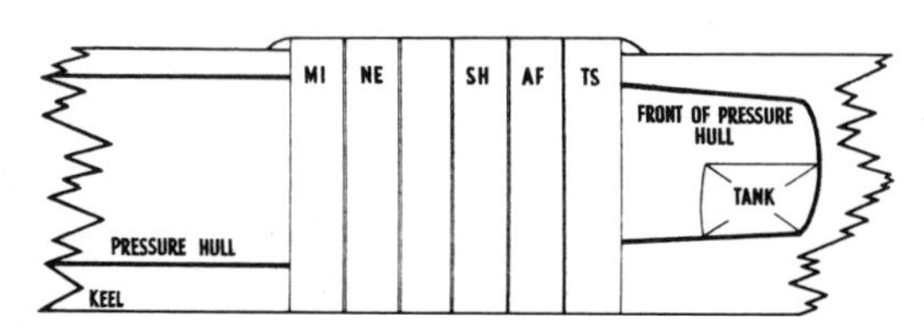

This shows how the six bow mineshafts projected above and below the pressure hull of the Type X B.

Minelayer Type X B. U 119

The raised section in front of the conning tower contained six shafts, each with three mines. There were also four sets of six mineshafts on the side of the boat. The two starboard sets are shown on the diagram, but the lids were flush fitting, so on a photograph one would probably only spot them when looking down onto the boat.

Easy identification feature: *This was the only type, which had that raised section on the deck in front of the conning tower.*

ing directly, a plane would circle, well out of range of the boat's guns, and call up the nearest surface submarine hunter group. Once these craft appeared on the horizon the U-boat had no choice but to go into the 'cellar'.

That was the moment where the 'Battle of Seconds' started. Liberators, Sunderlands or Catalinas would need about 40 to 50 seconds for their final 'run in' to kill the U-boat. Yet the fastest time for a U-boat of Type VII C, with its 'Wintergarden' in full use, to leave the surface was 30 to 40 seconds. This speed could only be achieved with a highly trained crew; therefore the margin between life and death was so narrow that many of the new crews just could not react fast enough, and could only add to the large number of U-boats which were lost during their first few patrols.

The underwater speed of U-boats was up to this time rather slow, but the addition of the larger gun platforms reduced this speed still further. Even if the boat was able to dive in time to avoid a direct attack from a plane, it was more difficult than before to escape the subsequent barrage of depth charges.

The most dangerous area for aeroplane attack was the Bay of Biscay, where the RAF was keeping a watchful eye over the lanes leading to German bases in France. To prevent losses in this 'Black Pit', several U-boats, commencing with U 441 (Kptlt von Hartmann), were equipped with another gun platform forward of the conning tower, giving the boat sufficient fire power to combat attacking aircraft. Dönitz, realising their potential, ordered that all U-boats should cross the 'Black Pit' in small groups, so that their combined anti-aircraft fire would be effective against aerial attack. These 'aircraft traps' had a splendid success until the RAF became aware of them and called up surface hunters instead of flying in low. Any external additions to the basic designs lengthened by precious seconds the time taken in diving, because many more men were required to operate the guns. These gun platforms were later removed and the U-boats converted back to carrying two platforms aft of the conning tower. The actual appearance of the modified gun platforms differed from boat to boat. The types illustrated were in common use, but by no means the only designs. However, two designs have been described in post-war publications which probably did not exist. One shows the entire conning tower reversed so that the gun platforms are forward and the other shows the upper gun platform enlarged to take four 37mm anti-aircraft guns. No reliable reference of these variations could be found and one can assume that they may have been planned, but were not built.

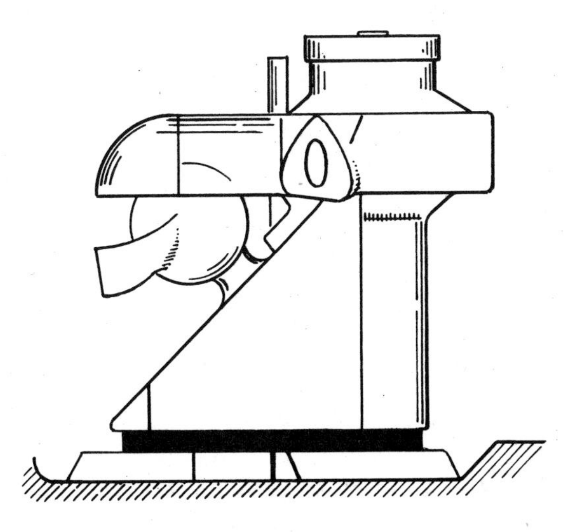

Periscopic Schnorkel Head Valve.

The Schnorkel

Germany's U-boats were designed to operate for most of the time on the surface and they only dived to evade the enemy or for a rare daylight submerged attack. They spent so much time on the surface during the first years of the war that regular checks had to be undertaken to ensure that a boat was still capable of diving and that the vital machinery had not 'seized up'. The introduction of radar and new anti-U-boat techniques made it quite clear that U-boats could no longer operate safely on the surface. As the existing boats were really only capable of operating on the surface, it was necessary to develop an entirely new breed of boat which could operate completely submerged. This could not be carried out over night and the air mast or schnorkel was brought in as a temporary answer.

This of course was no new idea, having already been suggested before 1881, with the first schnorkel probably having been installed on the American submarine *Argonaut I* in 1897. Several countries had experimented with similar ventilation masts, to supply fresh air to the crew, but they were considered to have no great future and research was not developed to any great extent. The Royal Netherlands Navy revived the idea in the early 1930s with the aim not only of supplying fresh air to the crew, but also of providing a means of running the diesel engines while the boat was submerged. Kplt tz J. J. Wichers developed the principle and the first schnorkels, with head valves, for bringing air to the diesel engines were fitted to the Dutch submarines 0 19 and 0 20 during 1938. Modified versions of this apparatus were later installed on 021–023. Some boats fell into German hands after the fall of Holland in 1940. At that time the *Kriegsmarine* considered installing air masts on German submarines, but it was thought that U-boats already had efficient ventilation systems and no one could see the need for running diesel engines below the surface, so the idea was dropped. It was revived again in 1943 when such a mast was fitted to U 58 and the equipment was tested in the Baltic Sea during the summer of that year.

The schnorkel was certainly not an answer to radar as it did not convert the U-boats' role from the defensive to the offensive. In fact it appeared to present far more difficulties than it solved and only provided the difference between death and meagre survival. It did enable U-boats to remain permanently submerged, to charge batteries below the surface and also to cruise on the diesel engines without surfacing. This, however, restricted the submerged speed to a maximum of six knots, otherwise the mast would break off. Such slow speed made it difficult to pursue convoys or indeed spot them in the first place, as the lookouts were restricted to the

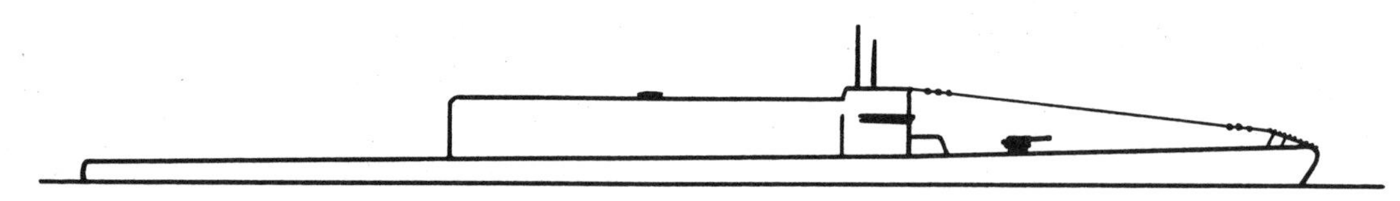

Type III

Designed in 1933, but never put into production. This boat was designed to carry two motor torpedo boats in a hangar behind the conning tower. The idea being that the submarine would partly submerge enabling the boats to float in and out, but this could only be performed in very calm weather.

periscopes' small field of vision.

Schnorkelling was also a highly uncomfortable and dangerous undertaking. At times the waves would shut the headvalve, which meant that the diesels would suck most of the air out of the boat before they were stopped, thus creating a near vacuum inside the pressure hull. This meant that the helpless crew would suffer intense pain and would be completely immobilized. U 1203 was fitted with a rigid schnorkel during October 1944 and it was tried out in Oslo Fiord. Two men did not manage to adjust to the terrific differences in air pressure and later had to be taken off the boat with damaged eardrums. This sudden vacuum was probably the worst of all schnorkelling experiences. One of the worst areas for using a schnorkel was around the Shetland Islands, where the water is exceptionally rough. In that area it was a real art to keep the boat 'hung up' at the correct depth.

On operational patrols the boat usually started to dive at the rendezvous buoy, where the escort through the minefield, protecting the base, departed. On return journeys the boat would surface there and await the escort. During the hours of daylight the boats proceeded with their electric motors at a depth of about 60 metres. During this period it was 'night time' on board with most of the men asleep. There was little to do as the boats were completely 'blind'. The only way of detecting the enemy was to stop every hour or so and listen with the sound detector. Apart from that the men were immune from all other stimuli.

The coming of darkness meant activity inside the boat. First would come food and then the boat would be "hung up" at periscope depth for a three-hour schnorkelling period. Everybody had to be awake by the time this started. Sleeping was prohibited because of the pressure problem and then the men could only sit or lie in their places. They were not allowed to move about too much because the balance of the boat was so delicate that even one man walking from one part to another would upset the trim. Normally this did not matter greatly as the LI would automatically counterbalance the difference. When schnorkelling, however, excessive movement could easily cause the headvalve of the 'nose' to close and create the unpleasant vacuum. For essential movement through the boat the men had to first obtain permission, so that the LI and the hydroplane operators could prepare for the new trim. Incidentally this was also the only time that the men could use the toilet. At a depth of 60 metres the water pressure would be too great to pump the contents out!

After the three-hour schnorkelling spell the boat would return to a depth of 60 metres to continue using only electric motors. All the necessary maintenance chores had to be carried out during this period, as much of this work was impossible while schnorkelling because of the vacuum danger and also because the boat was subject to wave action nearer the surface. Before daylight the boat would return to just below the surface for another three-hour schnorkelling spell to ensure that the batteries were fully charged for the daylight hours. The schnorkel head valve was easily visible as it left a prominent wake and it was therefore rarely used during the hours of daylight in case it was spotted by a passing aeroplane.

Using the schnorkel also presented a great rubbish problem. Before this 'miracle ventilatory invention' it was possible to throw 'gash' overboard while the boat was charging its batteries on the surface. Now the hatch was rarely opened and waste disposal became a real problem. Disposal via the torpedo tubes was one method used; however, care had to be exercised in case any waste material should foul the ejection system. The thought of a tube being out of action as a result of a blockage was too dreadful to contemplate. There was one other ejection method fitted to some boats. This was the device which pushed out the asdic 'foxer'. The 'gash' could be compressed into an empty tin and ejected. This was a tedious business as only one tin could be ejected each time and it could only be performed with tins of the correct size.

The men were left with only one practical choice – to stow the rubbish. One of the favourite places for this was the torpedo room, where it was possible to fill up the empty covers which protected the torpedo tails during loading. Forty to fifty men produced a vast quantity of rubbish. Potato peel and vegetable waste alone made huge heaps. The dampness of the interior usually made other products such as bread go mouldy, which then had to be added to the waste pile. Normally the atmosphere inside a U-boat was foul enough, but the additional garbage stench made life even more difficult for the crew, and all they could do was to cultivate an indifference towards it.

New U-boats are Planned

During 1943 U-boat losses reached such a pitch that one out of two boats did not return from patrol. These dreadful losses can be attributed to radar, 'Huff Duff' and successful anti-U-boat techniques. The Germans also contributed to their own losses in that ordinary boats, without schnorkels, were still despatched to carry out 'traditional' raids, which really meant that the men were sent out to their deaths. The new boats often had poorly trained men who just did not have sufficient experience in handling their complicated equipment. In wartime, training was too short and there were far too many emergencies when seconds separated life and death. Under such conditions every action had to be perfect and every man had to react instantly.

It might be obvious that these heavy losses made it clear that a new generation of U-boat was needed. As Dönitz first approached his superiors he was told that such boats would be impossible and he would have to make do with the existing types. The *Seekriegsleitung* made it quite plain that this request for new boats was considered a little impertinent. "At first he asked for VII Cs; then we gave him his VII Cs and now suddenly he wants a completely different type altogether". Eventually in 1943 the losses became so serious that it was realised that the entire fleet had become obsolete and that it would disappear completely unless something was done to produce a fast, truly underwater U-boat fleet.

There was no shortage of ideas. Professor Walter and Germania Werft had even carried out experiments with a boat which could do almost 30 knots submerged and it did not need air to run its engine (30 knots is faster than most Royal Navy ships could do on the surface). This revolutionary idea of doing away with conventional propulsion systems had been considered long before the war. Initially preference had been given to conventional designs which could be mass-produced.

The Walter Turbine had several drawbacks. First, two Type VII C boats could be built for the same price as one Walter Boat. Secondly, the fuel needed for the Walter Boat was concentrated hydrogen peroxide. This was consumed in such large quantities that the fuel gauge could easily be calibrated in hundreds of gallons rather than in units of ten. Thirdly, the special fuel was a scarce chemical which would require a completely new plant to produce it for submarine use.

One of the first questions from the committee considering a U-boat type to replace the VII C was: "Where was Professor Walter intending to store such vast quantities of fuel?" Walter had overcome this difficulty quite easily by designing a boat with two pressure hulls, one underneath the other, as in a figure '8'. The upper one would contain the turbine, accommodation and usual controls and the lower hull would be one large fuel tank. Someone on the committee immediately suggested that a new fast underwater U-boat could be produced much more easily by fitting a conventional propulsion system in the upper hull and filling the lower one with additional batteries. The additional electric power would provide a much faster underwater speed. Eventually it was decided to continue with experiments into new propulsion systems and at the same time commence mass-production of double-hulled Walter Boats with the additional batteries. Two different types of this 'electro boat' were put into construction, the large Type XXI to replace

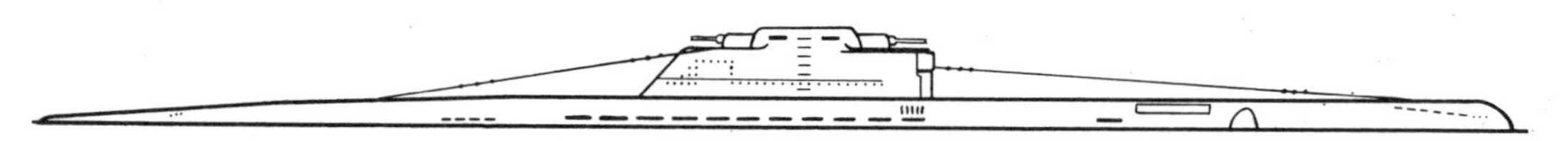

Type XXI

This boat was supposed to have replaced the Type VII C in the battle for the Atlantic, but the war stopped after two had left port for operational patrols. The long rectangular box between the conning tower and bows contained retractable hydroplanes.

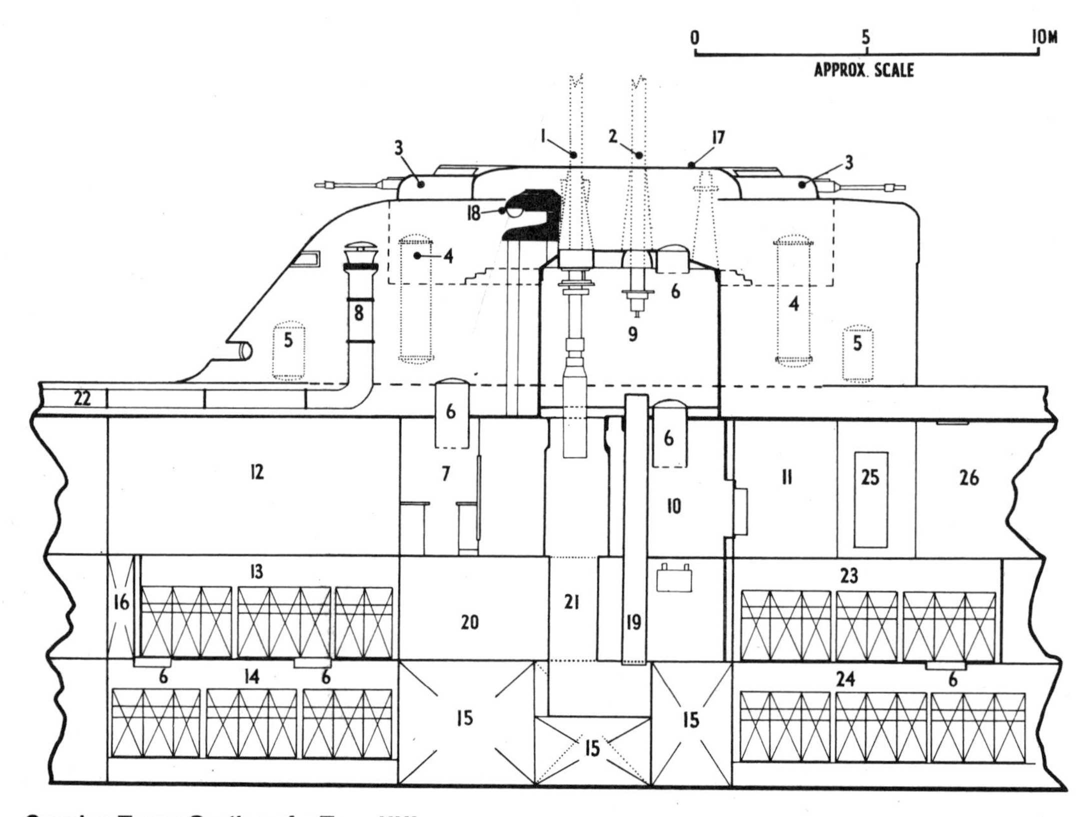

Conning Tower Section of a Type XXI

1 and 2. Periscopes. 3. Anti aircraft guns. 4. Water tight containers for AA ammunition. 5. Water tight containers for rubber dinghies. 6. Hatch. 7. Galley (kitchen). 8. Air intake (When boat is on the surface). 9. Conning tower room. 10. Control room. 11. Commander's cabin. 12. Crew accommodation. 13. Battery room. 14. Battery room. 15. Tanks for various purposes. 16. Drinking water tank. 17. Position of radio direction finder aerial. 18. Schnorkel (Periscopic). 19. Periscope well. 20. This section contained: munition room, potato room, deep freezer and tank for dirty water. 21. Periscope well. 22. Air duct to engine room. 23. Battery room. 24. Battery room. 25. Radio and listening room. 26. Accommodation.

the VII C and a small coastal boat Type XXIII.

The responsibility of building these boats was given to Dr Speer's Department of Military Armament, who concluded that it would be possible to produce about twenty Type XXI boats per month. However, the first of this type (U 2501) launched on July 17th, 1944, never saw active service because the war ended before trials could be completed. Several major problems hampered production. Skilled labour in the shipyards had been reduced by about seventy percent because most of the men had been called up to the armed forces. Most of the work was being done by old men, women and children and

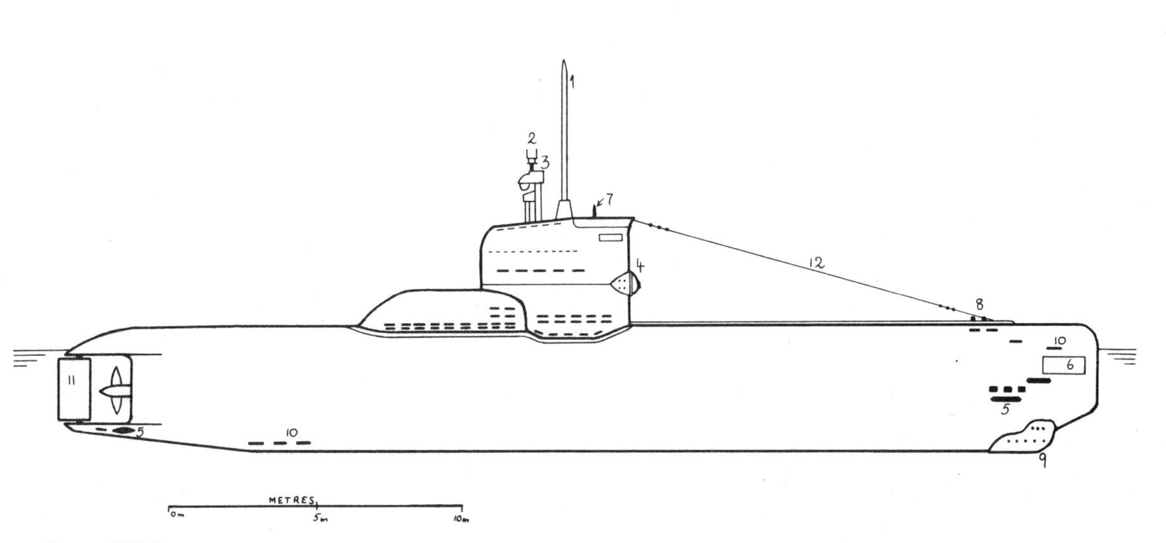

Type XXIII
1. Periscope. 2. Radar detection aerial. 3. Schnorkel head. 4. Container for rubber dinghies. 5. Hydroplane. 6. Torpedo tube door. 7. Position of periscopic aerial. 8. Bollards. 9. Balcony apparatus (for underwater sound detection). 10. Vents. 11. Rudder. 12. Jumping wire and aerial.

the boats lacked the touch of the German craftsman. The situation was made worse by not scrapping the Type VII C. Instead this obsolete boat was still being produced and it held back a large number of skilled workers who might otherwise have worked on the new types. It became impossible for the shipyard personnel to go out with the crew on the first trip and all the teething problems had to be solved by the crew, many of whom were never trained for such work. This difficult construction work was being done at a time when the RAF had gained air superiority over vast areas of Germany. Cities such as Hamburg and Bremen often received four to five separate waves of bombers each night, making construction work on ships almost impossible. The yards building U-boats were promised heavy defences by the Propaganda Ministry, but such defences did not exist anymore. It is interesting to note, however, that in spite of these difficulties the new boats were being produced at an astonishingly fast rate.

The Electro Boats—Types XXI and XXIII

XXI The following boats were *commissioned:—*
2501 to 2552
3001 to 3035
3037 to 3041
3044
3501 to 3530

XXIII The following left for operational missions
2321, 2322, 2324, 2326, 2329, 2336.

As the war ended, a further twelve boats were lying in Norwegian ports, awaiting orders to sail on operational patrols.

The following boats were *commissioned:*
2321 to 2371
4701 to 4707
4709 to 4712

A new method adopted for building Type XXI was to produce them in sections with different yards making the different parts. Each section took about three weeks to build; moving them to the riverside yard, about five days. Fitting the sections together was often completed in under eighteen days and then merely 10 to 14 days more were needed for fitting out and to carry out the initial tests. Such production methods might be excellent under peacetime conditions, but in wartime this system proved to be less than efficient.

The delays became so great that only four Type XXI boats were ready by January 1945 and two boats, U 2511 (commanded by Korv Kpt A. Schnee) and U 3008 (commanded by Kptlt Manseck), eventually left for operational patrols. U 2511 left on April 30th 1945 and waited north of Britain for a convoy. Later, in view of the imminent capitulation of the Third Reich, it received an order not to attack anything. On the way home Schnee met a fleet of warships and tried out a mock attack, merely to see whether the old methods still worked. Without being detected he made his way into a favourable shooting position, some 500 metres from HMS *Norfolk*. Then, remembering his orders not to attack, he slipped quietly away again.

This action only goes to show that the Type XXI might have been extremely successful against Allied shipping, had it been put into service a few years earlier. It was certainly a very much superior boat to its VII C predecessor. In addition to the general performance (given in the Table of Technical Data) provisions were made for a deep freezer to be installed to supply better food. A ventilation plant, to purify the air, was also installed for the first time during the World War II period, although such an idea was not new as it had already been used during World War I. Perhaps the most revolutionary device of direct help to the crew was the hydraulic torpedo loader with which they could reload all six bow tubes in twelve minutes (in a VII C it took about 10 to 20 minutes to reload *one* tube!).

The Type XXIII had no machinery for reloading torpedo tubes at all. The interior of the boat was so cramped that the torpedoes had to be loaded from the outside and spares could not be carried. There was also very little space for the crew, which meant that a very high standard of morale had to be achieved to avoid tensions. Only a few boats of this type were actually engaged against the enemy. These had a few successes, but they really appeared too late to make any great contribution towards the war effort.

Experiments which were not put into mass production

The performance and details of the experimental craft, so far as this is known, has been given in the Table of Technical Data. A number of these experimental boats fell into Allied hands at the end of the war, although unfortunately some of these special types were destroyed by the Germans.

Two projects, in addition to the new boats mentioned in other parts of this book, are worthy of further examination. First, one idea for a fast underwater submarine, apart from the 'closed circuit' system developed by Professor Walter, was a method of extracting oxygen from sea water to drive the turbine. It is not known to what extent this project was, in fact, developed. Secondly, Germany also experimented with the possibility of launching rockets from U-boats. One wonders what impact these might have had on the war had they been used to bombard New York. The whole idea of guided missiles and rockets originated just after the First World War when the Treaty of Versailles prohibited Germany from building or possessing heavy artillery. Instead the Germans started to experiment with alternative weapons. Hitler never really had any great confidence in rockets and was convinced that he could win battles without them. These new ideas were thus not developed to their fullest extent.

The connection between rockets and submarines came about unofficially, because Dr Steinhoff, a member of the Peenemünde Rocket Research Station, had a brother who was commanding U 511. This U-boat was detached from its usual duties for a short time so that it could aid the rocket research. Together the two brothers successfully launched, during the summer of 1942, a c. 210mm solid fuel rocket from a depth of twelve metres. Like many other inventions the hierarchy showed no interest and as permission for 'official' tests was not obtained, the project had to be dropped. The idea of launching rockets from U-boats was revived during the latter months of 1943 as it was suggested that a schnorkel-fitted U-boat might tow a special container with an A 4 (better known as V2) rocket to within 300 kilometres of New York and launch it. The rocket itself would be fitted into a special watertight container which would float upright, after being jettisoned, and act as a launching platform. A contract for three such devices, the total that one boat was expected to carry, was given to a building yard in Stettin during December 1944, but as with many other German projects the war ended before this could even go through the experimental stage.

Armament

U-boats were not always exactly identical and often minor differences, even among boats of the same class, appeared. Nowhere were these differences more noticeable than in the field of armament and radar.

This attack with depth charges and gun fire has missed its mark, although it appears unnecessary as the boat is already sinking. Several inflated life rafts have been thrown overboard and are floating near the bow of this Type VII C.

Torpedoes

All German torpedoes, including those used by the midget submarines, had the same diameter of 530mm. Experiments with smaller models for midget craft were carried out, but were never fitted to operational craft.

Germany used two basic torpedoes: Types G7a and G7e. The first was powered by compressed air[1] and was, soon after the start of the war, replaced by the latter, which was propelled by an electric motor. This propulsion unit remained in use throughout the war and was later fitted to the new torpedoes, such as *Zaunkönig* and *Flächenabsuch Torpedo*. Performances of torpedoes has always been 'top secret' and it is not certain whether the following data is correct, so it must only be used as a rough guide:

G7a. 30 knots for 14 Kilometres
40 knots for 8 Kilometres
44 knots for 6 Kilometres
} Carrying 380kg of explosive.

G7e 30 knots for 6 Kilometres carrying 500kg of explosive.

WEIGHT:	About $1\frac{1}{2}$ tons.
COST IN 1938:	About £2,000 each.

[1] Perhaps it should be explained that these were not 'jet' propelled, but the compressed air turned a propeller.

The torpedoes had different firing mechanisms. Either they exploded on impact or were activated by the target's magnetic field by means of a magnetic pistol. In this case the torpedo would explode directly under the target and one torpedo was normally sufficient to 'break' a merchant ship in two. Later the *Zaunkönig*, T5 or Acoustic Torpedo was introduced. This had a sound receiver and would home in automatically on propeller noise. The advantage of this obviously was that it only had to be aimed in the general direction of the enemy for it to find its own target. Another successful introduction was the *Flächenabsuch Torpedo*, which could be set to travel in a straight line for a certain distance before zigzagging about rapidly changing direction. These were especially effective against convoys, for sooner or later they were bound to collide with a ship and explode.

Handling and overhauling torpedoes was one of the dirtiest and roughest jobs on a U-boat. Torpedoes in the torpedo tubes had to be withdrawn every four to five days for overhaul. Usually one torpedo was pulled out each day, so that there were always three more ready for action. Reloading was hard work which could not be undertaken on the surface unless the water was dead calm. To load the reserve torpedoes they had to be winched up by chains from below the 'floor boards' and manhandled into the tubes. Such action would be too dangerous if the boat was rolling heavily. During this reloading period the boat would be trimmed slightly bow heavy, so that the torpedoes would slide more easily into position.

Right and below: *April 17th, 1943. A capture that did not come off! US Coast Guard Cutter* Spencer *is heading on a collision course towards U 175. The Germans abandon their still moving U-boat and can be seen in the upper picture.* Spencer *then changes course, stops and lowers a whaler. Lieutenant Ross Bullard managed to jump on to the conning tower, but the U-boat was already sinking and went down a few minutes later. Note: The radar detection aerial on the conning tower of the lower photo.*

A Type IX B, probably U 106, under attack from aircraft.

"....Boarders Away...."
–A Capture

The target which every Coastal Command crew prayed for: a U-boat stationary on the surface, blowing its tanks. The photo probably shows U 955, but Squadron Leader J. H. Thompson must have had a similar view as U 570 surfaced underneath his Hudson S *on 27th August, 1941.*

U 570 after her surrender. Keeping watch is HMS Burwell.

U 570. In the background is HMS Burwell.

Temporary Lieutenant H. B. Campbell (standing at rear) leading the boarding party to take over the surrendered U 570. The sea was too rough to lower a boat and the men crossed in a life raft.

The Canadian corvette Chilliwack *and the frigate* St. Catharines *with U 744 between them. Men from HMCS* Chilliwack *managed to get aboard the U-boat to hoist the White Ensign and also to collect a few secret documents.*

The total number of torpedoes to be carried was decided by the commander in co-operation with his superiors. The correct number were then brought to the boat by a special electric truck and loaded under the supervision of the torpedo mechanic or his mate. There were 'long' or 'short' rules that had to be followed. The 'long rules' meant that the entire torpedo received a check before being taken on board. The 'short rules' allowed the mechanic to merely check the vital points. Once on board the torpedoes had to be signed for and from then on they were part of the boat's expendable equipment.

Guns

Artillery

105mm WITH c. 4700mm BARREL.
88mm WITH c. 3900mm BARREL.

These were general purpose quick-firing guns, which could be used against surface targets, but could not be used as anti-aircraft guns. 88mm guns were usually fitted on Type VII and 105mm on Types I, IX & X. These were always situated forward of the conning tower. Photos which have been published in English books showing such a gun aft of the conning tower are in fact pictures of Italian submarines. The ammunition for these guns was stored in a special locker inside the pressure hull and the shells were passed up by hand via a 'human chain' through the conning tower hatch to the gunners.

AA 37mm This gun was usually situated on the lower gun platform behind the conning tower. Some boats, eg Types IX and XIV also had this one fitted directly on to the deck.

AA 20mm Fitted as single, twin or quadruple barrel guns. The single was the standard anti-aircraft fitting until aeroplanes became a real threat in 1943.

AA 15mm It has been stated, even by ex-U-boat men, that such guns were fitted to U-boats, but there is no reliable printed record of this.

AA 8mm It has been stated in an English book that such guns were fitted to U-boats. Germany did experiment with small calibre anti-aircraft guns, but there is no reliable record of 8mm guns having been fitted to U-boats during World War II.

Above left: *A US Navy Avenger torpedo bomber, with wing flaps lowered to reduce speed, is about to land on USS* Guadalcanal *while U 505 is in tow. Moving in U-boat infested waters meant that the carrier had to maintain flight operations throughout the four days during which she towed the captured U-boat. Later a sea-going tug appeared and took over the towing task.*
Above right: *Only one man (Gunner's Mate Fischer) was killed during the action when U 505 was captured. His comrades strapped him to a stretcher and here he is seen being brought aboard USS* Guadalcanal.

Ammunition carried: The usual number of rounds carried has been noted on the Table of Technical Data. Towards the end of the war, as aircraft attacks became more frequent, far more ammunition than stated was actually carried. Boats have been known to leave Brest with all the available space on the top of the conning tower filled with AA ammunition. Ammunition was stored inside the pressure hull; however, special water and pressure tight lockers were later fitted into the deck, next to the guns for easier and quicker access.

Boats also carried a variety of small hand weapons. The quantities and variety of guns carried varied and the following should only be taken as a rough guide for boats stationed in Germany. Boats serving abroad had their total number of light weapons increased, depending on where they were serving and what missions were undertaken:

6 Mauser pistols.
7 Rifles.
1 Single barrelled signal pistol.
1 Double barrelled signal pistol.
Demolition charges.

Type II

Guns fitted as listed. Some boats received heavier AA guns after 1943.

Types VII A, VII B, & VII C

The 88mm gun was removed during or after 1943 and the AA armament was strengthened. In a few cases, especially those boats serving in the Baltic, the 88mm was re-instated at a later date. The number of AA guns were increased so that the lower gun platform held either a single 37mm or a quadruple 20mm gun. The upper platform usually carried two twin 20mm guns. The 'plane traps', ie U 211, U 256, U 271, U 441, U 621 and U 953, were equipped with one 37mm gun, one quadruple 20mm and two twin 20mm guns. These 'plane trap' modifications only lasted for a relatively short time and later they were converted back to look like ordinary boats.

Type VII D

Plans have been published showing this type with an additional gun platform. There is no reliable evidence of this and it appears that these boats only had the normal single platform.

Type IX

The 105mm gun was removed during or after 1943 and the aircraft armament increased as in Type VII A to VII C.

Type XIV

Not fitted with a large gun such as 88mm or 105mm. This type only carried anti-aircraft guns.

Chance For Red?—The Toilet

Every U-boat, except midget craft, had a toilet. The larger ones even had two, except that on long voyages one would often be used as the larder as already described. Every action on a submarine had to be carefully planned – even a visit to the 'little room'. It has already been mentioned that toilets could be only used while the boat was somewhere near the surface, because once they went below 25 metres the water pressure became too great to pump the contents out. Of course during those early years of the war the boats spent most of their time on the surface, so this situation presented only a few difficulties. Later as the boats were forced to remain submerged for long periods, (those in the Mediterranean often remained up to twenty-four hours 'in the cellar'), a new special high-pressure toilet had to be installed. On the comfort of the crew, depended their safety; extreme concentration was very necessary and a functional 'head' could make all the difference between total and part concentration on delicate instruments.

As patrolling at great depths became more common, high-pressure toilets were fitted, but not universally. The operation of this equipment proved to be so difficult that men with technical aptitude were specially trained to learn about the new system. The sailors had a delicate expression for these toilet operators, perhaps the term 'Toilet Graduate' might suffice in English. These complicated 'Thunder Boxes', as they were often called, also took their toll. One U-boat, U 1206 commanded by Kptlt Schlitt, was sunk as a direct result of mishandling the toilet. Kptlt Schlitt tried the levers for himself and had some difficulty in ejecting the contents. The LI, guessing that the chief was not all that technically-minded, sent one of the 'Toilet Graduates' to rescue him. Somehow, with two brains on the job, the levers were pulled in the wrong order so that the toilet's contents, plus a thick jet of water, flew into the men's faces. The LI, seeing what had happened, took the boat up to periscope depth in order to relieve the high water pressure. This enabled the men to shut the valves. However, a large volume of salt water had entered the boat and found its way into the batteries below the toilet. Slowly poisonous chlorine gasses started to fill the boat and Schlitt had no choice but to surface in order to ventilate the interior. (Chlorine gas is produced when the salt from the sea water reacts with sulphuric acid in the batteries.) U 1206 was depth-charged by an aircraft as it broke the surface, making diving and further progress impossible and the boat had to be abandoned.

Foreign Submarines which were commissioned into the Kriegsmarine

U A	Built by Germania Werft in Kiel for Turkey, (as the *Batiray*) but not handed over.
U B	ex *HMS Seal*, captured by German forces.
U C1	ex Norwegian B 5 } Same type.
U C2	ex Norwegian B 6 } Same type.
U D1	ex Netherlands O 8
U D2	ex Netherlands O 12
U D3	ex Netherlands O25 } Same type.
U D4	ex Netherlands O26 } Same type.
U D5	ex Netherlands O27 } Same type.
U F2	ex French *La Favorite*
UIT 17	ex Italian CM 1
UIT 21	ex Italian *Giuseppe Finzi*
UIT 22	ex Italian *Alpino Bagnolini* } Same type.
UIT 23	ex Italian *Reginaldo Guiliani* } Same type.
UIT 24	ex Italian *Commandante Cappelini*
UIT 25	ex Italian *Luigi Torelli*

Experimental U-Boats

Type	*Number built*	*Remarks and the numbers of the boats launched*
VB 60	0	Similar to V 80, but very much smaller. Designed in 1939. There were no plans to build this boat.
V 80	1	A true submarine, propelled by a turbine which did not need air to operate. Designed from VB 60 by Professor Walter and Germania Werft. Launched January 19th 1940. About 100 experimental voyages were undertaken. V 80—no other number.
XVII A (V 300)	0	Building contract issued to Germania Werft in Kiel during 1942. Cancelled in 1944 before the boat was completed. U 791.
XVII A (V 300 II)	0	Further development of V 300. This type was not considered for building.
XVII A (V 300 III)	0	The final development stage of V 300. Building plans were scrapped in favour of Wa 201.

The aft torpedo compartment of U 505 after the capture. In front of the circular torpedo doors is the emergency steering wheel. The iron girder, used for hoisting torpedoes into the tubes, can be seen at the top. It could be pushed from side to side for use with either tube.

....Only the Lucky Ones Managed to Return....

Korvettenkapitän Lehmann-Willenbrock, commander of the 9th U-boat Flotilla, together with the Flotilla's mascot, awaits an incoming U-boat....

....U 377, under the command of Oberleutnant zur See Gerhard Kluth, entering Brest on October 10th, 1943.

Above: *Lehmann-Willenbrock welcomes the men back. Gerhard Kluth the commander (with white cap) was injured by gun-fire from a Liberator, which also killed two men.*

Top left: *U 377 coming into Brest.*

Left: *U 377's bows with close up of damage. The hole had just missed the diving tanks, so the damage was not fatal and the boat managed to crawl home from the Atlantic. The anchor chain is just visible at the front of the hole.*

Type	Number built	Remarks and the numbers of the boats launched
XVII A (Wa 201)	2	Experimental boats designed by Germania Werft, Blohm & Voss Werft and Professor Walter. U 792 & U 793.
XVII A (Wk 202)	2	As Wa 201. U 794 & U 795.
XVII B	5	Experimental boats designed by Ingenieurbüro Glückauf in 1941/42. The following were completed: 1405, 1406, 1407 The following were launched, but not completed: 1408 & 1409. (All built at Blohm & Voss in Hamburg.) The building contract for the following was issued to Blohm & Voss during 1943, but cancelled in 1945: 1410 to 1416.
XVII B2	0	Projected improvements of XVII B.
XVII B3	0	Projected improvements of XVII B.
XVII G	0	Designed in 1941/42 by Ingenieurbüro Glückauf. Building contract for twelve boats was issued to Germania Werft in Kiel during 1943, but all cancelled. This was a 350 ton boat, about forty metres long and with a crew of about nineteen.
XVII G2	0	Projected improvements of XVII G.
XVII K	1	An experimental boat which obtained its oxygen from the water and not from the air. Launched on February 16th, 1945 at Germania Werft in Kiel, but not completed. U 798.
VS 5	1 (?)	Designed 1939. Had a crew of seventeen and was considered highly dangerous. Details missing. No record of its fate.

U-Boats Which Were Planned, But Not Completed

Type	Remarks
III	Designed in 1933/34. A modification of the Turkish *Gür*, with a hangar to carry two torpedo boats. These boats could be launched while the U-boat was partly submerged, however this could only be carried out in calm weather and the project went no further than the initial design stage.
VII C/42	An improved version of VII C & VII C/41 with numerous minor modifications.
VII C/42A **VII C/42B** **VII C/43**	Modification of Type VII C/42. None of these were considered for building.
VII E	As Type VII C, but with a smaller engine to save space and weight. Project was abandoned at an early stage.
X A	A large, double hulled, 2500 ton U-cruiser designed in 1938. The project was abandoned and switched to Type X B.
XI	A large submarine cruiser that could have operated with the surface fleet. Four boats (U 112 to U 115) were planned for construction at the Deschimag Werft in Bremen, however the building contract was not issued. For further details see Table of Technical Data.
XII	A fast 1600 ton submarine cruiser, which was capable of about 22 knots on the surface. Project abandoned at an early stage.
XIII	A small, single hulled coastal submarine of about 400 tons. Project abandoned at an early stage.
XV & XVI	Huge submarine cruisers which were planned to carry provisions, fuel, and repair facilities to distant parts of the oceans. They were equipped with a workshop to repair operational U-boats.
XVIII	Designed by Ingenieursbüro Glückauf in 1941/42 to be similar in appearance to Type XXI. For further details see Table of Technical Data.
XIX	A 2000 ton submarine cruiser designed by Ingenieursbüro Glückauf. Abandoned at an early stage. Its top speed was not expected to exceed 14 knots.
XX	A large transporter for carrying cargo and fuel oil. Developed by Ingenieursbüro Glückauf for possible voyages to the Far East. For further details see Table of Technical Data.
XXII	A small coastal submarine, from which Type XXIII was developed. Project abandoned on August 14th, 1943. See Table of Technical Data.
XXIV	A 2000 ton ocean going boat, similar in appearance to Type XXI. Based on Type XVIII only with much stronger torpedo armament. Project abandoned.
XXV	A 160 ton coastal electro submarine which could only carry two torpedoes. It had an underwater range of 400 sea miles at 6 knots. Project abandoned at an early stage.
XXVI	A high sea submarine, without conning tower, fitted with a Walter turbine. There were various modifications to this design, but they were all cancelled at early stages.
XXVIII	A 200 ton coastal submarine designed to operate in the Mediterranean. It would have had a submerged range of some 2000 sea miles at 6 knots. Project abandoned.
XXIX A **XXIX B** **XXIX B1** **XXIX C** **XXIX F** **XXIX G** **XXIX K1 to K4 (?)**	650 to 1000 ton submarines without conning towers. Design stages were not fully developed.
XXX **XXXI** **XXXII** **XXXIII** **XXXIV** **XXXV** **XXXVI**	All these boats only reached the elementary drawing stage. Details have not been published.

Foreign Submarines Which Were in German Hands, But Not Commissioned into the Kriegsmarine

Boat number	*Remarks*
U F1	ex French *L'Africaine*
U F3	ex French *L'Astere*
UIT 1	ex Italian R 10
UIT 2	ex Italian R 11
UIT 3	ex Italian R 12
UIT 4	ex Italian R 7
UIT 5	ex Italian R 8
UIT 6	ex Italian R 9
UIT 7	ex Italian *Bario*
UIT 8	ex Italian *Litio*
UIT 9	ex Italian *Sodio*
UIT 10	ex Italian *Potassio*
UIT 11	ex Italian *Rame*
UIT 12	ex Italian *Ferro*
UIT 13	ex Italian *Piombo*
UIT 14	ex Italian *Zinco*
UIT 15	ex Italian *Sparide*
UIT 16	ex Italian *Murena*
UIT 18	ex Italian CM 2
UIT 19	ex Italian *Nautilo*
UIT 20	ex Italian *Grongo*

Midget Craft

A comprehensive submarine fleet, ranging from large cruisers, such as Type XI, to midget craft was due to have been constructed according to the *Kriegsmarine's* pre-war building policy. The latter were not planned to be added until the late 1940s at the earliest and the outbreak of the war did not increase the need for small submarines, because it became obvious that the decisive battle was going to be fought in the Atlantic, where much larger boats would be required. The early success in that theatre further diminished the importance of midget craft and none were even considered for building until the Allied invasion of Europe became a real threat. This led the *OKM* to form a new department, the *Kleinkampfverband* or *K-Verband*, to investigate the possibilities of small midget craft. This was a completely different department from the U-boat Arm and was also headed by a person of admiral status, who was solely responsible for the development of all types of small craft.

The *K-Verband's* initial task was by no means easy. They were not short of ideas, but in the past these had been ridiculed and now suddenly were supposed to be developed overnight as a 'last straw' to save the Reich. This was at a time when industry was suffering severe setbacks due to the lack of materials and labour and constant bombing attacks.

Midget submarines were not designed to be 'Suicide Weapons', but were expected to give the operator a fair chance of survival. The plan was to station them in concrete bunkers in a convenient hinterland position, from where they could be transported by road or rail to where they were needed. This idea in itself was quite good; the rather chaotic war situation, however, contributed a great deal to the failure of midget craft as an effective weapon of war. The chief reason for their failure was that these midget U-boats were produced so quickly and cheaply that they were far too primitive and were barely capable of being sent into battle. Some designs were so poor that operators were expected not only to carry out several jobs at once but to keep up a high level of concentration for up to sixty hours at a time. The mechanical quality of the craft was also exceptionally poor. This was mainly due to the lack of suitable materials and to the lack of skilled workmen. More than half of the vessels which arrived at their operation areas were incapable of being engaged because of mechanical breakdowns. Yet in spite of all these difficulties some midget craft found rewarding targets.

Mass Produced Midget Craft

Type Hecht (Pike) XXVII A

(Developed from Type Molch. About 3 were completed).

The original idea for the *Hecht* was to produce a small submarine, similar to the Italian 'Human Torpedo' (also called 'Chariots' in England), which could be armed with a powerful mine. The craft would then penetrate enemy harbours and attack stationary ships. The whole plan was abandoned before the boats were completed. The few which were actually finished were used only for testing and training.

Type Seehund (Seal) XXVII B

(Developed from Type Hecht. Over 300 were completed)

The *Seehund* proved to be the most successful of all midget craft. There are parts of this type in the Deutsches Museum in Munich.

Type Adam

A prototype which went into mass production as Type Biber.

All following illustrations of midget craft are to no special scale.

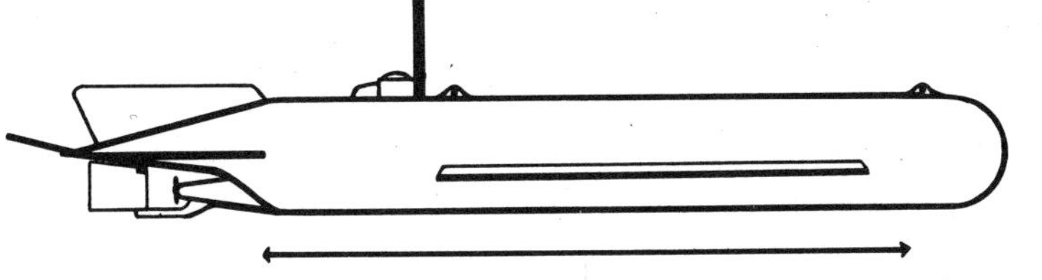

Midget Craft Type Molch. *The arrow under the boat indicates the approximate length of a German torpedo.*

Midget Craft: Type Hecht. *The arrow indicates the approximate length of a torpedo. The section at the front was designed to carry a mine.*

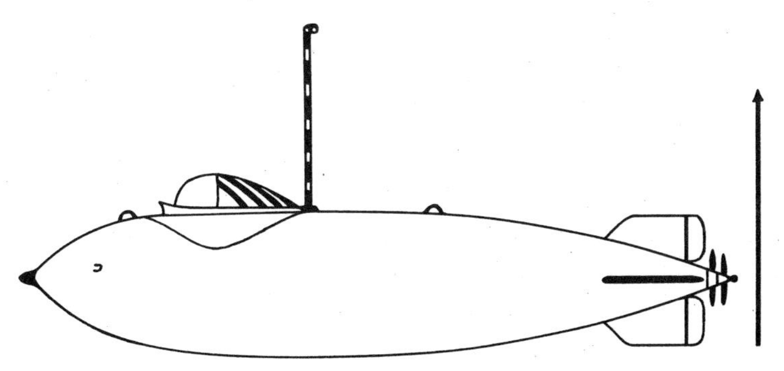

Midget Craft: Delphin. *Only the prototype of this fast underwater craft was built.*
The arrow indicates the approximate size of a man.

Midget Craft: Seeteufel. *Also called* Elefant *and* Projekt Lödige. *It could move on land to make its own way to water. Only the prototype was built. The arrow indicates the approximate length of a torpedo.*

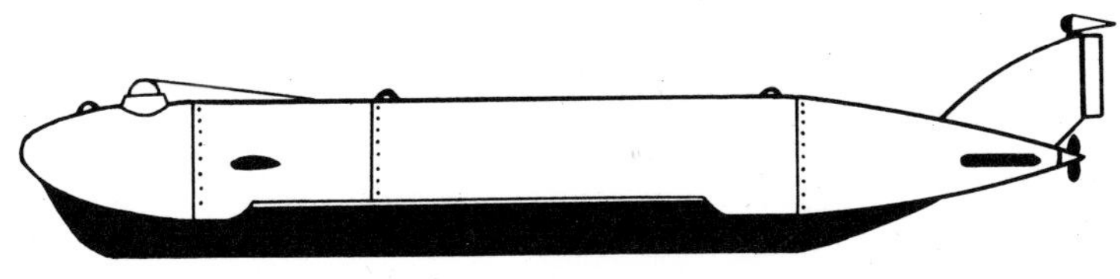

Midget Craft: Schwertwal I. *This was supposed to be an underwater "fighter craft", functioning similar to fighter aircraft. Only the prototype was constructed.*

Midget Craft: Schwertwal II.
This was supposed to be an underwater "fighter" craft, functioning similar to fighter aircraft. Only the prototype was constructed.
The arrow indicates the approximate size of a man.

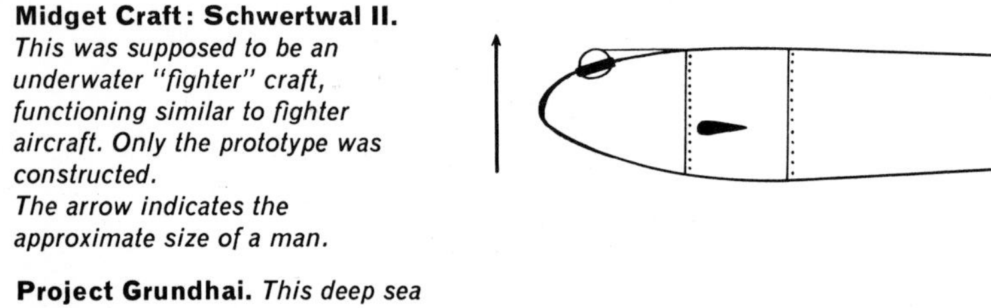

Project Grundhai. *This deep sea rescue craft was never built. It was designed to dive to 1000m.*
On the front are three circular searchlights. There are two electric motors, one on each side. On top of the craft is the hatch and an arm with an electromagnet grab. It had wheels and tracks so that it could crawl on the sea bed.

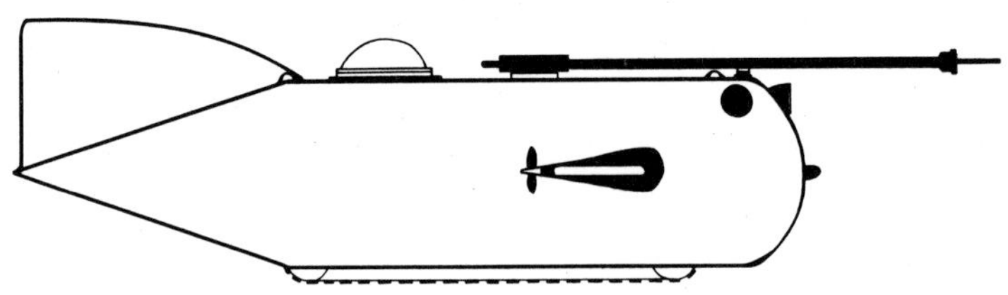

Type Seehund.

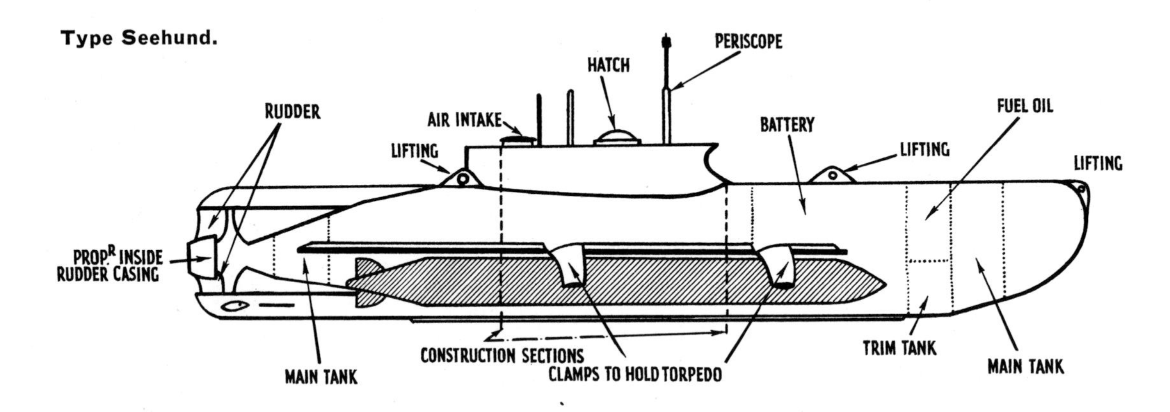

Type Biber (Beaver)

(About 325 were completed).

A one-man submarine of which about 300 were put into service. *Biber 90* is now at the Imperial War Museum in London. It was found in a sinking condition on December 29th, 1944, about 50km east of Ramsgate in Kent, with the operator dead. Provisions had not been consumed and it was concluded that carbon monoxide from the petrol engine had killed the occupant. *Biber 90* was successfully towed to Dover Harbour and later used for tests to supply the Allies with information about this type of craft.

Type Marder (Marten)

(About 300 were completed)

This was really a normal torpedo, slightly modified to carry an operator instead of a warhead, with another ordinary torpedo slung underneath it. It only had an electric motor, being designed to operate completely submerged. Once the operator had brought his deadly load within striking distance of a target he would detach the lower torpedo and make his get-away with the upper craft. About 300 were placed in service.

Type Molch (Newt/Salamander)

(About 390 were completed).

A one-man submarine designed to operate completely submerged and had only electric motors fitted. Just under 400 were completed.

Type Neger (Negro)

A one-man craft of which about 200 were completed. Reliable details missing.

Gültig für freie Urlaubsreisen auf kleinen Wehrmachtfahrschein.

1. Frei von ansteckenden übertragbaren Krankheitserscheinungen.

Schiffsarzt

Kriegsurlaubsschein

Der Ob. Masch. Jack Mallmann
(Dienstgrad, Vor- und Zuname)

von M 16791
(Truppenteil)

ist vom 7. Juni 1942 bis einschl. 27. Juni 1942 ... Uhr beurlaubt

nach Hamburg nächster Bahnhof Hamburg

nach nächster Bahnhof

nach nächster Bahnhof

Er reist auf kleinen Wehrmachtfahrschein. Die Inanspruchnahme von Wehrmachtfahrkarten oder Fahrkarten des öffentlichen Verkehrs für die im Wehrmachtfahrschein bezeichnete Strecke ist verboten.

Über die umstehenden Befehle ist er belehrt worden.

Flensburg 21. Jun 1942 Ausreise

9. Jun 1942

6. Juni 1942

Dienststelle Feldpostnummer M 16791

Inhaber gehört zu den Angehörigen der gegen den Feind eingesetzten Front U - Boote. Er ist berechtigt zu den zustehenden Reichsurlauber karten für die Dauer des Heimaturlaubs die Schwerarbeiterzulage in Form von Reise - und Gaststättenmarken sowie zusätzlich wöchentlich 2 Eier zu empfangen.

Kpt.Lnt. u. Kmdt.

Abgefunden mit Lebensmittelbezugs(Reise)-Marken bis einschl.

Abgefunden mit Feinseife bis einschl. 30. 6. 42, mit Rasierseife bis einschl. 30. 6. 42

Die Aushändigung hat die Kartenstelle hierunter zu bescheinigen.

9. Dieser Urlaubschein ist nach Rückkehr vom Urlaub der Wehrmachtdienststelle abzugeben.

10. Besondere Vermerke (z. B. über das Tragen bürgerlicher Kleidung am Urlaubsort u. a.):

Bescheinigung über Meldung am Urlaubsort:

gemeldet am

Kommandantur Hamburg

Hamburg, den 10. Jun 1942

Bescheinigung der Kartenausgabestelle:

Lebensmittelkarten für Normalverbraucher der Zivilbevölkerung sind ausgehändigt für die Zeit vom 7.6. bis einschl. 27.6.42

Tabakkarte vom 7.6. bis 27.6.42

Gemeindeverwaltung der Hansestadt Hamburg

A war time leave pass.
Top picture shows front, bottom picture shows reverse.

Top: *There were always great celebrations when a U-boat came home.*

Above: *The commander is presented with a bunch of flowers. Such celebrations died out towards the end of the war.... (Oblt. z S Kluth of U 377, white hat)*

U—Boat Bases

Top left: *Close up of conning tower. The 'horseshoe' on the tower wall is a life belt. (Otto Kretschmer's U 99 –* The Golden Horseshoe *had real horseshoes. They were fixed to the sides of the tower, in front of the navigation lights, about half way between the spray and wind deflectors.)*

Middle left: *A Type VII C backs out of the massive U-boat bunker at Brest.*

Bottom left: *U-boat pens at Trondheim after the surrender. The nearest boat is U 861 (Korvettenkapitän J. Oesten) and the further is U 953 (Oberleutnant zur See Herbert A. Werner). 37mm AA guns have been fitted to the lower gun platforms of both boats. U 953 has a rigid schnorkel with a 'beer barrel' headvalve of which only a limited number were introduced.*

Top right: *A Type VII C tied up to a depot ship. The diesel engine exhaust is clearly visible above the 5th vent from the left.*

Middle right: *Nine days before Christmas 1943: U 377 leaves Brest for its very last mission—its 13th! Above the bunker, towards the right, is the French Naval College, used as headquarters for the 1st U-boat Flotilla.*

Bottom right: *Interior of the U-boat bunker at St. Nazaire. The water could be pumped out of the basin, so that it could also serve as dry dock.*

VERSUCHSKOMMANDO 456 (Experimental Command)

The main drawback of the mass-produced midget craft was that they were too slow, their range too small and their weapons inadequate. Although they carried normal torpedoes, often half the batteries would be removed to make them lighter. Obviously, this also decreased the speed and range of the torpedo. It soon became clear that the midget crafts' success was small, compared with the resources needed to make them operational, and that much better midget weapons would be needed. In view of this Vice-Adm Hellmuth Heye, Commander-in-Chief of the *K-Verband*, founded this Experimental Corps during July 1944 to produce effective midget submarines. The *Versuchskommando 456* was stationed in Kiel near the Walter works and experimented both with midget craft and with weapons for them. The following experimental submarines were produced:

Type Delphin (Dolphin)

(3 were completed)

The *Delphin*, known originally as 'Apparatus 205', was designed over the Whitsun weekend of 1944 by Dr. Ing. K. Haug and the first boat was ready for testing by the autumn. These tests were carried out by Lt Ingenieur Wittgen. They came to an abrupt halt as the *Delphin* collided with its tender on January 18th, 1945! Two further boats had been built in Berlin by the same firm who had constructed the hulls for the V1 and V2 rockets. These were transported as far as the Trave Estuary, where they were destroyed just before the advancing British troops arrived.

Experts thought that the craft was too fragile to have been of any great use, but after the initial teething problems it proved to be quite reliable. The prototype reached a speed of 17 knots, with an improvised torpedo motor, instead of the closed circuit Walter Turbine. It dived dynamically and did not require diving tanks.

Type Hai (Shark)

Only 1 completed (?).

A five ton one-man torpedo which reached a speed of 20 knots. Only one prototype was completed. Type *Hai* should not be confused with Type *Grundhai*.

Type Seeteufel (Sea Devil)

(Also called '*Projekt Elefant*' (Project Elephant), because it looked so clumsy, or '*Projekt Lödige*' after its developer.)

The major problem with all midget craft was getting them into the water. They were too heavy to be launched by hand and port facilities, with cranes, were needed. Such equipment is in ample supply during peacetime, but by 1944 even the small ports had received their share of bombings and cranes were very scarce. To overcome this problem Diplom Ingenieur Alois Lödige developed a midget submarine with caterpillar tracks. The *Seeteufel* could be taken by rail or road to any part of the coast and the boat would then crawl, under its own power, into the water. The contraption looked rather unstable, but it reacted exceptionally well both on land and in the water.

The controls were similar to those of an aircraft. Once trimmed, the boat could dive and surface without use of air tanks. The problem of keeping the boat at schnorkel depth was overcome by painting a red line on the air mast, which the pilot could see through his plexiglass dome and could easily keep this in line with the surface. The top of the periscope could also hold a pair of binoculars, so that the commander, who was tied with a safety line to the air mast, could use it as a normal torpedo aimer. There was also a special speaking device enabling him to communicate with the engineer inside the boat.

Performance could not be verified with the prototype because only improvised motors were fitted. Instead of a powerful diesel engine a small 80 hp lorry engine was fitted and a torpedo motor was used to drive the propeller. The boats were put into mass-production at the Carl Borgward works in Bremen. It is not certain whether work started, but it is highly probable that none were ever completed. The prototype was blown up in Lübeck just before British troops moved in.

Type Schwertwal I & Schwertwal II (Swordfish)

The *Schwertwal* project was completely different to the other midget submarines in as much as these were intended to fulfil a similar role to fighter aircraft. With a maximum speed of

Top left: *Interior of the E-boat pens at Cherbourg showing the torpedo store. The photo was taken by American forces shortly after the Germans' hurried departure. The tin with a handle, on the far left corner of the nearest table, is a hand grenade.*

Top right: *This shows the state of some of the German bases in France during the summer of 1944. (Cherbourg)*

Above: *The roofs of the U-boat pens were designed to be three to five metres thick. Being composed of solid re-inforced concrete they were capable of withstanding any air attack until they were bombed by R.A.F. Sqdn. 617 with Barnes Wallis' special* Blockbuster *or* Earthquake *bombs. The Germans thought that these were special rocket propelled bombs and set hundreds of people to work to increase the thickness of the roofs to eight metres. This new additional concrete can be seen above the older, darker structure of the bunker at St. Nazaire.*

thirty knots the craft would zoom through the depths to destroy surface hunters. The two prototypes were fitted with automatic pilots, similar to those found in aircraft. This was a great aid to the operator because he did not have to waste time and energy keeping the craft on the correct course.

This type proved so promising that the Germans did not destroy it. Instead, the prototype was filled with vital plans and documents and then laid to rest on the bed of the larger of the Plön Lakes (Schleswig Holstein). After the war Royal Marine Engineers made a special point of salvaging it. Britain showed no more interest after examination of this unusual craft and it was later scrapped.

Type Grundhai (Ground Shark)

This project did not advance beyond the drawing board and model making stage. It was designed as a submarine salvage vessel which could assist in raising sunken boats, and possibly even help the occupants to get out.

Type Schwein (Pig)

No details.

10
The Men

The men who manned the U-boats were drawn from all over Germany and only volunteers were considered for service. It must, however, be emphasised that the recruiting campaign was backed up by an enormous amount of propaganda, which gave the impression that life on board U-boats was one of extreme luxury and did not reveal the horrors of submarine warfare. After volunteering at the local military office the men had to attend a thorough medical and undertook a short test to assess their mental ability. If this was successful the recruit would receive a free travel warrant together with instructions to report to one of the naval training establishments.

This was followed by a three months period of intense 'Initial Training' (*Grundausbildung*) with a 'Naval Infantry Unit'. Such training was given to all recruits, no matter which fighting force they joined. It consisted mainly of general infantry training to teach military discipline and to accustom the men to weapons and their new way of life.

During this period of initial training the men were usually issued with three types of uniform:

1. Good quality, blue naval uniform. This remained the recruit's property after the initial training period.
2. Grey uniform
3. Drill clothes or Denims.

} Infantry style clothing which was handed back after the *Initital training*.

After initial training the following clothes were issued to men going on to the U-boat Arm:

1. Blue naval uniform (Already in the recruit's possession.)
2. Blue naval uniform Same as 1, only made with inferior material.
3. White naval uniform. Two sets were issued to allow for one being worn while the other was being cleaned.
4. Denims. Looked similar to 3, only made with rough, tough linen.
5. U-boat uniform Brown. Two sets were issued. This was worn on land and not usually taken to sea. There were summer and winter sets available.
6. Leather coat Grey. Ordinary sailors had long jackets with lapels and technical staff had short jackets with standing collars.
7. Wet weather gear. This was issued, as ordinary non-expendable stock to the boat and not to individual personnel. Only a few sets were issued to each boat and it had to be shared.

Other gear such as life jackets, Dräger Lung (Escape apparatus), sea boots and special U-boat shoes were issued whenever the men went to sea. The golden rule in the *Kriegsmarine* was that all this gear had to be in perfect condition.

The three months initial training period was concluded with a full-scale manoeuvre and then the men moved on to their special training school. The length of this training varied from school to school and it also depended on the type of course. On average it lasted about three months. After passing the terminal examination the candidate was posted to one of the special U-boat schools, where he was taught numerous U-boat procedures, including how to escape from sunken boats. These schools were mainly near the towns where U-boats were built, in order that the men could easily move on to real boats to put into practice what they had learned. If the recruit failed the final examination then he was moved to a *Kriegsmarine* Front Command (shore-based). Often there were chances to re-take examinations.

On board the U-boat, men were divided into 'seaman' and 'technical' divisions, with radio operators and torpedo mechanics belonging to the former. The important posts on a U-boat were as follows:

Commander:

IWO: *Erster Wach Offizier* (Pronounced *Eins WO*)–First Watch Officer. This was an officer who would at some future date become a commander.

IIWO: *Zweiter Wach Offizier* (Second Watch Officer).

LI: *Leitender Ingenieur* (Chief Engineering Officer).

Obersteuermann: (Chief Helmsman) Also i/c provisions.

Diesel Obermaschinist: (Chief Diesel mechanic)

Elektro Obermaschinist: (Chief Electro Mechanic).

Smut or Smutje: (Cook) The only duty was to prepare food for all the men, no matter under what conditions the boat found itself, whether in rough seas or under attack. It should be remembered that only a few of the men had learned this as a trade and that most of them started to learn cooking after their initial training. The cook was usually assisted in chores such as peeling potatoes or cleaning vegetables. Sometimes he also undertook other voluntary duties such as keeping lookout.

Wireless Operator: He was responsible for receiving and sending all signals. When submerged he would also man the acoustic detector. (Radio signals could only be picked up as long as the aerial was above the water.) Acoustic detection had been developed to a fine art by the Germans and their apparatus was capable of detecting propeller noises long before they became audible to the ear. The drawback with this device was that it produced a continuous, monotonous noise over the earphones which could easily send the operator to sleep. The commander, whose bunk was close to the radio room, would often rest with additional earphones plugged into the receiver.

Torpedo mechanic: See Armament Section.

Lookouts: These were drawn from all over the boat and even the mechanics sometimes had to do a four-hour spell when they were not required below. Usually there were four lookouts, each covering a quarter of the field of vision. Due to the lack of sleep it sometimes happened that the lookouts fell asleep with the binoculars in front of their eyes. Of course there was hell to pay if this was noticed by an officer. Occasionally sleeping lookouts were accessories to their own deaths—eg when crash diving, it could be that in the rush to climb down through the conning tower they were not noticed and with movement restrictions inside the boat a man might not be missed for some time. If the absence was noticed quickly enough the boat might be able to return to the surface to search. Far too often, however, the man would be picked up dead. His life jacket would keep him afloat, but the cold water would have killed him.

On the whole accommodation was very poor, compared with that of English submarines. The commander had a small "cabin" that could be shut off from the rest of the boat with a heavy curtain. The officers and petty officers had bunks which could be curtained off. There were also some bunks for the other ranks, except that some of these were often used for torpedo storage and the men had to sleep where they could. Some, particularly the torpedo mechanics, always slept in hammocks.

The executive ranks were permitted a small amount of personal belongings, but the other ranks were often limited to only one spare set of underwear and one or two odds and ends. So many provisions were crammed into the boat, that such little luxury as had been provided for the crew was removed to make extra room for the stores.

Drinking water was often rationed. Consumption was determined before the boat left, and should the boat have to remain at sea longer than anticipated, perhaps because it had not used all its torpedoes, then the officers would first calculate how much fuel they had left and secondly how long their drinking water would last. Provisions and water would be further restricted even with the fresh water generator working full time. The product of this apparatus was really distilled water and it had a foul taste. Drinking water could only be obtained in the galley, so it was not easy to steal it. Under severe restrictions the officers might even remove the handle from the tap. The torpedo mechanic always had an opportunity to acquire some water from the hydraulic torpedo ejection system. This water

In Brest one of the special Grand Slam *bombs designed by Barnes Wallis, cut through the concrete roof and exploded inside the U-boat pen. Two U-boats immediately below, were demolished but the pens were so well constructed that the ten ton bomb did not seriously damage U-boats at the other end of the shelter. One of these U-boats put to sea shortly afterwards.*

The landward side of the U-boat pens at Lorient (?). The big doors were large enough for a VII C to be hauled through for repairs on land.

Schnorkels

Opposite page: *The forerunner of the German schnorkel: The Royal Netherlands Navy's submarine O 21 experimenting with a ventilation mast during February 1940. From left to right: Navigation or sky periscope. Attack periscope, Rod aerial, Diesel air mast with head valve, Exhaust pipe, (All 'periscopic').*

U 313 (Type VII C) with rigid schnorkel. When not in use the air mast was housed in the deck casing. It could be raised by special gear controlled from the inside of the boat. Note the Hohentwiel *(bedstead-like) radar aerial on the conning tower of the boat on the left.*

Type VII C boats at Lisnahilly after the war. In the foreground is U 826. Two types of schnorkel head valves can be seen. Also note the differences in size of the periscope head lenses. (Sky periscopes on the left and attack periscopes on the right.) The rectangular slot, above the horseshoe shaped lifebelt, is the hole for the Hohentwiel *radar aerial, which can be seen in a raised position on the second boat.*

Periscopic schnorkel and periscope of a Type XXI or Type XXIII. The arrow points to the exhaust holes in the rear shaft.

Close-up of the periscope schnorkel's head valve.

had to be mixed with syrup to make it drinkable because it also tasted foul. This, of course, was a severely punishable offence, but desperate situations breed desperate solutions.

U-boats carried two types of water. There was a drinking water tank and a washing water tank, and on trips it was possible to carry additional water in the spare torpedo containers. The only difference between these tanks was that the drinking water tank was cleaned better than the other tank. Drinking water would be obtained through a hosepipe from a tap ashore and washing water usually came from a fire hydrant. Washing water was not really contaminated and in emergencies washing with it was prohibited, so that it could be used for drinking. Washing water was only provided for officers and petty officers and other ranks had to wash with sea water or, if they were lucky, with cooling water from the diesel engines. Every man was provided with special salt water soap. This helped a little, but it did not really get oil and grime out of the skin. There was only one answer: the men had to cultivate an indifference to being dirty. "Tar your clothes—the white is showing", was a common U-boat men's phrase.

It has often been said that the U-boat Arm fought on with utter determination and dedication to the bitter end. This is of course true, but one or two additional points must be made.

Determination to fight to the end was encouraged by Hitler's SS and by the Secret Security Police. Such units were stationed behind the front line and they shot anybody who was either retreating or deserting. In the German towns, too, the SS was active in discouraging deserters. An out-of-date leave warrant was sufficient to classify a person as deserter!

Most of the U-boat men were not keen on fighting. The author has never heard of an ex-U-boat man who actually enjoyed going to sea after 1940. Had the men been given the chance to go home or to stay with the U-boats then Hitler would have been left with just a handful of fanatics. The new recruits joining the U-boat Arm were keen to fight, but this was due to the propaganda with which they had been indoctrinated and not to hearing depth charges explode! Extremely strong nerves were needed to cope with life in an operational U-boat and more than a few people were removed from sea-going duty after a few patrols because their nerves could not stand the strain. It is a small miracle that so many men remained determined and cheerful while their home towns were being reduced to heaps of rubble.

11
The Death of the U-boat Arm

The dramatic battle for supremacy in the North Atlantic shipping lanes came to a climax during March 16th to 20th, 1943 when forty ships of the fast convoy HX 229 caught up with 51 ships of the slower convoy SC 122. A total of 44 U-boats were sent into battle against this mass of merchant ships. The meagre escort fought hard to keep the sea wolves at bay, but in spite of their inspired bravery some nineteen U-boats crept in close enough to be able to fire. A total of 21 merchant ships of over 142,600 GRT sank to the bottom. These successes were announced to the German people by special news bulletins which interrupted normal radio programmes and gave the impression that German U-boats were ruling the Atlantic.

Only two months later the situation was completely reversed. The monthly U-boat losses dramatically increased – January, six lost; February, nineteen lost; March, sixteen lost; April, fifteen lost; and then May, 42 lost. During this period of 1943 the U-boat offensive totally collapsed and Germany turned to the defensive in the Atlantic. Never again were U-boats in a position to dictate the battles and the battle for the Atlantic was lost.

This was by no means due to any one special weapon introduced by the Allies, but to a combination of factors:

1 The most important, most deadly and most feared was radar. Especially the new short-wave apparatus that Germany could not detect with the Metox. This made it possible for the Allies to detect U-boat in all weathers, no matter how bad the visibility. Surface escorts could detect them before the U-boat lookouts could see the convoy.
2 High Frequency Direction Finders (Huff Duff) were installed and this enabled the Allied forces to pinpoint the source of any radio message even if the U-boat sent merely four coded digits.
3 The Allied navies were being equipped with new weapons such as the 'hedgehog' and later the 'squid'. These were capable of throwing a pattern of depth charges ahead of the vessel and they made destroyers more effective. Depth charges were being filled with the new explosive Minol, which was twice as powerful as the previously used Torpex and they also had special shallow and deep set pistols fitted to make them more versatile.
4 At the beginning of the war destroyers usually hunted on their own. This meant that they lost asdic contact during the last moment and had to drop their depth charges 'blind'. In addition to this the U-boat could also hear asdic, whence surprise attacks were impossible. The U-boats could also hear the destroyer coming in 'for the kill' and this gave the commander just sufficient time to move out of the way before the depth charges exploded.

Later during the war the U-boat hunters were arranged in special hunter-killer groups of three destroyers. Two could hold the U-boat on asdic contact while the third dropped the depth charges. These groups and convoy escorts were also equipped with VHF radio, which meant that it was possible for commanders to speak to each other, but the radio waves were not strong enough to travel all the way to Europe, so they could not therefore be picked up by the German monitoring stations. Previously the convoy commanders could only communicate with one another by using flash lamps or semaphore.
5 Aircraft-carriers, many of them being merely converted merchant ships, started to patrol the middle of the Atlantic and thus closed the 'air

U 776.
Close-up of the piston which raised and lowered the rigid schnorkel. The arrow points to the schnorkel pipe.

New Electro-Boats

Type XXIII, probably U 2326, in a British port after the war. This type was designed to operate completely submerged and it was not fitted with deck casings. A rack full of depth charges can be seen just to the right of the conning tower on the ship in the background and there is a loaded depth charge thrower aft of the superstructure.

Three Types XXI after the war. The middle boat is probably U 2511. Adalbert Schnee, her last commander, said that she was painted white because he discovered that light boats were more difficult to spot from planes than darker colours. The rumour that it had a connection with his name (Schnee means snow) came about later.

gap' which had protected U-boats until the spring of 1943.

6 More and more intelligence and scientific information was becoming available, making it possible for the Allies to intercept U-boats before they attacked.

7 German manpower was stretched beyond its limit, and many of the new U-boat crews just did not have sufficient experience. Many of the men were not aware of the dangers facing them in their complicated vessels and in emergencies just did not react quickly enough.

Why then were the U-boats still sent to battle after they proved to be obsolete and with such heavy losses? The *Seekriegsleitung* (Directors of Naval Warfare) had great faith in the new strengthened anti-aircraft guns and hoped that these would be sufficient to prevent losses to aircraft. Additionally, faith was put into new weapons such as the acoustic torpedo (*Zaunkönig*–T 5) and it was hoped that this would drastically alter the situation. Hitler insisted on U-boats being sent into the Atlantic to keep the Royal Navy and the Royal Air Force occupied to reduce the totals in men and materials available for use against Germany itself.

The D-Day invasion of 700 ships, 4000 landing craft, almost 400 minesweepers and 42 Divisions, supported by thousands of aircraft threw itself on to the French coast at dawn on June 6th, 1944. This was the greatest military invasion in history. U-boats had been specially assembled in their French Atlantic bases for invasion defence, but their commanders did not receive sailing instructions until some twelve hours after the Allied landings. This was not due to negligence by the regional commander, but due to the general confused situation. There had been numerous false alarms and at first the Germans did not know what was happening. The nearest U-boat base to the Allied invasion route was Brest, where the U-boat men had a sorry tale to tell. The following boats were definitely in Brest on June 6th, but there may, however, have been one or two more:

U 218 Kptlt R. Becker.
Left Brest on 10th August and managed to crawl into Bergen on 23rd September.

U 247 Oblt z S Matschulat.
Was attacked shortly after leaving Brest and had to return for vital repairs. Departed again on August 26th for the Bristol Channel but was sunk en route.

U 256 Oblt z S Boddenberg.
This boat had been modified with an additional gun platform in front of the conning tower to work as an aircraft trap. The modification proved useless and the platform was removed. The boat left during the evening of June 6th and it was back by midnight the following day. Being so heavily damaged it was withdrawn from service. Later it was repaired and sailed to Norway under the command of Heinrich Lehmann-Willenbrock.

U 269 Oblt z S Georg Uhl.
Left Brest during the evening of June 6th. Destroyed on June 25th.

U 373 Kptlt 'Teddy' von Lehsten.
Left for its 12th war patrol on June 7th to operate off Lizard Point and the Scilly Isles. It was sunk one day after leaving port.

U 390 Oblt z S Geissler.
Left port on June 27th. Sunk on July 5th.

U 413 Oblt z S D. Sachse.
Left Brest on June 6th and returned three days later with heavy damage. Tried to break out again on August 2nd. This time successful, but sunk less than three weeks later.

U 415 Oblt z S Herbert A. Werner.
The Flotilla Engineer ordered the IWO to take the boat out (the commander was not on board). The diesel engines activated a mine and the boat sank in front of the U-boat bunker.

U 441 Kptlt K. Hartmann.
Left during the evening of June 6th. Sunk less than two weeks later.

U 621 Oblt z S Stuckmann.
Left on August 13th for La Pallice. No schnorkel. Sunk on August 18th.

U 629 Oblt z S H. Bugs.
Left Brest during the evening of June 6th for Plymouth area. Sunk two days later.

U 740 Kptlt G. Stark.
Left on its 2nd war patrol on June 6th, to operate off Lizard Point and the Scilly Isles, but sunk en route.

U 763 Kptlt Ernst Cordes.
Left on June 10th. Returned three days later after accidentally penetrating the Royal Navy anchorage at Spithead. (The water between the Isle of Wight and Portsmouth.) Departed from Brest again on August 9th and successfully

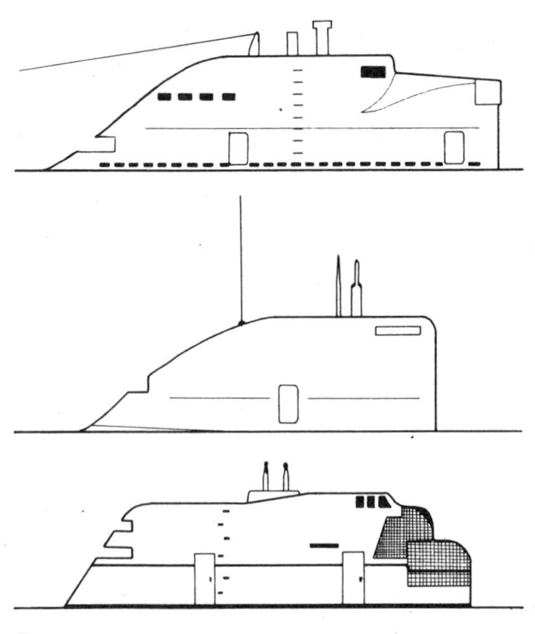

Top: *The conning tower of* Roland Morillot *(ex U 2518) after 1950.*

Centre: *The conning tower of U 3008 after conversion in U.S.A.*

Above: *Conning tower of* Wilhelm Bauer *(ex U 2540)*

reached La Pallice on August 14th. Left on August 23rd and made its way to Bergen, where it arrived on August 25th.
U 821 Oblt z S Knackfuss.
Left for its 2nd war patrol during the evening of June 6th. Sunk four days later.
U 953 Kptlt Heinz Marbach.
The commander went to Berlin to receive the Knight's Cross and could not return because the route had been cut off by Allied land forces.
Oblt z S Herbert A. Werner was given command of U 953 and the boat left Brest with important scientific equipment and about 90 people on board. The extra people and equipment were unloaded at another French base and the boat then sailed to Norway, using its schnorkel.
U 984 Oblt z S Hein Sieder.
Left during the evening of June 6th. Returned heavily damaged on June 9th. Departed again on June 12th and returned shortly afterwards. Tried to break out once more on July 26th and was destroyed by Allied forces on August 20th.

None of these boats reached their planned operation areas and those which managed to return to Brest were all damaged by enemy action. One boat, U 256, was so badly damaged that it was withdrawn from service. However, as there were sufficient spare parts and fairly good repair resources still available in France the boat was given a complete re-fit and later it was declared seaworthy again. The 9th U-boat Flotilla was dissolved and its last commander FregKpt Heinrich Lehmann-Willenbrock was ordered to take U 256 to Norway. The men waited for foul weather, so that rain, fog, high seas and strong winds would cover their departure. Eventually it was able to leave for its 5th war patrol on September 3rd, 1944, travelled on the surface through the English Channel, and arrived at Bergen on October 17, where it was withdrawn from service.

The crews which arrived in the French Atlantic bases with wrecked U-boats at first made their way across country to Germany and many of them were drafted to other boats. Once the Allied armies cut off the routes to Germany there was no choice, except to go to Norway by sea or to remain in the French bases and hope for the best. Those who had to remain on land were issued with army weapons and trained to defend the bases from the advancing armies. A bloody battle was fought for Brest, especially for some of the buildings which had been U-boat headquarters. There the men worked hard to destroy documents which might aid the destruction of more U-boats. From D-Day onwards the Channel and Atlantic bases in France were so heavily patrolled by Allied forces that they ceased to be effective.

Hitler never admitted defeat. He told the German people on January 1st, 1944 that the 'slight lapse' in the U-boat war was only due to one single English invention (Hitler referred to anything British or Allied as 'English') and that it would not be long before Germany introduced countermeasures. Later in 1945, as the situation became more desperate, Hitler ordered that "Every German will fight to the last drop of blood. No one will surrender and anybody who orders a retreat should be shot on the spot." He added that any person, no matter what rank, can take command and lead the fighting.

Type XXI boats being assembled near Bremen. In the background is the river Weser.

Pre-fabricated sections of Type XXI at Hamburg after the capitulation.

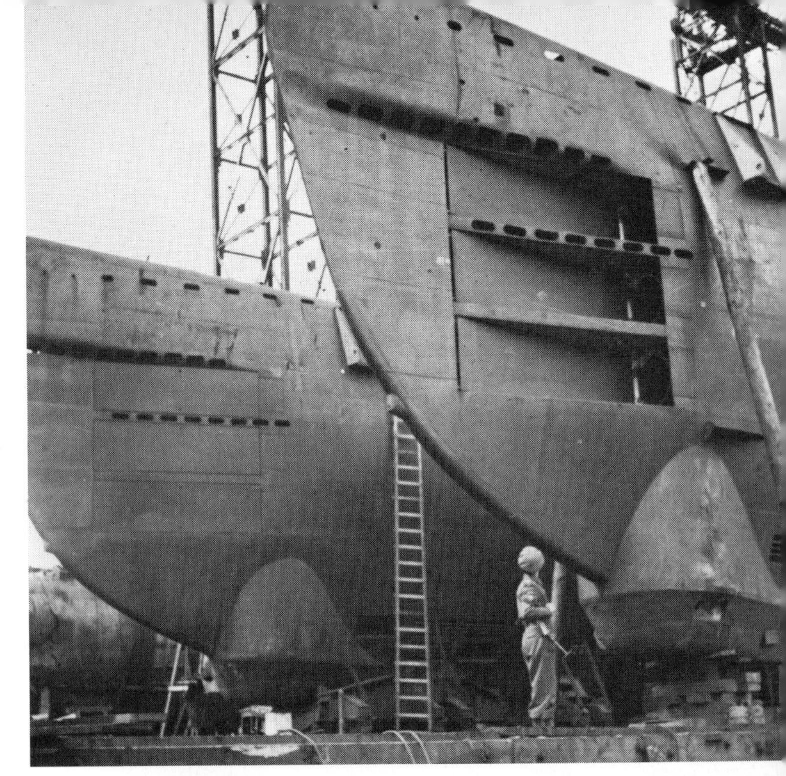

Bow torpedo tubes, open and closed, of Type XXI. At the bottom is the large, bulbous Balkon Gerät, *which houses the receivers of underwater sound detection gear. (The soldier is British.)*

Type XXI boats being built. The nose section, seen on the third boat, has not been fitted to the first two. (The soldiers are British.)

Midget Submarines

Below: *The inside of a concrete bunker used for the construction of Type* Seehund.

Below right: *A poor photo of Type* Marder, *or Type* Neger.

Bottom: *Parts of a Type* Seehund *at the Deutsches Museum in Munich.*

There is no doubt that these ruthless *NSDAP* policies led several authors to publish various strange statements about the U-boat Arm. For example, it has been hinted or stated that Dönitz used concentration camp and slave labour in the dockyards; that he gave suicide orders to U-boat commanders; that U-boats were sent out in poor mechanical condition so that the men had no chance of survival; and that Germany constructed suicide weapons similar to the Japanese. Perhaps it might not be inappropriate to discuss these points here.

Slave labour was used for the construction of U-boat pens, but that had nothing to do with the U-boat arm nor with Dönitz. This work was carried out by the Todt Organisation. Dönitz did agree to using concentration camp labour, but this was before the war and like most other Germans he was completely unaware of the atrocities committed there; he thought that these men were ordinary prisoners. It is not certain whether such labour was actually employed in the end.

I have been very interested in 'suicide' orders because my father disappeared with U 377 at a time when these were supposed to have been issued. I tried hard to prove the point, but could not find one single shred of evidence to support the idea. My conclusion, therefore, is that Germany did not give 'suicide' orders or construct 'suicide' weapons. Even midget craft, such as the human torpedoes (which is an English term and was not used in German), were designed to give the operator a good chance of survival. It has also been stated that U-boat commanders were ordered to follow Allied radar impulses to find the enemy. This idea was certainly suggested and it was a well-known way of finding convoys, but there is no reliable record of this having been an order; and it appears that the commanders who tried this method of finding the enemy did so of their own free will.

I also found no reliable record of U-boats being sent out in poor mechanical condition. Even the wreck of U 256 was re-fitted so that it was free from all major defects.

There was a noticeable change in the U-boat men's attitude from 1944 onwards. On arrival at the office the shore-based staff started to say "Good Morning" instead of the obligatory "Heil Hitler". Songs such as *Denn wir fahren gegen Engeland* ("We are sailing against England") or U 47's song *So klein ist das Boot und so gross ist das Meer* ("The boat is so small and the ocean is so large") were being replaced by far more cynical ones that lamented the poor weapons of the U-boats and the radar that was being used to hunt them. The men knew that they were beaten and that their end was inevitable – but no one knew how long Germany would last and there was always a faint glimmer of hope in Hitler's promises of new weapons.

The last bitter end came quite quickly and with little warning. U 1203, commanded by Oblt z S Sigurd Seeger, was just preparing for another war patrol when they received the order *Waffenstillstand* (Cease fire). U 1203 was re-fitting in the Lofiord, behind Trondheim, because there was no room at the base itself. At first everybody was astonished at the news. The men's first thoughts were of getting back to Germany and home. Some wanted to take the boat to the German coast, scuttle and then make their own way home. Others suggested that the boat should be scuttled immediately and some even suggested going to South America in it. In the end the men decided to stay put, obey instructions from their new superiors and hope for the best.

The *Kriegsmarine* Ensign was lowered from the small masthead, laid on the deck, soaked in petrol and burned. Then the men waited for their uncertain fate, but the enemy did not come swarming in as expected. After a few days a Royal Navy destroyer appeared and its crew checked that there were no scuttling charges. In doing so they looted the German lockers for valuables and then they departed again. They did not even take weapons away. The U-boat men were told to carry on as before, wear their uniforms with badges, only the swastikas had to be removed.

Some orders from the new chiefs were disobeyed. For example, some U-boat men were told to appear in Trondheim, fully armed, to help round up some Russian prisoners who had been set free by the Allied Forces and were looting and raping. The Germans did not wish to give trigger-happy soldiers an excuse to shoot them and they refused to carry arms. The men were also asked to volunteer for minesweeping duties. Not one man stepped forward. All the U-boat men wanted was to go home to their

Top: *Prototype* Delphin *being lowered into the water. This was a fast one-man craft.*

Above: *A prototype* Adam *that later went into production as Type* Biber.

Conning tower with G 7e torpedo.

Bow section.

Biber 90

Parts of Biber 90 *at the Imperial War Museum in London.*

Rear view of conning tower. The pipe coming from it is the exhaust pipe. It can be shut or opened by turning the small rod. (The strip of metal going from the exhaust pipe to the hatch has been fitted to prevent the hatch from being closed.)

families and forget U-boats for ever, but this wish was not granted. After a thorough interrogation, to search out war criminals, the men were marched off to prison of war camps.

The U-boats at sea also received the order to stop action against the enemy. Later they were told to surface, fly a black flag and then run into specified ports. This black flag has been a bone of contention among German sailors ever since, because they considered it to be a pirate's flag. This black flag was not intended to signify that U-boat men were pirates. In any case in Britain a black flag must bear the skull and crossed bones before it is considered a pirate's flag. In the eyes of the Royal Navy there was nothing humiliating about flying the Jolly Roger as it was always flown by Royal Navy ships when entering port to denote success, not failure.

The boats that had survived the war and had not been scuttled were assembled at continental and British bases. Those on the continent were made seaworthy and then moved by skeleton German crews to Britain. Most of these surviving boats were taken out into the Atlantic and sunk during 'Operation Deadlight.' A few were kept and distributed among the Allied navies.

12
U-boat Chronology

1933
1 Oct: Submarine Defence School founded in Kiel.
1934
20 Mar: First radio ranging (radar) experiments carried out by the Germans.
1935
16 Mar: Repudiation of Versailles Treaty and re-introduction of national conscription.
17 June: Anglo-German Naval Treaty signed.
29 June: U 1 is commissioned.

27 Sept: 1st U-boat Flotilla (Flotilla Weddigen) is founded and Karl Dönitz is appointed as Commander.
1936
7 Mar: German forces march into the demilitarized Rhineland.
12 Aug: U 27, the first Type VII boat is commissioned.
1 Sept: 2nd U-boat Flotilla (Flotilla Salzwedel) is founded at Wilhelmshaven.
3 Sept: London Submarine Protocol (Prize Ordinance) is signed.
22 Nov: The first U-boat sinks after the end of the First World War. U 18 collides, by accident with the tender T 156.
1938
4 Feb: Hitler appoints himself as commander-in-chief of the armed forces.
13 Mar: Austrian *Anschluss.*
4 Aug: The first Type IX boat is commissioned. (U 37).
1938
Sept: 'Z'-Plan was formulated.
29 Sept: The Munich meeting—Chamberlain 'Peace in our time'.
1939
27 Jan: Hitler gives 'Z'-Plan highest priority.
8 Mar: U 48 the most successful U-boat during World War II was launched.
27 Apr: Anglo-German Naval Treaty repudiated by Hitler.
22 July: Admiral Raeder meets heads of the U-boat Arm aboard the *Aviso Grille* in Swinemünde to tell them that Hitler had said there would be no war with Britain.
26 Aug: Admiralty in London assumes control of merchant shipping.
1 Sept: German forces invade Poland.
3 Sept: Britain and France declare war on Germany.
4 Sept: Passenger liner *Athenia* sinks after being attacked during the late hours of the 3rd by U 30.
14 Sept: U 39 commanded by Korv Kpt Glattes sinks. The first U-boat to be sunk by enemy action.
17 Sept: U 29 commanded by Korv Kpt Schuhart sinks the aircraft carrier HMS *Courageous* in the Western Approaches. This leads Admiralty in London to withdraw aircraft carriers from anti-U-boat duties.
1939
28 Sept: Hitler visits U-boats at Wilhelmshaven.
13 Oct/
14 Oct: U 47 commanded by Günther Prien penetrates the defence of Scapa Flow and sinks the battleship *Royal Oak.*
1940
19 Jan: V 80, the forerunner of the true submarine, is launched.
18 Apr: U 99 is commissioned under Otto Kretschmer, the most successful U-boat commander of World War II.
June: Air cover is extended to the Western Approaches, but not much further west than the 12th Meridian.

10 June: Italy joined the war on Germany's side.
25 June: French-German armistice.
17 Aug: Hitler declared a total blockade of the British Isles.
19 Sept: U 69, the first Type VII C boat, was launched.
19 Nov: The first time that a U-boat is detected by radar. The boat escaped.
1941
29 Jan: U 152, the last Type II boat was commissioned. It was used as a training boat for the whole of its life.
10 Feb: A Whitley aircraft was reported as sinking the first U-boat after detecting it by radar. The boat must have escaped as there are no records of a U-boat having been lost during this month.
1941
5 Mar: Hitler issues directive to give assistance to Japan.
7 Mar: Günther Prien's (U 47) last report.
17 Mar: Two U-boat 'aces' are lost. U 100 commanded by Kptlt J. Schepke is rammed by HMS *Vanoc* and U 99 commanded by Otto Kretschmer is sunk by HMS *Walker*. Schepke was killed. Kretschmer is still alive.
23 Apr: Oblt z S Zürn of U 48 is awarded the Knights Cross. The first one awarded to a U-boat LI.
9 May: 'The Secret Capture' U 110 is captured by the Royal Navy.
27 May: The battleship *Bismarck* is sunk.
2 July: Dönitz's son-in-law, Kptlt Hessler returns to Lorient with U 107 after the most successful operational war cruise during World War II.
28 Aug: U 570 is captured. (HMS *Graph*)
Oct: H/F D/F ('Huff Duff') is installed in fairly large numbers.
14 Nov: U 81 commanded by Kptlt Guggenberger sunk the aircraft carrier HMS *Ark Royal*.
15 Nov: U 459, the first Type XIV, was commissioned.
25 Nov: The battleship HMS *Barham* was sunk by U 331 commanded by Oblt z S Freiherr von Thiesenhausen.
26 Nov: The 'ace' Otto Kretschmer was awarded Oakleaves with Swords to the Knight's Cross. First one awarded to the U-boat arm. Kretschmer was in a British POW camp at the time.
7 Dec: Japanese forces attack Pearl Harbor, and destroyed part of the American Pacific Fleet.
11 Dec: Germany and Italy declared war on the United States of America.
1942
13 Jan: Pauckenschlag at America starts.
14 Mar: U 177, the first Type IX D_2, is commissioned.
27 June: Convoy PQ 17 leaves Reykjavik in Iceland.
5 July: PQ 17 scattered.
11 Aug: The aircraft carrier HMS *Eagle* was sunk by U 73 commanded by Kptlt Rosenbaum.
12 Sept: The liner *Laconia* was torpedoed and sunk in the South Atlantic by U 156 commanded by Korv Kpt Hartenstein.
Dec: *Hohentwiel* radar aerial introduced to U-boats.
1943
30 Jan: Grand Admiral Erich Raeder resigns and he is succeeded by Karl Dönitz. For the time being Dönitz also remained as Commander-in-Chief of U-boats.
2 Feb: Stalingrad fell to the Russians. The turning point of the Second World War.
12 Feb: Rotterdam radar apparatus crashed.
22 Feb: Research Corps Rotterdam is founded under the chairmanship of Dip. Ing. Leo Brandt.
16 Mar/
20 Mar: Largest convoy battle. (Convoys HX 229 and SC 122).
24 May: Dönitz tells Hitler that owing to heavy losses the U-boats must be withdrawn from the Atlantic for the time being.
31 May: U-boat production is handed over to Dr Speer's Department of Military Armament.
Summer: Naxos radar detector is introduced.
4 Aug: U 489, a Type XIV, sinks. Only two *Milkcows* remain afloat.
9 Aug: Kpt z S Wolfgang Lüth is the first member of the U-boat arm to be awarded Diamonds, Oakleaves & Swords to the Knight's Cross.
16 Nov: U 792, the first of the 'new' experimental true submarines with Walter Turbines is commissioned.
1944
1 Jan: Hitler tells the German people that the 'lapse' in the U-boat war is due to one single English invention and that the countermeasure would soon be introduced.

Tail end of Biber 90 *with G 7e torpedo. Note the primitive way of moving the rudder and hydroplane.*

17 Apr: U 2321, the first Type XXIII, is launched.
May: Schnorkels came into *widespread* use.
12 May: U 2501, the first Type XXI, is launched.
4 June: U 505 captured by United States Forces.
6 June: D-day, 'The Longest Day', 'The Invasion.'
11 June: U 490, the last *Milkcow*, was sunk.
12 June: U 2321, the first Type XXIII, is commissioned.
27 June: U 2501, the first Type XXI, is commissioned.
July: Versuchskommando 456, to experiment with midget craft, is founded by order of Adm Hellmuth Heye.
23 Aug: U 953 commanded by Herbert Werner leaves Brest. The last U-boat out of the base.
23 Nov: Freg Kpt Albrecht Brandi was awarded Diamonds, Oakleaves & Swords to the Knights Cross.
1945
18 Jan: The experimental fast midget craft Type Delphin collided with its tender and further tests were impossible.
15 Apr: Two Type Delphin craft arrive at the Baltic for trials.
30 Apr: Hitler committed suicide.
Dönitz became Head of State. The first Type XXI leaves for a war cruise. (U 2511 commanded by Schnee.)
1 May: The two new Type Delphin midget U-boats are blown up.
4 May: 18.30 hours. The German delegation signs the Instrument of Surrender.
5 May: Prototype of midget U-boat Type Schwertwal I is completed.
7 May: Unconditional surrender of German Forces.
U 320, commanded by Oblt z S Emmerich, is the last U-boat to be sunk by enemy action.
1965
19 July: Trawler *Snoopy* sank. The last ship to be sunk by a World War II German torpedo, which had been entangled in its net.

Top: *Tail end of Biber 90.*

Middle: *Rear part of starboard side.*

Bottom: *Starboard side without torpedo. (Looking forward)*

13
Submarine Warfare in the Early 1940s

The modern atomic submarines of today are capable of cruising submerged around the world. They can launch guided missiles from the depths and they can even travel under the North Polar Ice Cap. All this helps to spread the misconception that submarines during the Second World War were capable of similar feats, which they were certainly not. Those submarines should really have been called 'diving boats' or 'submersibles' as they usually operated on the surface and only dived to evade the enemy or to carry out a rare daylight submerged attack. These craft were certainly not capable of dashing through the depths at great speed! Supposing one would superimpose a map of Europe over the Atlantic. Then a U-boat in Berlin, Warsaw, Prague or Vienna might be ordered to attack a mobile object in London. The U-boat would travel there on the surface at a speed of a pedal cyclist. Once submerged its cruising speed would be cut down to walking pace.

Navigation and enemy detection aids were still in their infancy and the only noteworthy advantages the U-boats had over Nelson was a gyrocompass, a small calculating machine, radio and superb binoculars. Nearly all their targets were located by positioning lookouts on the conning tower, who scoured the horizon. Since the conning towers were not very tall these lookouts were restricted to a field of vision of about ten kilometres in radius. Once submerged the vision was still further restricted to a few kilometres, depending on how far the periscope stuck out of the water and on the height of the waves. A periscope was only a tube, with a few lenses and prisms. It enabled the commander to see what was going on at the surface without surfacing the boat. The small attack periscope had a very bad "blind spot" which could harbour a whole squadron of aeroplanes. These could be spotted with the sky or navigation periscope; however, this device had such a large head that it was unadvisable to use it during daylight in case it was spotted.

U-boats had the advantage at night-time on the surface, as they were surprisingly difficult to spot, even on a relatively light night. It is fairly easy to spot ships on the horizon, where they stand out against the slightly lighter sky and the low profile U-boat could easily spot the bulkier surface vessel. Then the U-boat would turn head on to the target, thus exposing the smallest possible silhouette. Once a U-boat has left the surface ship's lookouts' horizon it can be almost impossible to spot against the black waves. A Royal Navy destroyer has been known to pass within a hundred metres of a U-boat without spotting it.

There are two ways a conventional submarine can dive or surface. First, a series of tanks can be filled with water or air to make the boat light or heavy. The boat has main diving tanks and so-called "trim tanks". The trim tanks were used to balance the boat and also to adjust the bouyancy. Usually the submarine's trim was adjusted so that the boat had more or less neutral buoyancy when submerged. This meant that it would neither go up nor down, but remain at the same level in the water. On blowing water out of the main diving tanks the boat would suddenly become lighter and rise to the surface. In doing so the boat would use up electricity and compressed air and it would only surface this way during an emergency. Normally the hydroplanes would be used to do most of the work. These functioned similarly to the elevators on aircraft in making the craft go up or down. Once the boat came to the surface the diesel engines could be started and

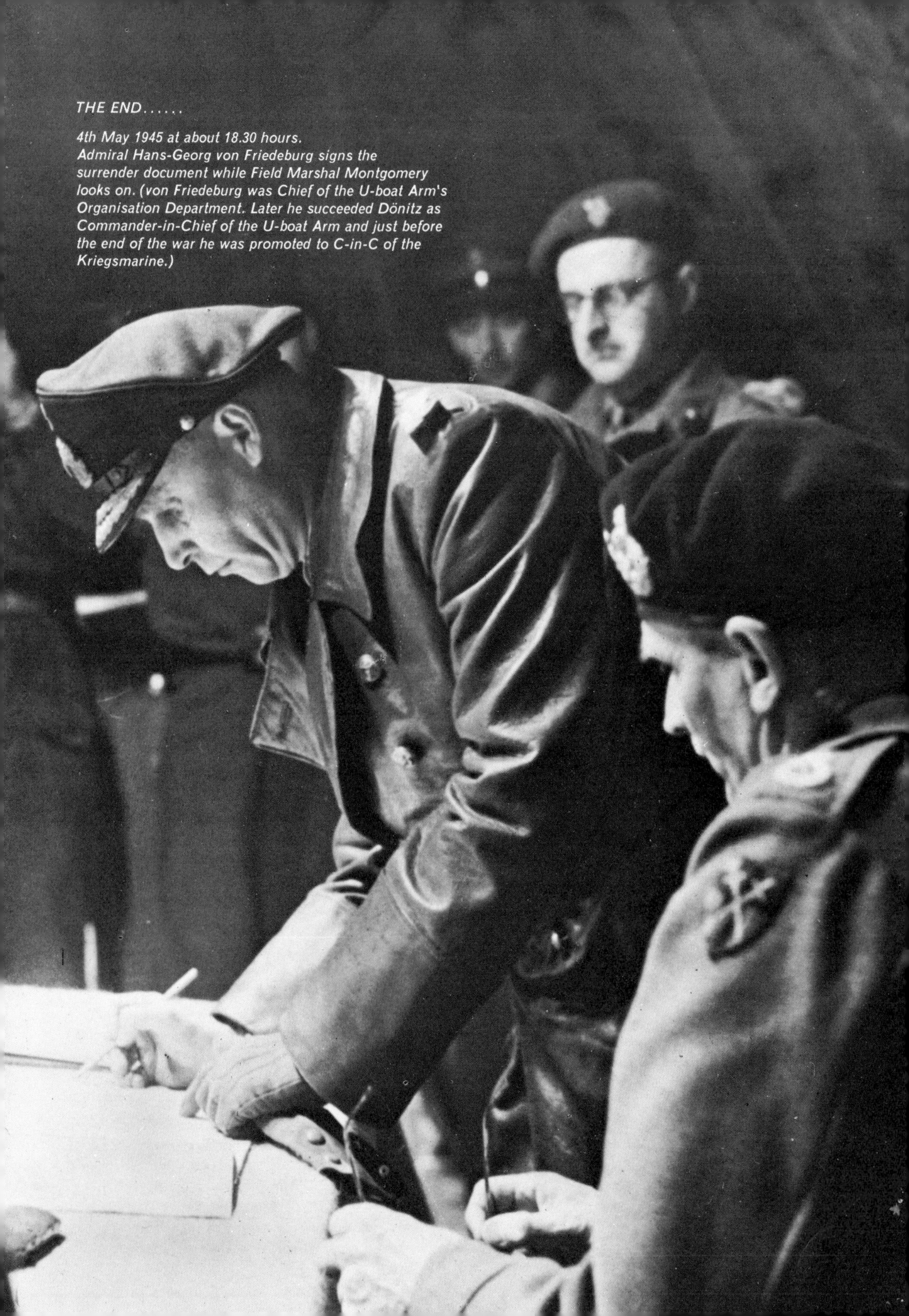

THE END......

4th May 1945 at about 18.30 hours.
Admiral Hans-Georg von Friedeburg signs the surrender document while Field Marshal Montgomery looks on. (von Friedeburg was Chief of the U-boat Arm's Organisation Department. Later he succeeded Dönitz as Commander-in-Chief of the U-boat Arm and just before the end of the war he was promoted to C-in-C of the Kriegsmarine.)

their exhaust fumes used to blow the water out of the main diving tanks to make the boat much lighter and float better.

The degree of trim or balance of a submarine is quite remarkable. It can be adjusted to within a fraction of a pound and even a man walking from one end to the other is sufficient to upset it. This is why so much concentration is needed once the boat is submerged, specially when schnorkelling. Firing torpedoes, say a salvo of three, will mean that the boat is suddenly four to five tons lighter and immediately would start to rise. The engineering officer must therefore pump water into the boat to counterbalance it and to prevent it from surfacing. A submarine is so complicated that exact neutral buoyancy is almost impossible to obtain. Usually the boat is trimmed slightly heavy. If it would therefore remain stationary while submerged it would slowly start to sink, like any other weight. The electric motors are used to propel the boat forward to prevent this. Only a few revolutions of the propeller are necessary to keep the boat at the required depth with the hydroplanes. Therefore it is dangerous to keep the boat submerged once the batteries are exhausted.

The diesel engines, which are a conventional submarine's main power source, cannot be used once below the surface because they require air to operate. They have to be switched off the moment the vents are shut. At the same time a pair of powerful electric motors are engaged to propel the boat. These motors obtain their power from large storage batteries, weighing several tons, but functioning similar to car batteries. On the surface the diesel engines could be used to turn the electric motors, which then behaved like a dynamo to generate electricity and charge the batteries.

These batteries ruled the life of a submarine in more ways than merely limiting under water endurance. The men in the U-boats were only allowed to smoke on deck because batteries give off a mixture of hydrogen and oxygen gases when being charged. This is not harmful, but it is the same mixture which causes domestic gas explosions!

Should sea water get inside the batteries and mix with the sulphuric acid then chlorine gas is given off. This choking gas is highly poisonous and it was the submariner's nightmare as its presence gave them no alternative but to surface and ventilate the boat. Such action could be highly impractical if the enemy was waiting on the surface.

The U-boats' main weapon was the torpedo. This was really a miniature little submarine itself. At the front of the torpedo was a warhead, containing explosives, and the stern section contained an electric motor to push it along. Early torpedoes were propelled by compressed air, but these were replaced by the other type once the war started. On reaching the target the warhead could be detonated by various methods, depending on the type of torpedo. It was not easy for a torpedo to explode inside the U-boat because there was a small safety device that only made the torpedo "live" after it had travelled through the water for a certain period.

At first the submarine hunters were no more sophisticated than the U-boats. In fact, in many ways, their equipment was far inferior to that of the U-boats. Before the advent of radar the destroyers depended entirely on sight for detecting surfaced U-boats. Once their target was submerged they could locate it with their asdic. This apparatus transmitted a sound impulse which sounded as a metallic 'ping' to the men inside the U-boats. The sound wave would be reflected by any object in its path and be picked up by the asdic. On contact the angle of a submarine's position could be read off on a scale, and the distance calculated from the time taken for the sound echo to travel to and from the target. It did not function when the U-boat was on or near the surface and it became unreliable once the destroyer came too close to the target.[1] The 'ping' was also reflected by whales, shoals of fish and differences in water temperature or differences in salinity. Considerable training was therefore needed to operate the set effectively.

Once the hunter had detected a U-boat it would have to run in and drop depth charges. The asdic 'pings', the change of speed and the splash of the depth charges could be heard inside the U-boat. This gave it a little time in which to accelerate and move out of the way of the main blast. U-boats have been known to evade such

[1] This is because at short distances it becomes difficult to distinguish between the impulse and echo, since the time between the two is too short.

Ten days later.... May 14th, 1945.
The first U-boat, U 858, surrenders to United States Forces. The American boarding party is just going aboard.

depth charge attacks for more than twenty-four hours, with anything between 100 to 300 or more depth charges being dropped.

Nothing is more nerve-wracking than being at the receiving end of one of these attacks. Lights would go out, the boat would rock, throwing things all over the place, glass in the gauges would break, crockery would shatter, nerves would be frayed. It was impossible to see or to know when the next pattern would come. Whether that would be the end or whether the boat would withstand the attack. The men would keep up their morale by betting how many charges would be thrown down on them.

Depth charges were either just dropped off a rack into the water or they could be thrown clear by a special depth charge thrower. When just dropping them over the side, the ship had to move at a fair speed to avoid being caught by the subsequent explosion, which could easily

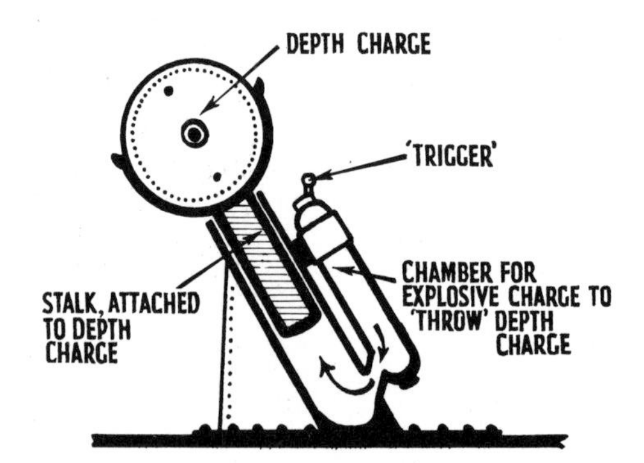

blow a destroyer to pieces. Later, during the war special ahead-throwing devices, such as 'hedgehog' and 'squid', were introduced and these proved to be more successful than the conventional depth charge. These had the advantage because a number of them could be thrown at the same time and they only exploded on impact, so asdic contact was not lost by useless explosions.

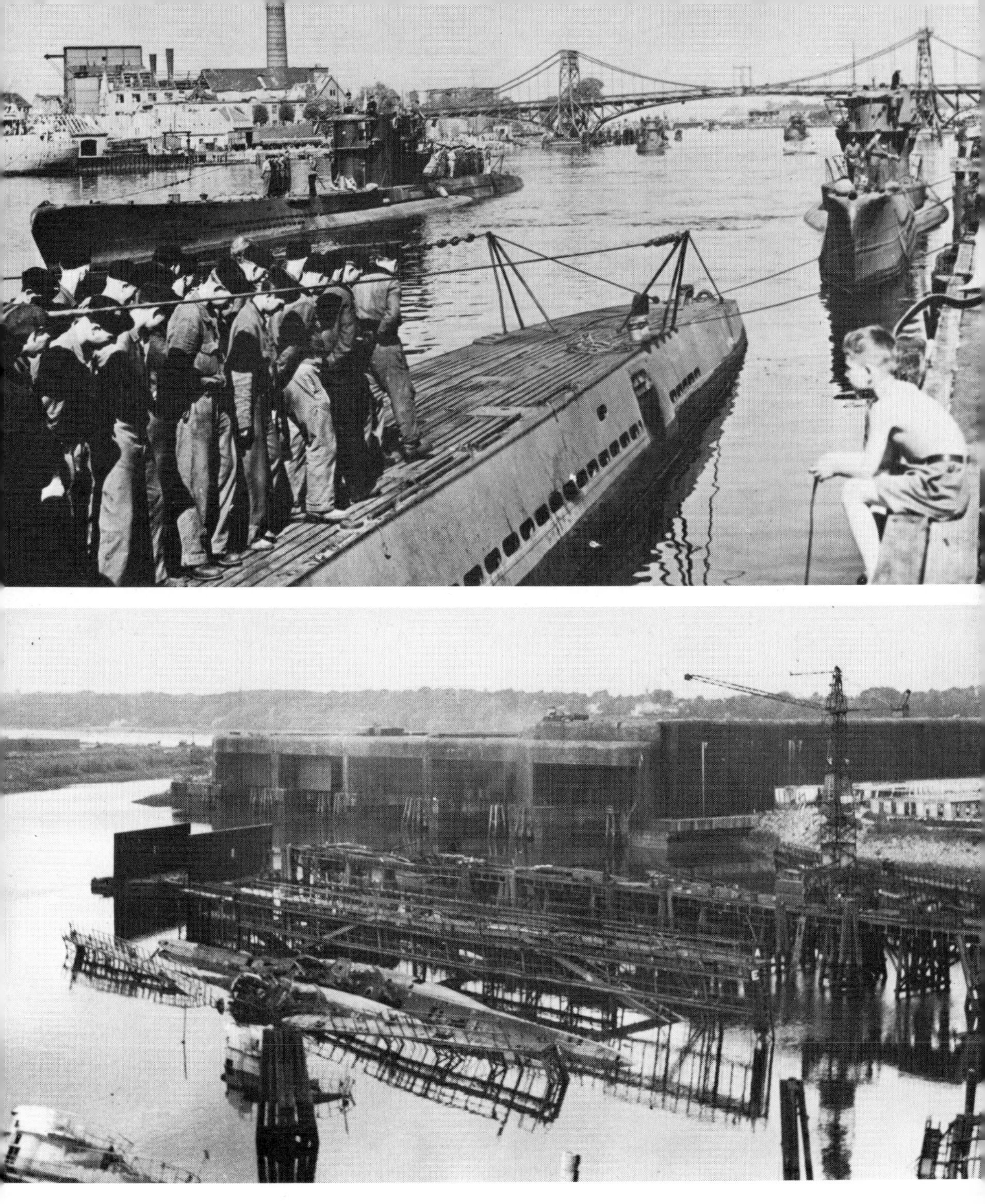

Top: *Type VII C boats coming into Wilhelmshaven to surrender.*

Above: *Hamburg, U-boat pens at Finkenwerder with river Elbe; Sülberg and Blankenese in the background. Many men defied the order to surrender and scuttled their boats, as can be seen in the foreground.*

23rd May, 1945. (Dönitz's Government is arrested) Dr Speer (left) – Head of the Department for Military Armament, with Admiral Karl Dönitz. Dönitz became Head of State after Hitler's suicide.

Insignias

A few insignias have been included in this book because they are useful for the identification of u-boats on old photographs. Many of them have quite a colourful history, which would be difficult to trace without personal knowledge of the individual boats. For example, U 201 had a snowman painted on the conning tower because the commander's name was "Schnee", meaning "snow", and thus the boat was called the "Snowman's Boat". The Knight's Cross around its neck also had a special significance—it appeared after Adalbert Schnee had been awarded the medal. U 99 had a horseshoe on each side of the conning tower. They were pulled up, out of the harbour, by the anchor chain. Taking them as a sign of good luck they were painted yellow and fixed to the boat, whence "The Golden Horseshoe". Some boats, for example, U 108 and U 208, were paid for by public subscription and bore the coat of arms of their sponsors the towns of Danzig and Köln.

The insignias were either the boat's private badge or sometimes all the boats of the same flotilla carried a similar badge. There was no hard and fast rule about this. A flotilla might adopt the badge of a famous boat. The "Snorting Bull", for example, was first painted on U 47 and later it was also adopted by all boats of the 7th U-Flotilla.

Some of these badges were painted freehand on the tower, but the boats with complicated symbols, or those with no "artists" on board, carried a large stencil. It must be emphasised that the badges were often re-painted and there were startling differences in detail. Theoretically, according to *Kriegsmarine* rules, the insignias had to be removed before a patrol, but this appears not to have been enforced because many boats carried their badges proudly into battle.

Insignias should not be confused with "tactical marks", which were painted on the boats for easy identification during naval exercises. These marks were usually just simple geometric symbols.

Insignias not illustrated
Coat of arms of Köln: U 208
Coat of arms of Duisburg: U 73
Coat of arms of Düsseldorf: U 557
Coat of arms of Salzburg: U 205
Coat of arms of Innsbruck: U 202
Coat of arms of Nürnberg: U 453
Mermaid with bow and arrow: U 332
Edelweiss: U 124
Playing cards—four aces: U 107
Black devil: U 552
Black cat with "3 x" underneath: U 564
German eagle with swastika: U 132
Steel helmet with crossed swords behind it, enclosed in circle of oak leaves: U 123
Jumping Goat with horns with star underneath: U 67
Row of flags and laughing cow: U 69
Viking ship with wail: U 83
White swan: U 178

U-25, Korvettenkapitän Schütze.

U-9, Oberleutnant zur See (later Kapitän zur See) W. Lüth.

U-404.

U-47 commanded by Günther Prien later it was used by 7th U-Flotilla.

U-108 (Danzig Coat of Arms).

U-201 commanded by Korv. Kpt Adalbert Schnee.

U-99 commanded by Otto Kretschmer.

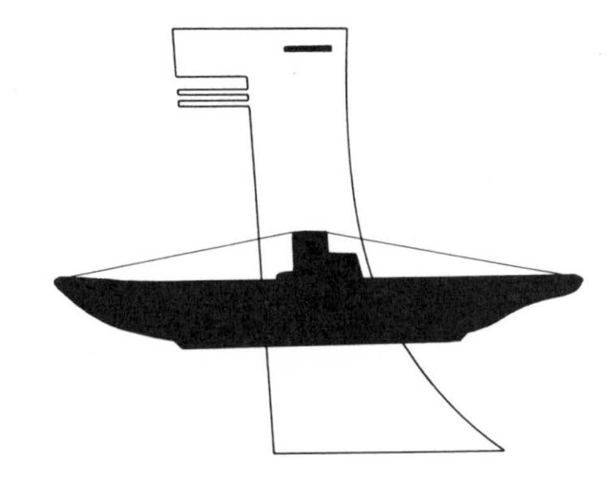

U-270 on front of tower

U-763 in 1944

U-100 Kptlt. J. Schepke

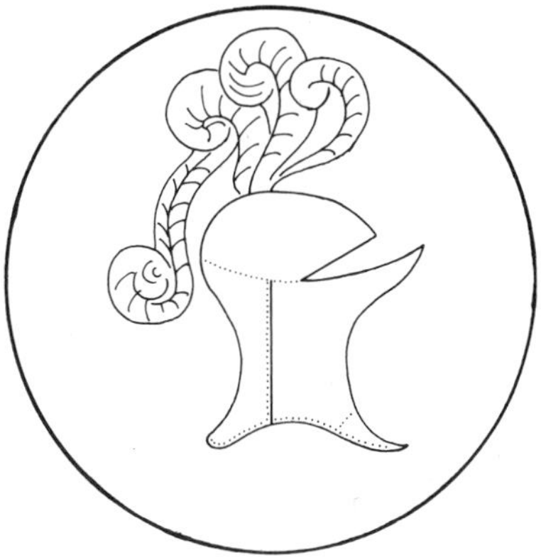

U-130 Korv. Kpt. Kals.

U-271 Kptlt. Barleben, at front of tower.

Insignia of 9th U-boat Flotilla

U-106

U-163, at side of tower

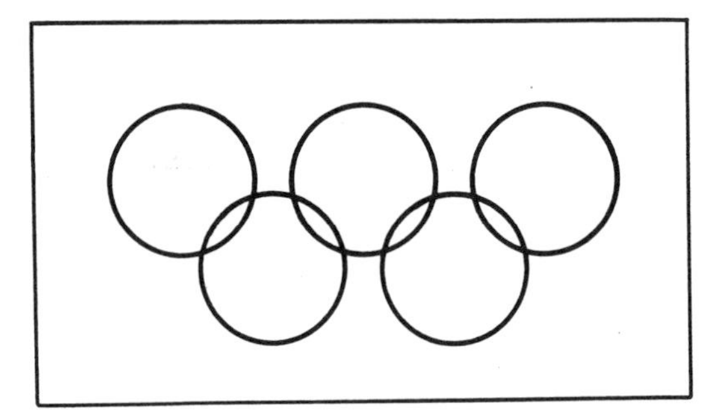

U-537, at front of tower

U-97 (Kapitänleutnant U. Heilmann)

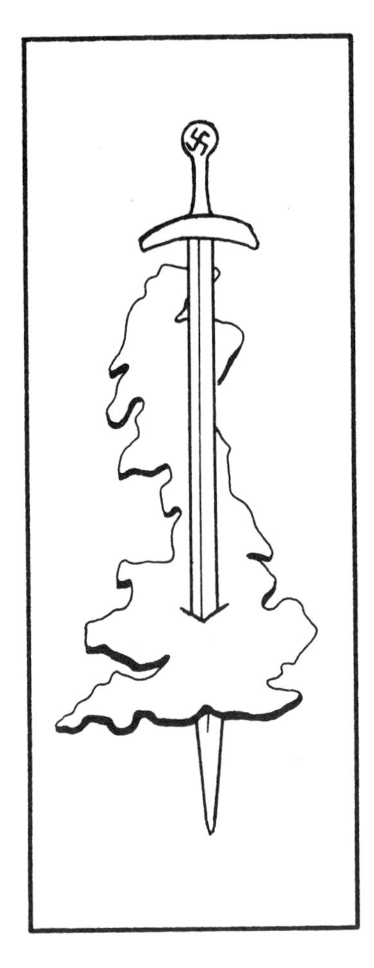

U-505

U-216, at front of tower

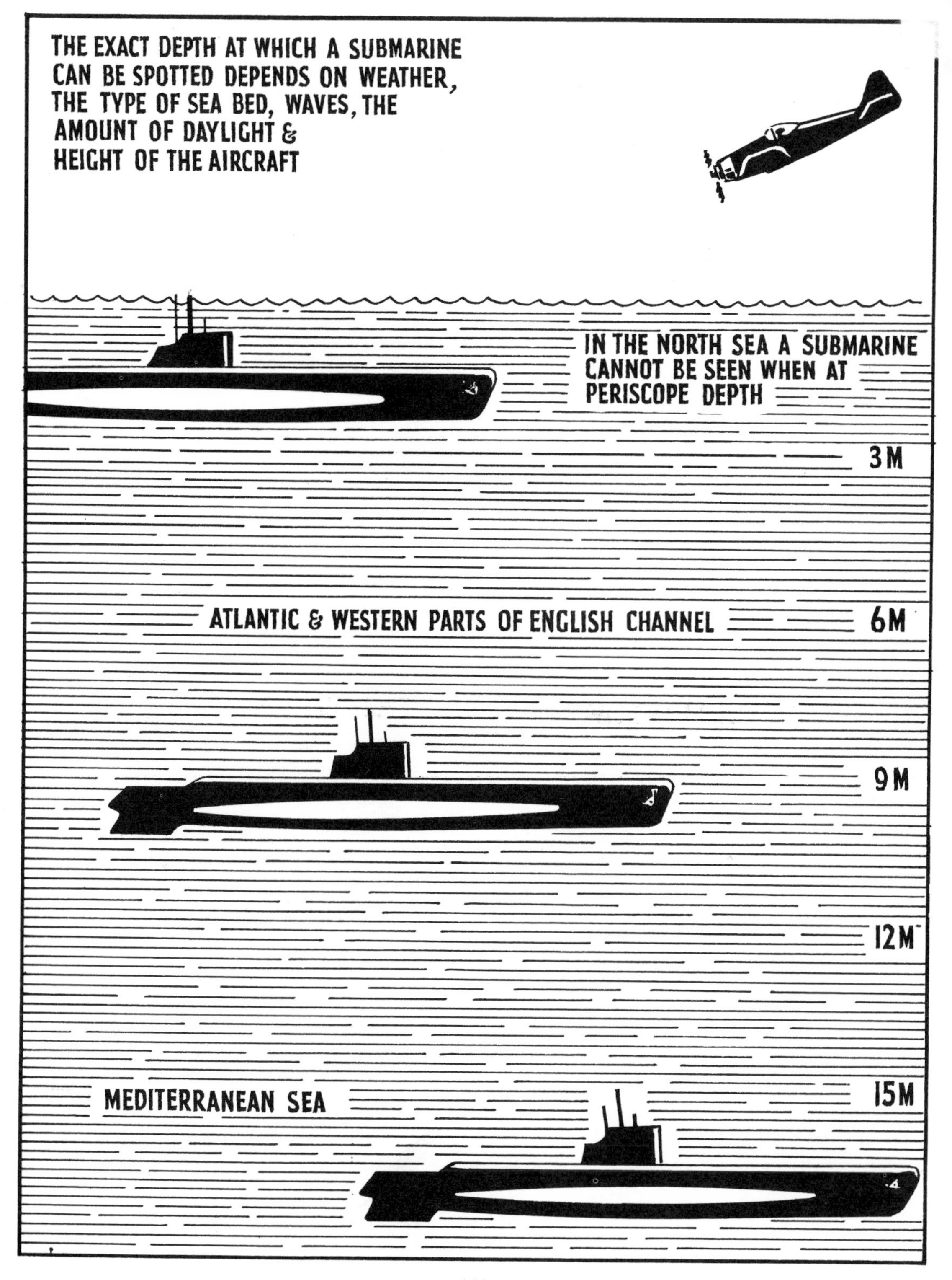
THE EXACT DEPTH AT WHICH A SUBMARINE CAN BE SPOTTED DEPENDS ON WEATHER, THE TYPE OF SEA BED, WAVES, THE AMOUNT OF DAYLIGHT & HEIGHT OF THE AIRCRAFT
IN THE NORTH SEA A SUBMARINE CANNOT BE SEEN WHEN AT PERISCOPE DEPTH
3M
ATLANTIC & WESTERN PARTS OF ENGLISH CHANNEL
6M
9M
12M
MEDITERRANEAN SEA
15M

Glossary

AA Anti aircraft.
aD/ausser Dienst Retired or withdrawn from service.
Abt/Abteilung Department.
AGRU Front *AusbildungsGRUppe Front:* A technical branch to train the men and to test the mechanics of the boats before they go on operational war service.
AO/Artillerie Offizier Artillery officer.
Aphrodite A German device for *foxing* British radar. It reflected radar impulses.
Asdic Initials of *Allied Submarine Detection Investigation Committee.* Called *Sonar* in America. A device for detecting submerged submarines.
Asparagus Translated from *Spargel,* a nickname for periscopes.
Athos A capstan shaped radio detection aerial. The upper ring detected 3cm and the lower ring detected 9 cm radio waves.
ASV Initials of *Air to Surface Vessel:* Radar.
Autobahn Motorway.
Bachstelze Nickname for *Focke-Achgelis,* a gliding helicopter that was towed by U-boats.
Bali Aerial for detecting radar impulses.
Bauwerft Ship building yard.
BdU Initials of *Befehlshaber der Unterseeboote:* Commander-in-Chief for Submarines.
Befehlshaber Commander-in-Chief.
Bewaffnung Armament.
Biscay Cross Nickname for the first radar detection aerial used on U-boats. It consisted of a rough wooden cross with wires strung around the outside.
Borkum Gerät Radar detector.
BRT Initials of *Brutto Register Tonnen:* Gross Register Tons.
Bundesmarine Germany's equivalent of the British Royal Navy. This name was used between 1848 and 1852 and again after 1956.
Destroyer The Germans called all small fighting ships *Destroyer.*
DDR Initials of *Deutsche Demokratische Republik:* German Democratic Republic, founded after World War II.
Dienst Duty.
Dienstgrad Rank.
Dienstelle Headquarters.
D-Maschine Diesel Engine.
Dräger Name of a German firm that developed submarine escape apparatus and air purification systems.
DT or DeTe Gerät Abbreviation of *Drehturm Gerät* = Dezimeter-Telephoniegerät: A radio rangefinder.
Einbaum Dug out canoe, nickname for Type II U-boats.
EK/Eiserneskreuz Iron Cross.
E-Maschine Electric Motor/Generator.
Englisch Everything Allied or British was called *Englisch* by the Germans.
FdU Initials of *Führer der Unterseeboote* Chief/Leader/Head/Commander of Submarines.
Feindfahrt War cruise/patrol against the enemy.
F.D./Fischdampfer Fishing boat.
Flak Word made from *FLiegerAbwehrKanone* or *FLugAbwehrKanone*: AA gun.
Fliege A later development of the *Naxos* radar detector.
Flug Flight/air travel.
Flugzeug Aeroplane.
Front U-Boot A U-boat used to fight the enemy as distinct from a training or experimental boat.
Führer Chief/leader/head/Commander, and in the case of Hitler—dictator.
FuMB From *FUnkMessBeobachtung*: Radar detection.

FuMO From *FUnkMessOrtung*: Radio detecting or Radar.
Funk Radio.
Funkmess Radio/Radar detector.
Funkpeilgerät Radio direction finder.
Gesunken Sunk.
GRT Gross Register Tons.
Hakenkreuz Swastika.
Hauptquartier Headquarters.
Hedgehog A device for throwing depth charges ahead of the ship. Used by Royal Navy.
HF/DF Pronounced 'Huff Duff'. Initials of *High Frequency Direction Finder*. A device that could pin-point the source of radio messages.
HK/Hilfskreuzer Auxiliary cruiser.
HMAS His/Her Majesty's Australian Ship.
HMCS His/Her Majesty's Canadian Ship.
HMIS His/Her Majesty's Indian Ship.
HMS His/Her Majesty's Ship.
Hohentwiel A German radar aerial that looked like a bedstead. (One side was a radar aerial and the other side detected radar impulses).
Hondo
Honduras } A type of Metox aerial.
Huff Duff See HF/DF.
Hundekurve Dog's curve. A path that a U-boat took when attacking, so that the smallest possible profile was exposed to the enemy all the time.
Hydroplane A type of rudder that makes a submarine go up and down.
iD/Indienststellung Commissioning.
Indienstgestellt Commissioned.
IWO Pronounced 'Eins WO' (One WO) 1st Watch Officer.
IIWO As above only 2nd Watch Officer.
Kaiserliche Marine Germany's equivalent of the British Royal Navy. So called between 1871 and 1919.
Kaleu or Kaleunt Short for Kapitänleutnant.
Kalipatrone A device for breathing into. It absorbed carbon dioxide.
KdO/Kommando Command.
KF/Kriegsfischkutter Fishing boat used for fighting duties.
Kleinkampfmittel Small weapons.
Kleinkampfverband/K-Verband A corps that experimented with small weapons.
KM/Kriegsmarine Germany's equivalent of the British Royal Navy. So called between 1935 and 1945.
Km Kilometre.
Knot The speed of ships is measured in *knots*. 1 knot is 1 sea mile per hour. (A sea mile is a little longer than a land mile.)
Kommandant Commander.
Korfu Similar to Naxos.
Krieg War.
Kriegsmarine See KM.
Leigh Light A powerful searchlight fitted under aircraft wings.
L.I. Initials of *Leitender Ingenieur*: Chief Engineering Officer.
Löwe Lion. A nickname sometimes used for Dönitz and also for the British Lion.
Luftwaffe Air Force.
Marine Navy.
Mark German currency.
Meddo Gerät Like Rotterdam Apparatus on 3cm waves—shot down at Meddo/Holland.
Metox A radar detection device.
Milchkuh A nickname for a Type XIV U-boat: Milkcow.
Mücke A radar aerial.
MS or **M/S** Motorschiff: Motor ship.
Naxos A radar detection device.
ObdM *OBerbefehlshaber Der Marine*: Commander-in-Chief of Navy.
OKM *OberKommando der Marine*: The equivalent of Britain's Admiralty.
OKW *OberKommando der Wehrmacht*: High Command of the Armed Forces. No British equivalent.
Operation Deadlight Code name for the action during which German submarines were sunk in the Atlantic after the war.
Paukenschlag A roll on the kettledrums.
Peilgerät Direction finder.
RAAF Royal Australian Air Force.
RAF Royal Air Force.
Radar From *Radio Detection and Ranging*. See chapter on the subject.
Radio Direction Finder A device for determining the source of radio waves.
RCAF Royal Canadian Air Force.
Reichsmarine Germany's equivalent of the British Royal Navy. So called between 1919 and 1935.
Reichsmark Old German currency.
Rentenmark Old German currency. Both preceded the present *Deutsche Mark*.

Ritterkreuz Knight's Cross (of the Iron Cross).
Rotterdam Gerät A German name for British radar. See chapter on radar.
Schiff Ship.
Schlüssel M Radio Key M.
Schnellfeuerkanone Quick firing large gun.
Schnorchel Schnorkel/Snorkel.
Sea Cow From the German *Seekuh*. See *Seekuh*.
Sea Mile 1.852km.
Sea wolves Nickname for U-boats and for U-boat men.
Seekriegsleitung The Directorate for the war at sea or the Admiralty.
Seekuh Nickname for the large U-boats.
SKL Initials of *SeeKriegsLeitung*.
Sonar American name for Asdic.
Sonar Buoy A buoy dropped by the Allies in waters where U-boats were suspected. It could transmit propeller noises.
Sonderführer Special commander.
Spargel Nickname for Periscope: Asparagus.
Spatz Nickname for a rescue buoy that was fitted to U-boats before the war: Sparrow.
Squid A device that throws depth charges ahead of a ship. Used by Royal Navy.
Stapellauf Launch.
T5 The German acoustic torpedo (Zaunkönig).
Sumatra, **Samoa**, **Samos** } Aerials for detecting radar.
Tauchboot Submersible boat.
Tauchretter Submarine escape apparatus.
Tauchtiefe Diving depth.
Tauchzeit Diving time.
T-Boot Torpedo boat.
TEK From *TorpedoErprobungsKommando*: Command for testing torpedoes.
Thetis Either the name for several German ships or the code name for a radar foxer.
Trim dive A dive to establish the proper balance of the submarine.
Tunis Radar search receiver. Probably never installed.
Turm Tower (conning).
TVA From *TorpedoVersuchsAnstalt*. Institution for experimenting with torpedos.
Typ Type. In English the term *class* tends to be used.
UA Germany built a submarine (*Batiray*) for Turkey, but this boat was not handed over. Instead it was commissioned into the German Navy as UA.
UAA From *Unterseebootsausbildungabteilung*: A department for training men to become submariners.
UAS From *Unterseebootsabwehrschule*: A school for teaching men anti-submarine warfare.
UB German name for HMS *SEAL*, (which they captured).
U-boot In German U-Boot means *Unterseeboot*, which is a submarine from any nation. In English the term U-boat is used only to refer to a German submarine.
UD Dutch submarines used by the Germans.
UIT Italian submarines used by the Germans.
UJ *Unterseebootsjäger*: Submarine chasers.
ULD *U-Bootslehrdivision* U-boats Training Division.
USAF United States Air Force.
USCG United States Coast Guard.
USS United States Ship.
US-FL *U-Bootsschulflottille* Submarine flotilla attached to submarine school.
Verb./Verband Unit.
verlohren Lost.
vernichted Destroyed.
versenkt Sunk.
VHF Very High Frequency (Radio).
Wabos Nickname for *Wasserbomben*: Depth charges.
Waffe Weapon.
Waffen Weapons.
Wanze From *Wellenanzeiger*: A radar detection device that automatically searched through various radar wavebands.
Werft Ship yard/dock yard.
Wintergarten Nickname for gun platform.
Wintergärten The plural of Wintergarten.
Wolf pack Translated from the German *Rudel*.
Wollhandkrabbe A nasty looking fresh-water crab that has been introduced into European rivers from the Far East. Nickname for Swastika.
Zaunkönig Code name for T5, the acoustic torpedo.